Province
Councillor's Office for S[...]

Travelling in the Province

Itineraries in the Province of Rome

Texts by
Alessandro Sagramora

FRATELLI PALOMBI EDITORI

PROVINCE OF ROME
Coucillor's Office for Tourism

By care of
Dipartimento VI Servizio 4 "Turismo"
with the collaboration of Dott.ssa Elena Manni
and Dott.ssa Rosella Masini

Photographic references
Archivio Fotografico Fratelli Palombi
L'Argonauta s.n.c.
Luca Sorrentino
Soprintendenza Archeologica per l'Etruria Meridionale
Soprintendenza Archeologica per il Lazio

The photographs of the works in the Museo Manzù at Ardea on pages 32-33
are drawn from
L. VELANI (by care of), *La raccolta Manzù, Catalogo delle sculture*, Latina 1994;
the photographs of the mosaic and the marble figure on pg. 59
are drawn from A. M. SGUBINI MORETTI (by care of),
La villa dei Volusii a Lucus Feroniae, Rome 1998;
the photograph of the frescoes in the church of San Leonardo at Montorio
Romano on pg. 75
is drawn from the brochure of the parish
of the Santissima Annunziata e Cristo Re at Montorio Romano;
the photograph of the bronze herma at the museo delle Navi di Nemi on pg. 136
is drawn from G. GHINI & S. GIZZI,
Il Lago di Nemi & il suo Museo, Roma 1996;
the photographs of the Triade Capitolina and the Nilotico mosaic
at the museo Archeologico di Palestrina on pg. 145
are drawn from S. GATTI, *Il Museo Archeologico di Palestrina*, Roma 1996,
the photograph of the painting by G. B. Rositi on pg. 134 is drawn from R. SANSONE
(by care of), *Museo Diocesano di Velletri*, Geneva-Milan 2000

© 2000 Fratelli Palombi Srl
Via dei Gracchi, 183
00192 Roma

All rights reserved to the
Amministrazione Provinciale di Roma

Edited and coordinated by the publisher

Translation by Stephen Scott

ISBN 88-7621-096-2

Presentation

In the year of the Jubilee, the Assessorato al Turismo della Provincia di Roma (Councillor's Office for Tourism of the Province of Rome) has made available to the general public the first true guide for that area which is the Province of the capital.

This guide has above all been thought of as an agile and stimulating tool for those who, although they may be also attracted by the charm of the Eternal City, anyway wish to be enriched by an equally stimulating contact with the realities of its Province.

The presentation in four distinct geographical areas, in turn entitled *From the ancient Lake Sabatino to Torre Astura*, *Along the meanderings of the Tiber amongst oases of greenery and memories of the past*, *From the Tiber to the Aniene following saints and hermits*, and *From the vinyards of the Castelli Romani to the woods of the Monti Lepini*, each with its naturalistic, archaeological and oeno-gastronomical itinerary, proposes a completely new approach in getting to know the culture, history and daily events of these places.

Following the different itineraries proposed, the tourist will be able to discover one by one the municipalities which constitute the whole of this metropolitan area and, at the same time, see the characterizing elements which exalt their individuality.

Beyond more traditional contents such as information on hotel accomodation, useful addresses and the itineraries, this guide aims to be a useful travel companion for a more modern form of tourism, capable of at once helping the tourist to get to know the more famous places and also all the other less famous but for that no less important ones, for a better understanding of the history of the territories of the Province of Rome.

Paolo Barelli
Coucillor for Tourism of the Provincia di Roma

The Province of Rome
Echoes of the past, charmed landscapes, myths, legends, traditions and gastronomic proposals

Introduction

A point of attraction for the inestimable wealth of its art treasures, Rome, with its millenary culture, has always overshadowed its Province. However, looking at the diaries of such famous people as Byron, Goethe, Gogol or, for that matter, anonymous travellers from all parts of Europe, exponents of that XVIII and XIX Century fashion which was the *Grand Tour*, we discover that a number of them ventured beyond the Eternal City's confines in order to explore the exotic and rather wild roman countryside, those hills and mountains crossed by the Tiber and the Aniene, describing in an at once disconserted and fascinated way the desolation of the landscapes full of signs of their ancient splendour, basking in the serene vision of the waters of a lake or in the contemplation of a work of art. To guide the tourist in the discovery of the Province of Rome is the scope of this publication, which intends illustrating all aspects of the territories of the Province which may interest those who wish to spend a day, weekend or a longer holiday far from the traffic of the city, in contact with nature or in search of ancient traditions. The Province of Rome, surrounded by the other provinces of the Region of Lazio and with its coast-line on the Tyrrenian Sea, thanks to its size and its particular geographical position, can offer something for virtually everyone's taste. Indeed, crossed by the Tiber, the second longest river in Italy, and by its confluent the Aniene, this area steeped in millenary history is a combination of green lowlands crossed by volcanic hills in the craters of which beautiful lakes have formed. There are also chains of mountains which are part of the Appenines, which despite their modest height are none the less charming, and purched upon which we find ancient 'borgos' which preserve lasting memories of ages past, such as cyclopean walls, the ruins of ancient roman buildings, castles, fortresses, palaces, baroque abbeys and churches. One hundred and nineteen municipalities, if we exclude Rome, where one has but to choose between archaeology, art and history, but where one can also discover ancient pagan legends which time has been unable to delete, in many cases linking them to miraculous events which could not but prosper in such a strong religious tradition as that in which the Benedictine and then the Franciscan orders were born. And because the numerous citadels of the Province are set within an environment of considerable interest, despite being near Rome and being heavily built up in parts, those who wish to spend a holiday in contact with nature, where they can contemplate the landscapes or dedicate time to healthy sports, from trekking to mountain biking, from free climbing to horse riding, will also find what interests them. Indeed, the Province of Rome is one of the greenest parts of our country as, for that matter, Rome is the greenest municipality in Europe. Parks, natural reserves, oases and protected areas have been given birth to in the last decades, and they continue to be created for the purpose of protecting the immense arboreal and wildlife patrimony which, in any case, is but a distant memory of the immense forest which Lazio once was, when the mythical Aeneas, the Trojan hero destined to give progeny to those who were to found Rome, reached its coasts. Given its pastoral and agricultural origins, roman cuisine disdanes manipulation and refinement, but has for centuries created simple and tasty dishes prepared with wholesome products and capable of winning over the most demanding of palates. The many wines, the extra-virgin olive oil, the typical cheeses and cured meats, the typical pasta dishes and cakes, all still home made, are a sure attraction for those tourists in search of wholesome flavours.

Thus, wishing to offer something for everyone's taste in this guide book, we considered it appropriate to divide the Province into four areas which broadly speaking reflect its four salient characteristics: the *sea* with its history and its culture tied to the Etruscans, who would seem to have come from there, and to the Ancient Romans,

Some history

If the Province of Rome appears to be so rich in testimony of ages gone by it is not only because it h been inhabited since Paleolithic times, it also soon became a melting pot for populations which we very different from one another, given its strategic position as a crossroads between the valley of t Tiber, Etruria, Campania, the Appenines and the sea. The Volscians, Equians, Faliscians, Sabines a Etruscans are but a few of the peoples who inhabited this area. With the assertion of the power Rome some of these cultures ended up disappearing, others were assimilated, and several of the peoples were obliged to migrate to new territories. Rome's encounter with etruscan culture was wi out doubt the most important, a process of fusion which went on for centuries and which really o ly ended in the reign of Emperor Augustus who, as a matter of fact, had amongst those closest to h the noble etruscan Maecenas, munificent friend of the poet Horace. Despite the destruction it s fered at the hands of the Barbarians during the invasions and, subsequently, at the hands of those w utilized parts of villas, thermal baths, temples and acqueducts as construction materials for new bui ings, the heritage of Roman civilization, from the times of the Republic to those of the Empire, is eve where visible in the Province. Indeed, the Ancient Romans used to love leaving what they, alrea then, must have considered a too chaotic city in order to take refuge in the villas which they had h built on the gentle hills near lakes and rivers, in the middle of woods or olive groves, not to ment the many places of worship such as the temple of Jove at Alba Longa.

With the decadence of the Empire, the barbarian invasions first and the Saracen ones later, the a which is today the Province was abandoned to total desolation and, for the subsequent twothousa years, its history was entirely that of Rome and the Papacy which, from the VIII Century on becam true and proper state. Due to invasions, in particular those of the Goths and Longobards and, later, Saracens, not to mention the perennial feuds between Papacy and Empire, between the IX and the Century, the citadels of the area were for the most part fortified. Given the presence of impervious a inaccessible places, many castles were built, often where before there had been *castra* (ancient r who made of it one of the fundamental means of communication for commerce and for the conquest of the world as it was then known; the river of Rome, the *Tiber*, with its surrounding environment, where nature is still in part uncontaminated and where the local culture is based on pasturing; the area of the *Sabina* and the *Aniene Valley*, full of a mystery tied to the birth of monastic life; the *Castelli Romani* and the area of the *Prenestina*, where tourism was already common centuries ago. Within each of these areas some itineraries based on more themes have been drawn. These are at once archaeological, monumental, naturalistic, religious and gastronomic and, without in any way pretending to be omnicomprehensive, are simply intended to offer a general over-view of what there is to be seen, visited, admired, and how to reach it. Lastly, we have also included information on hotels and places to stay in general, museums, palaces and other places worth visiting, also including a calendar for the most important feasts and "sagras", always divided by areas so as to make finding them easier. And so this is a practical and easy to use guide intended to stimulate curiosity and constitute a useful tool with which to face a *tour* of the Province of Rome.

man military camps), and it was around these that, little by little, the "borgos" that in many cases we can still today visit were built. It was in this period that the monasteries were also born, often as a consequence of the phenomenon of hermitages. After the foundation of hermitages by Saint Benedict (end V Century), the Benedictine and Cistercian (from Citeaux, in France) communities rapidly developed, often to become important centres of power (such as the case of the Abbey of Santa Scolastica and the Abbey of Grottaferrata), this too contributing to the birth of fortified "borgos" where the local population could find protection. This phenomen was to guarantee the survival of Greek-Roman terary tradition which would otherwise have been in great part lost, and also of more materialistic traditions such as that of the cultivation of vines and olives. However, the precariousness of life and of the economy remained a dominant characteristic of the area at least until the XVIII Century, this because the havoc caused by the invasions was followed by bloody feuds between noble families and the Papacy which caused poverty and destruction.

Despite the consolidation of the power of the Papacy at the end of the Renaissance, despite the reforms put into effect in the XVII Century and the fact that there continued to be the patronage of the arts and of architecture connected to the ostentation of the papal court and of the noble families which gravitated around it, the most part of the area remained a land of shepherds and brigands. A reality which was to cohabitate with the artistic fervour mentioned above. Indeed, from the XIII Century onwards the area saw the passing of those artists who, in their careers, monopolized both private and official commissions, in Rome but all the more so in the Province, the names of which are to become familiar to the readers of these pages. This from the dynasties of marble craftsmen to painters such as Antoniazzo Romano in the XV Century, the Zuccari brothers in the XVI Century, not to mention universally famous artists like Bernini or Pietro da Cortona. The province too lived through the epic events of Garibaldi's wars, to which it sacrificed more than one life, and, during the last war, many of its citadels were alas directly involved with the result that invasions and bombings in many cases damaged , and in some totally destroyed, works of art and buildings of considerable architectural worth.

Summary

From the ancient lake Sabatino to Torre Astura — 13
The naturalistic itinerary — 17
The archaeological-monumental itinerary — 30
The religious itinerary — 39

Along the meanderings of the Tiber — 43
The naturalistic itinerary — 47
*From Vejo Park to Soratte Natural Reserve,
following the Via Cassia and the Via Flaminia* — 47
*Following the meanderings
of the River Tiber along the Via Tiberina* — 58

From the Tiber to the Aniene — 67
The itinerary of olive oil and wine — 71
The way of olive oil of the Sabina — 71
The way of Cesanese di Olevano — 83
The archaeological-monumental itinerary — 87
The religious itinerary — 103

Castelli Romani - Monti Lepini — 119
The naturalistic-monumental itinerary — 123
The religious itinerary — 155

Useful information — 165

Parks and naturals reserves — 168

Places worth visiting — 168

Sagras and fairs, museums, accommodation — 171

Index of places — 197

Bibliography — 198

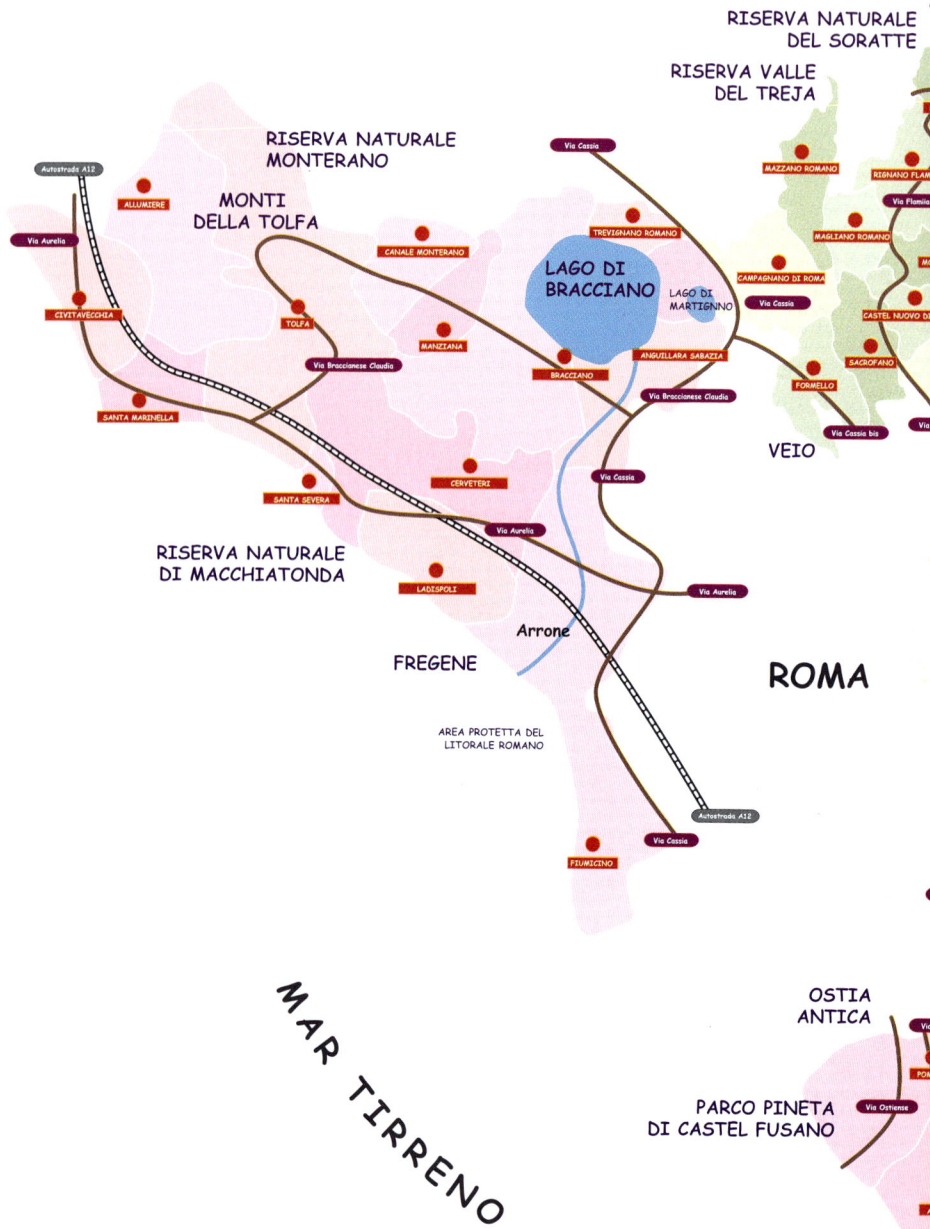

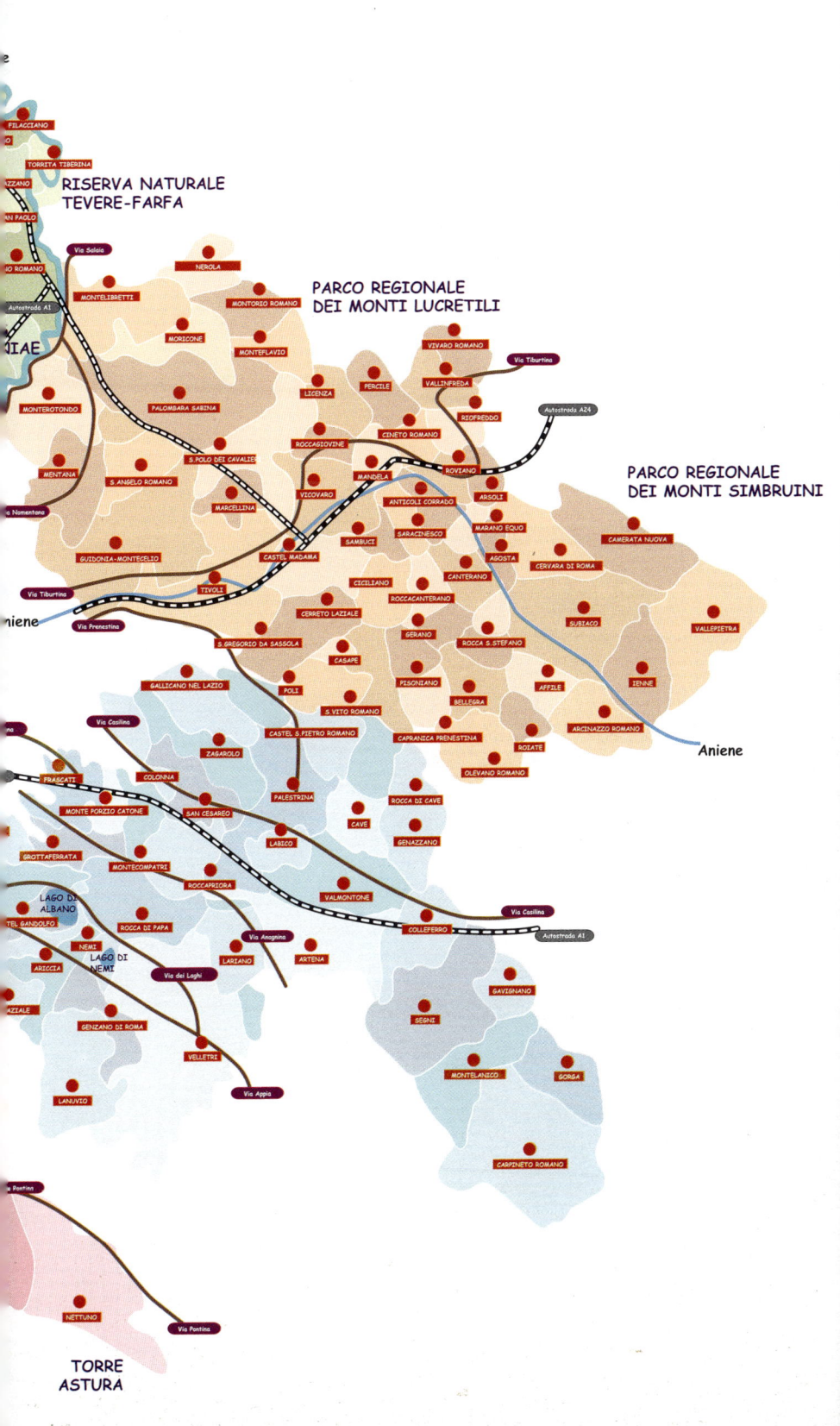

From the ancient lake Sabatino to Torre Astura

The coastline near Anzio

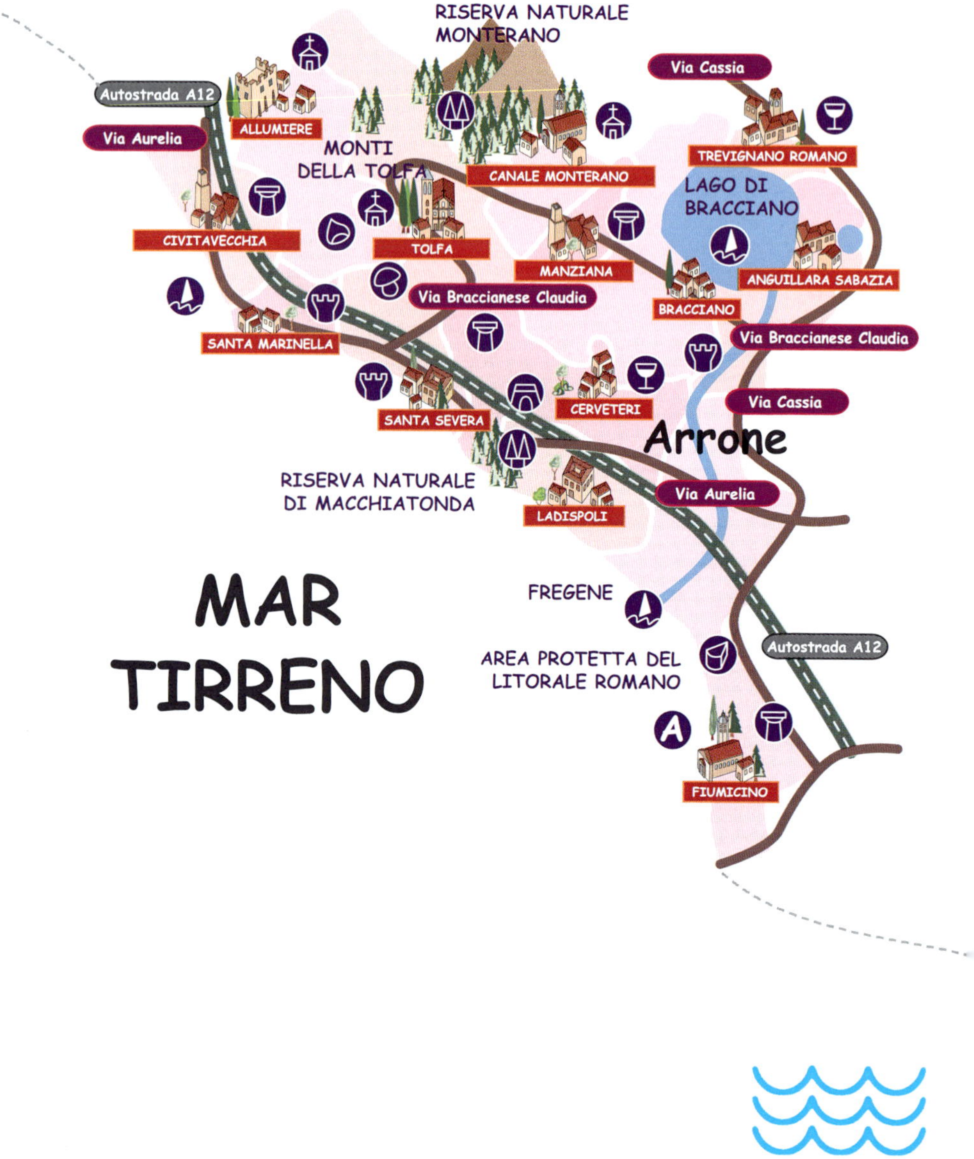
RISERVA NATURALE MONTERANO
Via Cassia
Autostrada A12
Via Aurelia
ALLUMIERE
MONTI DELLA TOLFA
CANALE MONTERANO
TREVIGNANO ROMANO
LAGO DI BRACCIANO
CIVITAVECCHIA
TOLFA
MANZIANA
ANGUILLARA SABAZIA
Via Braccianese Claudia
BRACCIANO
SANTA MARINELLA
Via Braccianese Claudia
Via Cassia
CERVETERI
SANTA SEVERA
Arrone
RISERVA NATURALE DI MACCHIATONDA
Via Aurelia
LADISPOLI
MAR TIRRENO
FREGENE
AREA PROTETTA DEL LITORALE ROMANO
Autostrada A12
FIUMICINO

- Water sports
- "Roccas" and castles
- Archaeological sites
- Places of worship
- Etruscan remains
- Parks and natural reserves
- Chestnuts
- Mushrooms
- Cheese
- Wine

ROMA

From the ancient lake Sabatino to Torre Astura

The areas in the North-East and along the southern coast of the province of Rome – amongst which there is Ostia (Rome Municipality), the modern Romans' favourite beach, with the interesting excavations of the ancient town – first and foremost share an element so typical of tourism in our peninsula: the sea. From Civitavecchia to Torre Astura run kilometre upon kilometre of flat sandy beaches, this with the exception of the rocky area of Capo Linaro in the vicinity of Civitavecchia, somewhat damaged by the frequent presence of buildings. The sea always has its charm, especially when in its waters, no longer as clean and transparent as when the Etruscans and Romans sailed them, one can see the reflection of the remains of ages gone by, shreds of history which relate true stories and distant legends. But the tourist attractions of this area are not limited to this: at the frontier with the area of Viterbo there are the Tolfa Mountains and, farther East some reserves and then lake Bracciano, one of the biggest volcanic lakes in Lazio. Be it for the size of the area and for the variety of things one can do, it seems opportune to indicate at least three itineraries each based on a theme even though they are not entirely disconnected from one another: one naturalistic, one archaeologico-monumental and one religious. Transversal to these will be the gastronomic itinerary, in no way secondary and closely linked to local "sagre" and feasts which still today keep up traditions which progress has been unable to suppress.

How to get there
Area Nord Ovest
By car: via A12 Motorway, Via Aurelia and Via Braccianese Claudia
By bus: CO.TRA.L. bus lines (tel. 800-431784), departing from Via Lepanto bus Terminal (Metro Line A, Lepanto Station - tel. 06/3214827-3244724)
By train: FF.SS.trains from Termini to Fiumicino, trains from any station on the Fara Sabina- Fiumicino line to Ladispoli, Cerveteri, Santa Marinella, Santa Severa, and trains from Termini to Civitavecchia on the Rome-Pisa-Genova line

Litorale Sud
By car: via the Via Pontina, the Via Ardeatina and the Via Nettunense
By bus: CO.TRA.L. bus lines (tel. 800-431784), departing from EUR Fermi bus Terminal (tel. 06/5920402) or Anagnina (tel. 06/7222153)
By train: trains for Pomezia, Anzio and Nettuno from Termini and Tiburtina railway stations (tel. 147888088) Roma Laziali railway lines (tel. 06/47303050)

The naturalistic itinerary

From an environmental point of view, one of the greatest riches the Lazio Region possesses is its lakes. In the province of Rome there are three: Bracciano, Albano and Nemi, plus the little lake of Martignano, which are respectively part of the municipalities of Anguillara, Campagnano and Rome. Known to the Romans as *Sabatinus Lacus*, name taken from the city of Sabate which legend has it sank into its waters, Bracciano occupies two craters – 57 kms^2 – with a perimeter of 33 kilometres surrounded on the one side by the Sabatini Mountains and on the other by the Tolfa Mountains. Its waters have for centuries reflected the images of the lovely villages of Anguillara, Bracciano and Trevignano, but its depths hide testimony of life there in protohistoric and perhaps prehistoric times, which the underwater investigations conducted by the Soprintendenza per l'Etruria Meridionale are trying to uncover. It must also be remembered that the lake has acted as a water reservoir for Rome for almost two thousand years, feeding the Pauline Acqueduct built by Pope Paul V Borghese (1605-21). Recently, a modern water purifying plant built by ACEA has made the waters, the blue colour of which gives a picturesque contrast to the green vegetation which surrounds it, drinkable. Woods of various types of oak, chestnut, willow and poplar trees, and olive groves, as well as market gardens and pastures are the ideal place for different species of animals and birds, whilst in the lake there are pike, whitefish, perch, trout and eels. Lovers of sport will find facilities for windsurfing, sailing, canoing and also archery, tennis, mountain bikes, whilst those who seek contact with nature can go for walks or take a horseback ride to the beautiful lake of Martignano only 1.5 klms

A view of Lake Bracciano

Fish Recipies

The numerous restaurants in the area serve many different dishes based on fresh water fish caught in the local lakes. One might start with spaghetti with eel sauce or fettucine with coregone sauce, and continue with crisp fried white-bait, grilled salmon trout or, in order to get a taste of the selection of fish dishes the area offers, try a mixed grill, of course cooked with local olive oil and washed down with local Cerveteri white wine. The fish "sagra" (feast) held at Anguillara in the first week in July should not be missed.

Anguillara: view from the lake

wide and so isolated as to represent a true miracle of environmental integrity. If a trip around the lake on the motor vessel *Sabazia II* has stimulated curiosity for a visit to the three medieval *borghi*, one could start with **Anguillara Sabazia** which gently rests upon a rock which slopes down to the lake. The name probably derives from that of one of the baronial families, Anguillara, who for a long time fought for the dominion of this area and whose coat of arms sports two intertwined eels ("anguilla" in Italian) which allude to one of the lake's typical products. However, authoritative sources make reference to one of the many ancient roman villas in the area known as *Angularia* for its location in a place where the coast forms an angle. In 1019 there was here only a military installation of the Anguillara family who, thanks to cruelty and prevarication, held on to the territory until the XI Century when the Orsini, who were no less arrogant, took over as is demonstrated by the graffiti in the cells of the prison once situated in the tower of the fortress which is today the seat of the local municipality and which towers over the Palazzo Baronale (XVI Century).

A view of Bracciano

Bracciano: frescoes in the apse of the church of San Liberato

Into the historic centre, still medieval in its appearance, one enters through XVI Century gates passing under an ashlered arch in which is set a clock. Of interest inside the **Church of Assunta**, rebuilt at the end of the XVIII Century, the painting representing the *Assunzione* by Girolamo Muziano (1528-1592) and the so called *Madonna di Roccamaggiore* of the XV Century. Also worthy of note is the **Church of San Biagio**, patron saint of the village, and, on the shores of the lake, that of **Santa Maria della Rana**, linked to a miracle: in 1976 the effigy of the Madonna kept there would appear to have moved its eyes. Between Bracciano and Anguillara, on the shores of the lake, one can visit the **Museo Storico dell'Aeronautica Militare** (Vigna di Valle) with original planes, prototypes and relics of our airforce from its beginnings to today. Proceeding in a clockwise direction we reach **Bracciano**, once inhabited by the Etruscans. During the ancient Roman period this small urban area, the small *Forum Clodii*, was in the vicinity of where there now is the **Church of San Liberato**, the bell tower of which – the oldest in Lazio (XI Century) and unique in its style – towers over the lake. The architectural complex, also dedicated to the saints Mark and Marcianus, is of great historico-artistic interest as it dates back to medieval times and shows clear signs of the presence of an earlier church, perhaps of the IX Century, as well as the remains of a Roman villa partly utilized for the portico. Inside, from the austerity of the stone and tufa, springs an unexpected patch of colour, the fresco of the absis (XV C.) representing the Madonna with child surrounded by putti and cornucopias. Also truly splendid are the gardens –

The Odescalchi Castle

Having passed, in dramatic circumstances, from the Prefects of Vico to the Orsini family in 1437, the ancient fortress was turned in to a splendid fortified castle by Napoleon Orsini and his son Gentil Virginio. Today it is one of the best examples of fortified military architecture in the country. Although the difference in style of the more ancient original late medieval "rocca" and the subsequent renaissance addition is evident, the whole, with its romantic mantle of ivy which changes colour with the seasons, is striking for its elegance and for the way in which it blends with its surroundings. Today the property of the Odescalchi family, the castle has an irregular quadrilateral shape and six imposing towers of which five are cylindrical and one square. The whole of the top of the castle has battlements. The rooms on the first floor are without doubt the most interesting, with frescoes and decorations which date back to the various periods of construction. In the **Camera Papalina** – where Pope Sixtus IV stayed when he fled from Rome in order to escape the plague – there are frescoes by Taddeo and Federico Zuccari (1561), and in the study next to it the *Storie di Alessandro Magno* and the *Amore e Psiche* are harmoniously alternated to decorations in the "grotesque" style. In hall V we find the **Ciclo delle Figure Femminili** by artists of the school of Antoniazzo Romano, to whom the great fresco with scenes depicting the life of Gentil Virginio Orsini, transported from the court-yard entrance hall where it originally was to the **Sala dei Trionfi di Caccia,** is attributed. Family history is also depicted in the works in the Hall of Isabella, where legend has it that this noble lady used to receive her lovers then to get rid of them by throwing them through a hatch and into the lake. On the floor above, one should visit **the Sala di Ercole** where the myth of this semi-god, symbol of the *virtus romana*, is depicted, and also the **Sala delle Armi** which contains splendid XV and XVI Century suits of tournament armour. Finally, one should take a walk on the battlements in order to enjoy the splendid view of the lake.

Taddeo Zuccari, frescoes and stucco-work in the Studiolo next to the Camera Papalina; at the sides of the coat of arms, the Allegory of Peace and Victory

Trevignano Romano

born between 1965 and 1975 of the good taste of the Counts Sanminiatelli and their architect Russell Page – with hedges of laurel and avenues of magnolia, rose gardens and borders with all manner of plants. But the true attraction is the **Castello Odescalchi** which dominates over the village and the lake. In the historic centre, where houses of the XV and XVI Century still survive, there are the **Church of Santa Maria Novella**, with its beautiful cloister of the XVI Century, and the **Chiesa Parrocchiale di Santo Stefano** with its baroque façade and XVI Century bell tower; it contains a painting by Jean Baptiste Wicar (1762-1834) known as the *Martirio di Santo Stefano*. We end our tour of the edge of the lake with **Trevignano Romano**, which stands on the sight of an ancient etrusco-roman centre which some experts consider to be the ancient Sabatia, and is not far from the still visible remains of the acqueduct which Emperor Trajan had built in 109 A.D. and which was subsequently restored by Pope Paul V. The history of this citadel, the fortress of which would seem to date back to the period of contrast between the powerful Prefects of Vico and Pope Innocent III, is also tied to the bloody battles between Pontifs and local lords. An aura of the past envelopes the historic centre with its lanes, small houses at the top of steep stairs, stamp sized courtyards, all leaving intact the original medieval structure of the borgo. Dominated by the emperious remains of the *Rocca Medioevale*, almost completely destroyed in the XV Century by the seige of the Borgias, is the **Church of Santa Maria Assunta** dated 1500 and extensively rebuilt in the XVII Century, in the apse of which there is a large fresco (1517) known as the *Transito della Madonna, l'Assunzione e l'Incoronazione*, the work of an artist belonging to the school of Raphael. In the **Palazzo Comunale**, which one reaches through the gates under the clock tower, there is a small museum which contains Etruscan funerary remains, and a little way further on there is the **Church of Santa Caterina** built using what was probably an ancient Roman building, still well preserved in parts.

> **The Apollinarian Thermal Baths**
> Dedicated to the god Apollo and famous in ancient roman times, they are situated between Bracciano and Trevignano in the locality of Vicovaro. In the last century, excavations brought to light walls and precious silver goblets (II and III Century A.D.) which are today at the Museo Nazionale Romano. The 48° Celsius waters contain bicarbonate and sulphate which make them particularly effective in the treatment of rheumatism. The baths are currently being refurbished.

The Caldara at Manziana

Continuing in the direction of the sea, we will come across a vast area where nature is undoubtedly dominant. Once, the Tolfa Sabatini and Ceriti mountains were covered by luxurious *Sylva Mantiana*, now only present in the **Macchia Grande di Manziana**, a protected oasis of 530 hectares, characterized by the presence of ancient oak trees, which includes part of the municipality of the same name at the foot of Monte Calvario (541 mts.). From here we can reach the unusual scenario of the **Monumento Naturale della Caldara**: here is the hot water pool which gives off sulphurous gas which has formed as a consequence of eruptive activity and, quite unexpected, a birch wood. As it is that from sulphur gas to hell the step is short, it is not surprising that the Etruscans should have thought that this was the home of the god of Hades, Mania, from whence the names Manziana and Monterano. The earliest information on Manziana, where Gustav King of Sweden often stayed as he was very interested in archaeology, go back to a *Castrum Sanctae Pupae* of the Prefects of Vico (late medieval period) which, in the early 1600's, was renamed *Castrum Mantianae* because of its forests.

Manziana

To be seen is the **Church of San Giovanni Battista** (XVI C.) designed by Ottaviano Nonni, better known as Il Mascherino, a pupil of Vignola, who was also author of the town plan.

Should we want to see suggestive landscapes where the silence and greenery of the woods echo centuries of history, we should not miss the opportunity of visiting, only a few kilometres away, the **Riserva Naturale di Monterano**, run by the municipality of Canale Monterano. Courses on the environment, summer camps, guided tours on foot, by bicycle or on horseback will allow us to best see this reserve which is not only interesting from a naturalistic point of view as it contains the ruins of the medieval Monterano which was abandoned after the pest of 1656 and then destroyed by the French in 1799. But history has also left signs of a more distant past, not far from the

Ruins near Canale Monterano

The Riserva di Canale Monterano

The place offers a varied landscape, from pastures where wild maremman horses and cows live, to the "forre", the geological formation typical of the Tuscia produced by the erosion of the tufa cliffs by the River Mignone and its confluents. The local climate produces a strange phenomenon, the cold of the lower areas produce conditions favourable to beech and maple trees which are normally to be found at higher levels, whilst in the areas more exposed to the sun we find arbutus berry, durmast, alder, poplar, weeping willows, hazelnuts and, in the undergrowth, holly, and even wild orchids. The animals which populate this area are wild boar, foxes, martens, hares, porcupines and wild cats. The shores of the Mignone River are instead populated by moorhens, coots and mallards, whilst the waters are populated by chubs and other fresh water fish.

ruins of the citadel there are an Etruscan necropolis (VIII-III Century B.C.), the Ponte del Diavolo (I Century A.D.) and the thermal baths of Stigliano.

Founded in the VI Century by woodcutters from Tuscany and Umbria, **Canale Monterano** has the *Fontana del Leone* by Bernini, once in ancient Monterano, and the *Chiesa dell'Assunta*, by Mattia de' Rossi, perhaps designed by Gian Lorenzo Bernini, inside which there is a wooden statue of the Madonna also from the dead citadel. But the true part of Maremma in Lazio starts starts with the *Tolfa Mountains* and continues into the province of Viterbo.

The scenery offered by these not so high mountains is unique (the highest, Monte delle Grazie is a mere 616 mts.) as they are one of the wildest and best preserved parts of Lazio, full of charm for their asperity but at once beautiful in their change of seasonal colours. The pastures, populated by the typical cows with lute shaped horns and by maremman horses, alternate with woods of chestnut, beech, oak and juniper, whilst in the undergrowth there are wild berries and aromatic herbs, as well as cyclamins, violets and orchids. Nor is wild-life less rich: heirs, boar, foxes, badgers, weasels, roe and hedgehogs inhabit the ground whilst in the air fly buzzards, kestrel and harrier eagles, a small rapacious bird which feeds on snakes. Typical of the area is the *buttero*, a sort of local cowboy who still lives according to past tradition, wearing leather thigh guards and boots, and always on horseback in order

The Thermal Baths of Stigliano

In the gardens of today's modern thermal baths, which utilize the sulphureous waters of the springs of Bagno Grande, Bagnarello and Fangaia, and which are used for the treatment of respiratory ailments, rheumatism and skin deseases, one can see the remains of a temple to Apollo and of the *Thermae Stygianae* which date back to about two thousand years ago and which were discovered by chance in 1928.

The produce of the woods and ancient recipes

The area of the Tolfa Mountains has some interesting gastronomic proposals, from the fragrant wholesome bread which marries so well with the local ham and cheeses, to the products of the woods. In autumn there are blackberries, arbutus berries and chest nuts, as well as excellent mushrooms and, when in season, that precious ingredient of so many recipes which is truffle. One should try even the most simple of the area's traditional cuisine, 'acquacotta', and pasta with beans are another must.

Pastures in the mountains near Tolfa

Tolfa: the "rocca" Frangipane

to follow and control his herds. What better way of getting to know the area than a horse ride along the routes indicated by the "butteri"?

Two are the towns to be visited in this area which has been inhabited since prehistoric times and where the many Etruscan centres are very well documented. The birth of **Tolfa** dates back to the period of the terrible saracen sieges (IX C.) which forced the people to take refuge on inland heights, the ruins of the *Rocca Frangipane* are clear evidence of this. But the economic growth of this town is tied to the discovery of allum (1462), a chemical which is indispensable for the tawing of leather and the dying of cloth. We could visit the Palazzo Comunale – originally designed to be a diocesan seminary – seat of the *Museo Civico* in which there are many archaeological remains from different periods: Etruscan, Roman, medieval. Further, there are the *Convento dei Cappuccini* (XVI C.) with its cloister so beautiful in its simplicity, the *Collegiata di Sant'Egidio* at the foot of the "rocca", which was restructured and dedicated to its patron in the middle of the XVII Century and where we can see paintings by Pastura (XV-XVI C.) and by Andrea Camassei (XVII C.), and finally the *Church of the Madonna della Sughera*. Next door to Tolfa is **Allumiere**, which owes its name and birth to Giovanni da Castro's discovery: allum. Thanks to this mineral, exported to all of western Europe via Civitavecchia harbour, it was possible to finance the war against the Turks. Of interest is the *Palazzo Co-*

> **On the Tolfa Mountains**
> Countless are the possibilities of excursions for those who love birdwatching, trekking and horse riding and, above all, want to forget hectic city life, smog and noise. One can follow naturalistic-archeological itineraries such as the **Sentiero del Biancone** South of Tolfa, where in summer one can see harrier eagles, or the **Vie dell'Acqua** itinerary, along which one can meet kingfishers, grey herons and brown kites in summer, or the **Sentiero dei Ginepri** where one can see an interesting environmental system which extends itself over an area of 10 hectares and is populated by junipers, and various types of moss and lichen.

> **Excursions on horse back**
> There are many horse riding centres in the area: at Anguillara, *I Due Laghi*, between Bracciano and Martignano (tel. 06/9969686); at Bracciano, the *Centro Ippico Macchia Grande* (tel. 06/9986392); at Canale Monterano, the *Associazione Equestre Caino* (tel. 06/9964137), the *Associazione Butteri Canale Monterano* (tel. 06/9963249), and the *Associazione Nazionale dei Butteri della Maremma Laziale* (tel. 06/99838416) with offices at Montevirginio; at Tolfa, the *Centro Natura e Cavallo* (tel. 0766/570202) which organizes horse trekking and courses in maremman style horse riding, and the *Cooperativa Monti della Tolfa* (tel. 0766/93524). Another two centres are the *Associazione Sportiva il Branco* in Fregene (tel. 06/6650689) and the *Centro Ippico Eldorado* at Fiumicino (tel. 06/6523366).
> Dal 1282 si svolge a Tolfa il Torneo dei Butteri (inizio agosto-ferragosto) che comprende gare ed esibizioni di butteri provenienti da diverse regioni.

munale, finished in 1580, which contains the *Museo Civico* with an archaeological and a naturalistic section. Next to it is the **Chiesa Camerale** which contains two beautiful paintings: the *Madonna dell'Assunta* and *San Giovanni Battista*. And finally a true jewel is the beech wood on the North-East of the citadel, near the quarries, scattered all over the place, are the archaeological remains of a prehistoric village.

As we go towards the sea the landscape changes, urban centres are more frequent, but along the coast it is still possible to find oasis and protect-

Kantharos kept in the museo Civico di Tolfa

Piazza della Repubblica at Allumiere

Civitavecchia: the Forte Michelangelo

The Pallio delle Contrade at Allumiere

The event takes place on the Saturday and Sunday after Ferragosto (in mid-August). There is a parade in XVI Century costumes and the "palio" where the six "rioni" or neighbourhhoods of the citadel, the colours of which are born by donkeys ridden bare-back, challenge each other to a race on horseback. The occasion is made all the more festive because there is music and because the various "rioni" offer all kinds of deliscious snacks.

ed areas which allow one to enjoy the coast. It is difficult to imagine that so close to Rome there can be places such as the *Oasis of Macchiatonda*, the *Natural Monument of Torre Flavia*, the oasis of the *Bosco di Palo* and of *Macchiagrande* and, South of Rome, the *Tor Caldara Reserve* and of *Villa Borghese at Nettuno* (closed to the public) and, finally *Torre Astura*.

Let us then start at **Civitavecchia**, the harbour of which, with a marina and a commercial and industrial section of international importance, has taken up an important role in maritime Europe for its position and climate. It was here that in the II Century A.D. *Centumcellae*, so called for the many bays the coast offered ships protection in, developed. In 813 A.D. it was destroyed by the

The pleasure marina

Saracens and its people fled to the Tolfa Mountains where they founded the villages of *Leopoli* and then *Cencelle*. Legend has it that, having beaten the Saracens in 889, the popular assembly, meeting under a giant oak, decided to return to the ancient city thanks to the incitement of an old seaman called Leandro, whose *optimum consilium* has come to posterity on the emblem of the city: an oak tree on a blue background with the letters O.C. The old *Centumcellae* thus became *Civitas Vetula*, from whence Civitavecchia. Closely tied to the history of this harbour is that of the Fortezza, the most significant edifice in the city, begun by Donato Bramante for Julius II in the early 1500's and finished mid-century by Antonio da Sangallo the Younger. In the middle of the XVII Century Pope Alexander VII ordered Gian Lorenzo Bernini to build a six nave arsenal from which six ships could be launched at the same time. A grandiose building of considerable originality, it was alas destroyed during the last war. It was this selfsame building which was later to inspire the great architect in his conception of the colonnade of Saint Peter's Square, as a symbol indicating how the Church of Peter was a port in which souls could take refuge. Instead, according to an unconfirmed tradition, the great octagonal keep is attributed to Michelangelo Buonarroti.

Of interest is the **Cathedral of San Francesco d'Assisi** (XVII C.) where there is the *Natività di Nostro Signore* attributed to Domenichino (1581-1641) and, in the medieval "borgo", the **Church of Santa Maria dell'Orazione e della Morte**, built in the XVII Century and restructured in the XVIII Century, which contains parts of the frescos known as *Anime del*

The Padellone

At Civitavecchia on the feast-day of Ferragosto in mid-August there are the festivities in memory of the victorious resistence to Saracen attacks and for the birth of the city, with an enormous fry-up of fish cooked in the central square in a giant sized pan (*padellone*). As well as eating the fish, one should not miss tasting the delicious local cakes: *nociata, pangiallo, tozzetti* and *torrone*. And if one is there at Easter, one should not miss the soft *pizza pasquale*.

Civitavecchia Harbour

In 106 A.D. Emperor Trajan built a new harbour at Capo Linaro in order to substitute those of Ostia and Anzio which were both subject to constant silting up. The task was assigned to the famous architect Apollodorus of Damascus and, in order to follow the works more closely, the emperor built a grandious villa nearby, from whence also the historian Plinius the Younger was able to follow the construction which he then recorded in his writings. Archaeologists think that the remains of the villa are to be found in the area of excavation of the **Terme Taurine** which were built at the same time as the harbour. One of the key strongholds against Saracen invasions, the harbour underwent numerous processes of modernization as of the XVI Century, at the hands of Pope Julius II. The most famous architects of the time, amongst which Donato Bramante, put their hand to the task. During World War II the port, but for the ancient Roman basin (which is today a pleasure marina) and the Lazzareto harbour wall, was almost completely destroyed.

Artichokes

Recommended since the XVI Century as being diuretic and aphrodisiacal and, more recently, as being beneficial to the circulation of the blood and to the liver, the "romanesque artichoke" cultivated in the area of Ladispoli and Cerveteri is truly delicious. The two famous recipes for its preparation are "*carciofi alla romana*" with parsley, a particular local mint, garlic, lemon juice and olive oil, and the deep-fried "*carciofi alla giudia*" which are a real gastronomic delight. Since 1950, at Ladispoli there is the "*sagra del carciofo*" which celebrates this delicious vegetable.

Purgatorio by Errante da Trapani (1788), the two VII Century wooden statues *Gesù Crocifisso* and *Gesù Risorto*, as well as the remains of its patron saint Firmina. Worthy of mention are also the **Church of Santa Maria Maris Stella** with its painting the *Adorazione dei Pastori* of the Cinquecento, and the **Church of the Santissimi Martiri Giapponesi** (1870), dedicated to the franciscans martyred at Nagasaki, with frescos and mosaics by the painter Lucas Ha Segawa.

Continuing down the coast along beaches and rocky bays we reach **Santa Marinella**, so called after the young martyr saint Marina to whom the Basilian monks, who in the year 1000 gave birth to a village there, were devoted. Today this is one of the most frequented seaside resorts in the province thanks also to the mild climate it has because of its vicinity to the Tolfa Mountains. Further along the Aurelia we come across **Ladispoli**, founded by Prince Ladislao Odescalchi in 1890, the beaches of which are known for their therapeutic qualities as its volcanic sands are excellent for treating rheumatism and arthritis.

Between these two seaside resorts we find the *Riserva Naturale di Macchiatonda* (information on visits at the centre inside the Castello di Santa Severa) and the *Monumento Naturale di Torre Flavia*, true paradises for those who love birdwatching. At Macchiatonda there are special itineraries with huts from which to watch about 214 species of birds, amongst which wild ducks, cormorans, oyster catchers, and rare birds such as the bittern and the gannet. Torre Flavia, the name of which derives from a perhaps medieval coastal sighting tower which Cardinal Flavio Orsini had restored in the 1500's, is intriguing for its position which, due to the advancement of the sea, is now near to a 100 mts. from shore so as to make it look as if it rises magically out of the waves.

Where to more - pleasure marinas

CIVITAVECCHIA:
Capitaneria di Porto di Civitavecchia (Civitavecchia harbour master's office) tel. 0766/35993
SANTA MARINELLA:
tel. 0766511834
LADISPOLI:
tel. 0699220174
RIVA DI TRAIANO:
private marina
FIUMICINO:
Capitaneria di Porto di Roma (Rome harbour master's)
ANZIO AND NETTUNO:
tel. 069846235

Ladispoli, in the background the Oasi di Palo

Positioning oneself in the beds of rushes and fields of saltwort one can hope to see coral gulls, coots, snipe, marsh-harrier and other birds which have their natural habitat here. Past Ladispoli we find the ***Oasi Faunistica di Palo***, 140 hectares of mediterranean macchia with turkey oak, holm oak, ash and sessile oak. It is a public park as well as a WWF bird sanctuary and contains a caravaning and camping sight. Porcupines, weasels and birds such as the hoopoe and tawny owl live in this surviving corner of forest where there are also swamp tortoises and Hermann turtles. The WWF has organized didactic itineraries and a museum for the purpose of initiating primary school children to the love and respect of nature. Further down the coast is **Fregene**, already chosen by the ancient Romans as long ago as 245 B.C. as a place where to build their villas, with its splendid pine groves planted by Pope Clement IX in 1667 in order to protect the coastline from wind and, since 1920, a national monument. Between this locality and Focene there is another area under the tutelage of the WWF, the ***Oasi di Macchiagrande***, so close to Fiumicino airport that the planes almost touch it when landing but without perturbing its inhabitants, perhaps because they too are winged: white and red herons, teal, bee-eaters, red kites, large areas of grassland, forest and mediterranean macchia. We are by now at the doors of Rome, the echos of which we can hear from afar as we progress down the last tract of coast of the province where, once again, history and nature live together in charming harmony. In the middle of the 1800's one of the many men of letters taken by Rome, Ferdinand Gregorovius, in his work *Passeggiate per l'Italia*, spoke of the area around the villa of the Borghese Prince, now the natural reserve of ***Tor Caldara*** in the municipality of Anzio and comprising 44 klms of coast line which have been saved from the onslaught of cement, as being populated by oak, cork trees and white myrtle. Certainly it is no longer the coast line that the German writer was able to admire, but the thick holm oak and cork tree forests, the mediterranean macchia, the little lakes generated by sulphurous springs and the rocks of tufa stone where wild birds nest all contribute to keeping alive a truly extraordinary landscape. Finally, we reach ***Torre Astura***, southernmost limb of the province of Rome inside one of the Ministry of Defence's shooting ranges and from whence we can turn back in order to start our archaeologico-monumental itinerary.

The archaeological monumental itinerary

Nettuno: Torre Astura

Situated close to the estuary of the River Astura, the tower by the same name, situated where once the Volsci had a harbour, is one of the many towers built along our coasts as of the IX Century in order to contrast the invading Saracens. It was here that the unlucky Corradino di Svevia took refuge and, betrayed by Giovanni Frangipane, was captured and consigned to Carlo D'Angiò who had him decapitated (1268). Almost entirely under sand one can also see the remains of an ancient Roman rural villa dating back to the republican period part of which is on dry land and part insular, the two parts being connected by an aqueduct bridge. About sixty centimetres underwater one can also clearly see a complex of fish-breeding basins and passages. The historian Plutarc deemed it the place where Cicero met his end whilst in fact he died in Gaeta. This part of the coast is often termed Coast of the Caesers or Aeneas' Riviera, as there are many interesting roman and pre-roman archeological remains there. *Torre Astura* is within the precincts of **Nettuno**, the original nucleus of which, according to a somewhat intriguing hypothesis, is the mythical Neptunia dedicated to the god of the sea and now under water but visible in part at low tide. However, today's town rises upon the ruins of Antium (IX-VIII Century B.C.), a Volscian city which the ancient Romans chose as a seaside resort as, in the words of Cicero, "no place is calmer, cooler and more pleasant". Undoubtedly of interest is a visit to the *Antiquarium Comunale* which contains findings

The forte Sangallo at Nettuno

The Imperial Villa and Anzio lighthouse

from the various civilizations which have in time lived in the area. The ancient Roman period then gave way to later ages, as the medieval borgo and Sangallo fortress testify. In the borgo there are the *Palazzo Baronale* with the the Orsini coat of arms in marble – a rampant lion and a rose – the *Palazzo Pamphili*, now *Borghese* (1650) and the *Collegiata di San Giovanni Battista ed Evangelista* (1738-1748) which substituted an older church in turn built on the ruins of a temple to Neptune. A prototype of renaissance military architecture for its admirable balance between beauty and functionality is the *Forte Sangallo* built by Alexander VI Borgia (1501-1503) on a cliff over the sea. Finally, a testament to more recent history is the *American Memorial Cemetry*, the American War Cemetry which contains the bodies of soldiers who died in the landings at Anzio, in Sicily, at Salerno and in the advance to the North. A short distance away there is also the British War Cemetery. Next to Nettuno, which has a 150,000 m² marina, **Anzio** too vaunts mythical origins. Legend relates that it was founded by Antheus, son of Ulysses and the sorceress Circe. It is however certain that the citadel was conquered by the Volsci in the V Century B.C. and later by the Romans who destroyed and rebuilt it. Here were born the emperors Caligula and Nero, who had a grandiose villa built on a drop over the sea, the imposing ruins of which can be seen from the beach and from above. It was here that some true masterpieces of sculpture such as the *Apollo del Belvedere*, now in the Vatican Museum, and the *Fanciulla d'Anzio*, kept in the Museo Nazionale Romano, were found. Also of great interest is Nero's port.

However, the places which most evoke history and legend are **Ardea**, built on the sight of the city of the Rutuli with the same name, and Pratica di Mare, the ancient *Lavinium*, in the municipality of Pomezia, where Aeneas, the Trojan hero sung by Virgil in the *Aenead*, landed, and whose progeny gave birth to Rome.

Anzio Harbour

The original harbour, built by Nero and well known until medieval times, was situated North-West of the present harbour built by Pope Innocent XII (1691-1700), the construction of which caused the definitive silting up of the old one. It is connected to numerous events in history: in 538 A.D., during the gothico-byzantine war, all sea traffic was rerouted there due to the occupation of *Portus* and, in 1190, the English King Richard Lionheart passed by on his way to Palestine. Today the harbour is frequented by pleasure boats and racing yachts, it is where one takes the ferry to the Pontine Islands (tel. 06/9845083-9845004), and at the local yacht clubs one can go sailing and windsurfing.

Ardea and its legends

Myth, which probably reflects a moment of Greek colonization, has it that Jove fell in love with the King of Argus's daughter Danae and that in order to have her he turned himself into a rainfall of gold. It was thus that Perseus was born, but the king had both mother and child put to sea in a wooden arc which the waves luckily brought to rest on the italic shores. It was here that two Rutulian fishermen found them and took them to their king, Pilumnus, who married Danae and founded Ardea with her. One of the descendants of Danae was to be Turnus the unfortunate antagonist of Aeneas who took from him both his spouse and his life. It was with him that the history of ancient Ardea came to an end, the burning of which was to inspire Ovid to write about another legend. In his *Metamorphosis* he wrote: "from amidst the rubble, seen then for the first time, a bird sets off in flight and, beating its wings, shakes off the ashes". The bird, symbol of the burnt but not destroyed city is, in reality, the Ardea Cinerea or grey heron, the swamp-land bird of majestic flight which is the symbol of today's municipality. The last legend, in terms of time, relates that in the Palazzo Sforza Cesarini (XV C.) which was seriously damaged by bombings during World War II, there is the ghost of Ludovico Colonna who was stabbed to death by his brother in law in 1436.

A very powerful people, the Rutuli also dominated over Anzio, Satrico and Lavinio and were in contact with the Etruscans. Amongst the cities which promoted the Latin League for the purpose of contrasting the power of Rome (V Century B.C.) was Ardea, which later joined Rome in its fight against the Volsci and the Gauls. There are remains, only in part accessible, which testify to this period in the historic centre of the city such as the archaic fortifications of the ***Acropoli***, of the ***Civita Vecchia*** and of the ***Casalazzara***, an important example of defensive structures, the remains of the IV Century city walls which were in part restructured in the Renaissance, and four of the temples amongst the many we know existed there. These remains are all the more important in that Ardea is the only example of urban structure extant in Lazio. The ***Church of Santa Marina***, of the frescos of which very little alas remains, is instead medieval. To the saint is also dedicated a fountain of the Seicento with an acephalous statue representing her and an inscription which defines her "goddess" as demonstration of the fact that Christian cult is born of pagan traditions hard to suppress, given that Marina is the appellative of Venus the goddess born of the sea. Also of the XII Century is the ***Church of San Pietro***, almost entirely rebuilt in the last

Giacomo Manzù, Ribbon (silver, 1973), Ardea, Museo Manzù

Century with the exception of the marble doorposts (II Century A.D.) and the frescoes inside (XV Century), whilst the font and tabernacle are by Giacomo Manzù. To the great sculptor, who died in 1991, is dedicated the *Museo Manzù* with 462 works the fruit of the various techniques used by him between 1950 and 1970. Outside the town one can admire, alas only from afar, the *Torre di San Lorenzo*. Situated inside the grounds of a farm the property of the duchi Cesarini, it is a guard tower, nick named "la Pomposa" (the pompous) by pirates for its beauty, built in the second half of the 1500's and perhaps designed by Michelangelo. Nearby there are the *Giardini della Landriana,* built in the Seventies by the English landscape architect Russell Page and comprising over ten hectares of gardens, lawns, avenues, woods, valleys, and lakes with heaths, olive, orange and apple groves, and rose gardens. In the municipality of **Pomezia**, born of the reclaiming of the Agro Romano once a swamp (1938), and today one of the few industrial centres of the province, is the "borgo" of *Pratica di Mare*, built upon the acropolis of ancient *Lavinium*, probably founded in the XII Century B.C. in honour of Lavinia, Aeneas' second wife and soon to become an important religious centre as testifies the *Santuario delle XIII Are* and the *Heeroon di Enea*. The sanctuary, only living example of Italic religion, was very important in cohesing the peoples who joined the Latin League. The thirteen altars in tufa stone, once painted, were built between the VI and IV Century B.C. Approximately 100 mts East is the Heeroon, a sepulcral monument said to be the tomb of Aeneas and venerated already in the VI Century B.C. In this archaeological area we can also admire the *Church of the Madonnella* or *Santa Maria delle Vigne,* an enchanting example of paleochristian architecture (VI Century) built upon the ruins of an ancient Roman villa.

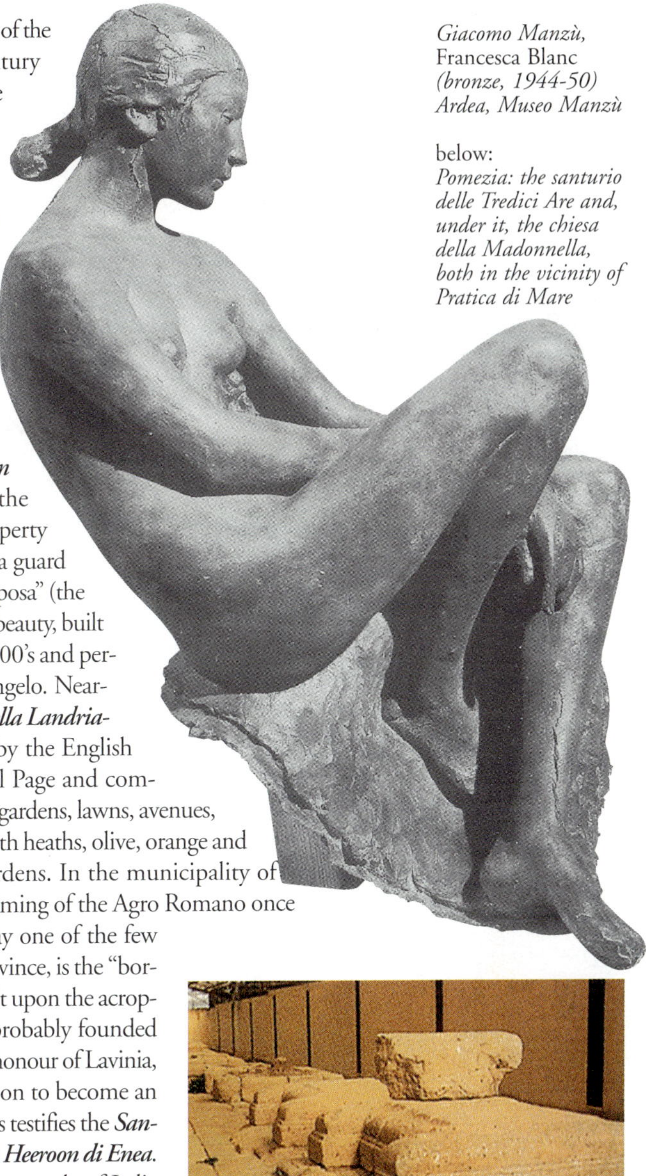

Giacomo Manzù, Francesca Blanc *(bronze, 1944-50) Ardea, Museo Manzù*

below:
Pomezia: the santurio delle Tredici Are and, under it, the chiesa della Madonnella, both in the vicinity of Pratica di Mare

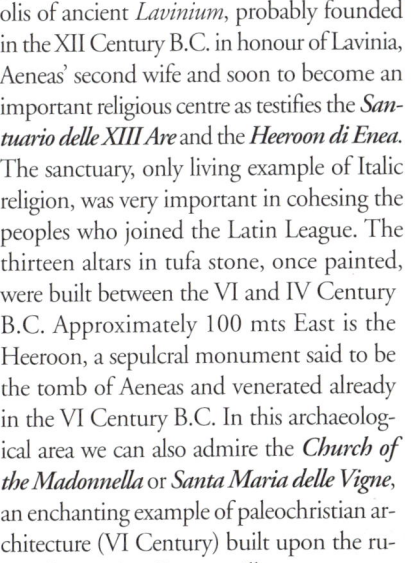

Fiumicino: the estuary of the Fossa Traiana at sunset

Fiumicino: the church of Santa Maria della Salute

Fiumicino too, which owes its notoriety to the presence of Leonardo da Vinci Airport, has roman origins. In order to cope with the shortcomings of the port of Ostia, Emperor Augustus thought of building another farther North, then actually built by his successor Claudius (42-54 A.D.) and around which the town of *Portus* was born. We have been able to learn a lot about what this area was like between the II and IV Century A.D. thanks to the findings at the necropolis in the nearby Isola Sacra, where there are about a 100 well preserved tombs. In modern Fiumicino, the nucleus of which was designed by Valadier in 1822 but which was only realized in 1940 by an unknown architect, there are the **Basilica di Sant'Ippolito** (XIII C.) of which only the romanesque bell tower remains, the **Church of Santissimo Crocefisso** at Isola Sacra and the **Church of Santa Maria della Salute** with an interesting fresco of the XIX Century which portrays the harbour as it was at that time. A must is a visit to the **Museo delle Navi Romane**.

As we head North from Fiumicino we come into contact with the mysterious Etruscan civilization. Indeed, along the coast there used to be the ports of the powerful city of Caere, the forerunner of today's Cerveteri: *Alsium*, where there is now Palo, *Pyrgi*, todays' Santa Severa, and *Punicum*, where today stands Santa Marinella. Near *Alsium* have been found the remains of a villa of the imperial period with marbles and polichrome

The Museum and the Archaeological Park

The remains of the city of **Portus** and of the Claudian and Trajan ports are to be found behind the **Museo delle Navi Romane** in the area of Fiumicino Airport. This small museum of ancient Roman ships contains four ancient Roman vessels of the III-IV Century A.D., reliefs representing harbour scenes and various other objects of the time, as well as a fully equipped boat made in oak wood known as the **Barca del Pescatore**. In visiting the 300 hectare archaeological park one will be able to see the remains of the enormous artficial harbour built by Claudius and finished by Nero in 64 A.D.. Claudius's harbour was built in a very short time but, as had been forseen by experts of the time, it soon silted up to the extent that, fifty years later, Trajan built his famous hexagonal inland harbour connected to the sea by canals and capable of containing as many as twohundred large ships, which was in use right up until the end of the empire. Trajan's harbour is situated on private property and visiting it is only possible by guided tour. It too is now silted up and so it is only possible to see the basin and the everian warehouses.

The interior of the museo delle Navi

mosaics, and statues of Mercury, Cupid and the philosopher Seneca and, close by, the sepulcral areas of Monteroni and Casali Vaccina, perhaps the city's necropolis. Carrying on up the Via Aurelia we reach the *Castello di Santa Severa*, in the municipality of Santa Marinella, right on the sea and situated within the archaeological area of *Pyrgi*, an important commercial harbour frequented by Greek and Phoenician ships. Here there was also an ancient sanctuary from whence have come the famous golden plates with Etruscan and Punic inscriptions (500 B.C.) which have proved of great importance for the understanding of the Etruscan language, and which are now kept at the Museum of Villa Giulia in Rome. The castle, called after the martyr Se-

The castle at Santa Severa

The Odescalchi Castle at Santa Marinella

vera who was buried close by the sea in 298 A.D., was built in the XIV Century, whilst the Norman Tower dates back to the XI Century. Inside it there is a pretty medieval and renaissance "borgo" set in time, with its cistern, mill and the XV Century *Chiesa-Battistero* with fresco by pupils of Antoniazzo Romano. Of interest is a visit to the *Museo Civico Archeologico*, at the entrance to the castle, which contains findings and documentation from the excavations of the Etruscan sanctuary, a copy of the gold plates, archaeological findings from the sea, as well as reconstructions and didactic materials which help us understand what life was like at the time. A few kilometres further on we reach **Santa Marinella**, once the ancient *Punicum*, the name of which would seem to derive from *malum punicum* which in Latin

Two attractive "borghi"

Ceri is today an attractive medieval "borgo" which, encased in its battlements and from the height of a tufa rock spur surrounded by woods and vineyards, looks down upon the valley of the Sanguinara. The gates to the citadel carry a marble inscription put there by the Torlonia family (1883) which erroneously identifies it with the ancient citadel of *Caere*. Of interest are the XIII Century castle and the **Parrocchiale dell'Immacolata Concezione** which contains the spoils of the martyred Pope Felix II and, even if changed in time, contains some fine XII Century frescoes. A true oasis of silence is **Sasso**, lost in greenery amongst trees and pastures. A mere handful of houses around a piazza, the Corte of the fortified Palazzo Baronale, and a church with sloping roof and steeple dedicated to the Holy Cross, it is the personification of that poem which all Italians have studied at school, *Rio Bo*. Perhaps it was indeed this protovillanovian centre that was in origin *Caere*.

Gate and battlements of the "borgo" of Ceri

means pomegranate. Here, in roman times there was a great seaside villa called Ulpiano from the name of the presumed owner (III C.) where statues and mosaics have been found. There are also remains in the gardens of the **Castello Odescalchi** which looks over the marina and has been transformed from castle into a princely home. Leaving the Via Aurelia, we head towards **Cerveteri** – the fulcrum of Etruscan civilization – which rises upon a tufa rock. *Kysry* for the Etruscans, *Agylla* for the Greeks and *Caere* for the Romans, the city was one of the most populous of the time, an important cultural and commercial centre capable, in alliance with Carthage, of contending the Greeks their dominance of the Tyrrenian sea. Its annexation to Rome in 273 B.C., Saracen incursions, malaria determined an irreversible crisis which forced the population to move to what is today *Ceri*, then called *Caere Nova*, whilst the abandoned city was renamed *Caere Vetus* which gave origin to the current name of Cerveteri. Excavation of the Etruscan city began in the 1800's and led to the discovery of the first tombs in the **Necropoli of the Banditaccia** very close to Cerveteri itself. However, it was only at the beginning of the 1900's that excavations became systematic, bringing to light tombs and materials from the villanovian period (IX-VIII Century B.C.) through to Roman times and in particular the VII and VI Century. Most of the findings are in the Vatican Museo Etrusco Gregoriano in Rome, in the museum at Villa Giulia and, in part, in the **Museo Nazionale Cerite**, in the XIII Century **Rocca** of palazzo Ruspoli in the heart of the city. Funerary apparels including bronzes, pottery, both local and Greek ceramics, jewels, urns and amphoras, can be seen in the museum but it is also worth paying a visit to the nearby necropolis with the large tumulus tombs laid out in such a way as to seem to conform to some kind of city plan so as to create the impression that the city of the dead is very similar to that of the living. On the square of the Rocca there is the modern **Church of Santa Maria**, built on the ruins of a previous romanesque church (XII C.) and inside which there are a renaissance altar (XII C.), a XVI Century fresco of the school of Perin del Vaga and a painting by

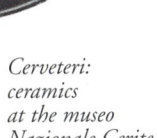

Cerveteri: ceramics at the museo Nazionale Cerite

Cerveteri: etruscan necropolis

The Necropolis of the Banditaccia

The most ancient are the sepulchral and the well tombs, followed by the chamber tombs surmounted by mounds of earth and lastly, in terms of time, the hypogean tombs similar to the houses of the living. Of particular interest are the Tomb of the Capitelli (VII Century B.C.), that of the Letti Funebri/Funeral Beds (VII-V Century B.C.) with beds shaped like an arc cut from the stone and upon which the bodies of the dead were laid, and the contemporary tombs of the Vasi Greci/Greek Vases, and of the Capanna/Hut shaped

The interior of a tomb

like a hut, as well as the famous tomb of the Rilievi/Reliefs (IV-II Century B.C.) which belonged to the Matuna family which contains household implements, weapons, animals and figures of the world beyond made in painted stucco work. There are also the tomb of the Scudi/Shields and that of the Sedie/Chairs, so called because of the drawings it contains, that of the Sarcofagi/Sarcophaguses (IV-I Century B.C.) which used to contain four alabaster sarcophaguses, and those of the Triclinio/Triclinium and of the Iscrizioni/Inscriptions, with many inscriptions in both Etruscan and Latin. Lastly, in the locality of Sorbò, one kilometre South-East of Cerveteri, there is the tomb of the Regolini-Galassi (VII C.) In part cut out of tufa rock.

The Wine of Cerveteri

Already the Etruscans new and appreciated the art of making wine which the Romans were also quick to learn. In an epigram, the poet Marzialus called for the planting of the vines of *Caere*, as its wine was lauded for its quality. "Cerveteri" is D.O.C. wine (a wine subject to controlled origin and denomination) which comes from the vineyards of Cerveteri, Ladispoli, Santa Marinella, Civitavecchia, but also from Tolfa, Allumiere, Anguillara and Trevignano. There is a dry sparkling or sweet white, and a red wine as well as a rosé and so it can be served with a variety of dishes. The white is particularly good with fish from the sea or the lake and with the typical local artichokes. The red is best served with first courses with mushrooms or truffles or with the cured meats of Tolfa. The sweet white is perfect with the local home made cakes. On the last Sunday of August there is the *Sagra dell'Uva*, during which grapes and wine are distributed and when there are traditional games and fire-works.

Lorenzo da Viterbo, the *Madonna col Bambino e i Santi Michele e Pietro* dated 1472. We end our itinerary with **Civitavecchia**, where we can vist the *Museo Archeologico Nazionale* in the Guarnigione Pontificia Palace (XVIII C.) which contains findings from the port, the Villa Ulpiano and the necropolis at Scaglia, Acque Tauri and Allumiere, and the *Terme Taurine or di Traiano*, a complex of Roman buildings the name of which comes from a legend: Jupiter, having turned himself into a bull (taurus), beat his hooves on the ground and gave birth to a spring in this self same place.

The Thermal Baths

For the ancient Romans they were places where one took care of one's health but also places where to meet and enjoy oneself. The **Terme Taurine** were built upon a preceding structure which, as always, had a *tepidarium, frigidarium* and *calidarium*. This last is of particular interest given that it has a basilica shaped structure with nine marble pools set around a central one, and travertine columns. The constructions of the imperial period, North-East of the preceding ones, are much larger in size, are richly decorated and have a library with twelve marble columns and niches which contained bookcases. The Terme della Ficoncella – about five kilometres from Civitavecchia – are instead modern and have waters with sulphuro-alcaline-terrous qualities.

The religious itinerary

Our final proposal is for a spiritual itinerary which, covering the same areas as the others, is directed at sacred places which have a particular atmosphere about them either for their setting or for their history. Between Canale Monterano and Montevirginio, in the quiet of the woods, there is the *Eremo di Montevirginio* (1651-1668) built by Virginio Orsini, son of the duke by the same name and a carmelite monk. An imposing rectangular building, the hermitage had in its basements a cellar, an oven, laboratories and a carpentry shop, and was soon to become a flourishing farm which also produced a wine of such quality as to be cited by Sante Lanciero, Pope Paul III's wine expert, who wrote of it in his book *Vini d'Italia* remarking on its violet aroma and ruby colour. Today's production is however limited to the small community of friars' needs. In the area of Tolfa we instead find the **Church of the Madonna della Sughera,** which we reach passing by the convent of the Capuchin monks, the contruction of which is tied to a miracle. It is told that in 1051 two hunters saw an icon of the Madonna with child on cork tree. They took it to the Church of the Misericordia but it disappeared and reappeared on the tree. Having heard of this, Agostino Chigi, who had the mining concession for allum in the area, had the church and the convent built in order to give custody to the sacred image. But in 1552 a murder was committed in the sanctuary so that for six years it was closed. In 1799, having become the local French military headquarters, the church was used as a prison for the insurgent people of Tolfa who were then shot outside it. The altar complex created to contain the miraculous icon is impressive but the icon disappeared forever at the time of the French occupation. On the road to Allumiere, in the charming if aggressive scenario of the Tolfa Mountains, we come across the **Church of the Madonna di Cibona** (1647), it too tied to the local mining industry in that it was built by another concessionaire in order to give custody to another miraculous image of the Madonna of the XVI Century. The church and convent, once a sober and harmonious place which gave lodgings to the hermits of Monte Senario, began its decline with the French siege of 1798-99 and is now totally abandoned. Always at Allumiere, there are also the *Eremo della Trinità* and the *Santuario della Madonna delle Grazie.* Amidst chestnut trees and oaks is the hermitage, probably built upon the remains of an ancient roman villa, which tradition has it hosted Saint Augustine who is said to have written *De Trinitate* there. It is the most ancient of sanctuaries in the area (IX C.), rebuilt in the XV Century but closed two centuries later despite the fact that there was still a hermit living there. In 1818 it was abandoned definitively. And finally the *Santuario della Madonna delle Grazie* appears before us against a rock in the Parco della Rimembranza. In origin it was one of a number of small chapels dedicated to the veneration of the Virgin

and built near the allum mines, but soon it developed considerably to be transformed in the XVII Century upon occasion of the transfer of the Madonna. Recently restored, the hermitage has become a diocesan sanctuary and the object of pilgrimages, also due to the incoronation of the image of the Virgin by Pope John Paul II in 1986.

We will conclude our itinerary with the *Santuario di Nostra Signora delle Grazie e di Maria Goretti* at Nettuno, close by the sea. The image of the Madonna here worshipped is tied to legend: right in the middle of Henry VIII of England's iconoclastic persecution, the ship sailing to Naples which had onboard and was carrying to safety the sacred images of the Virgin, Saint Rocco and Saint Sebastian met a storm in the vicinity of Nettuno but came out of it unscathed. The seamen, out of gratitude to these sacred images, decided to give them over to the custody of the local people who put them in the Church of the Annunziata and later transferred them to the Sanctuary of the Madonna delle Grazie. Here rests Maria Goretti, the 12 year old girl killed during an attempt at violence and for her sacrifice sanctified.

In the preceding page, above: Canale Monterano: ancient walls in the vicinity of Montevirginio

below: Allumiere: Hermitage of the Trinità

The imposing façade of the Santuario di Nostra Signora delle Grazie at Nettuno

Along the meanderings of the Tiber

The Tiber in the vicinity of Nazzano

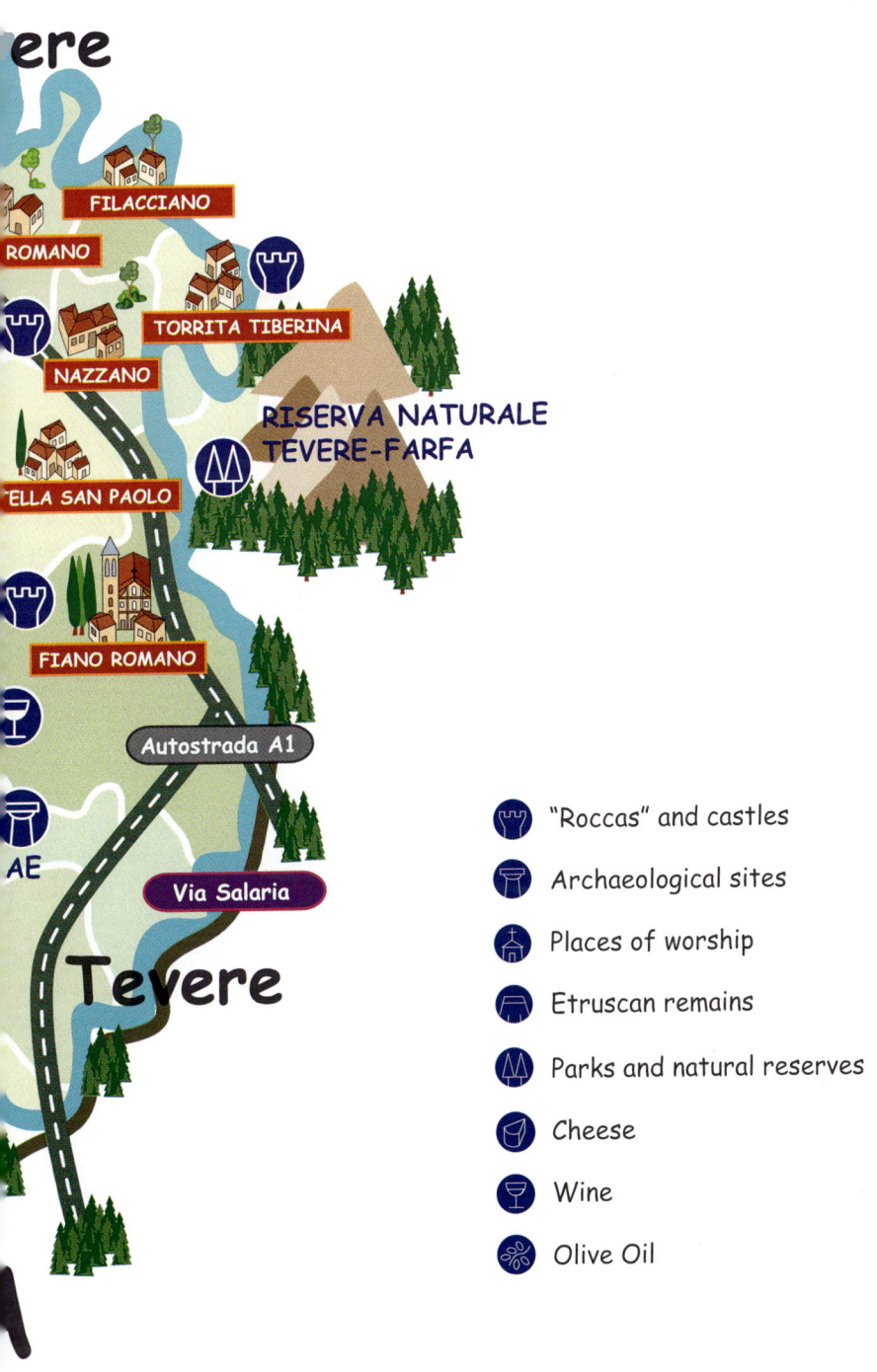

Along the meanderings of the Tiber

We leave lake Bracciano behind us and go East into the valley of the Tiber where the typical colour is green: green are the natural reserves it hosts, green the waters of the river which cross it, even if in history it has always been called the "blond Tiber". Cited by Virgil in the *Aeneid*, sung by Goethe and Belli, the river of Rome saw the birth of the city, was stained with blood during the fights with barbarians and Saracens, and has seen its waters parted by the boats which brought supplies to the city from the sea and the North. The source of this, the second largest river in Italy, is in Romagna at a height of a full 1268 metres.

The centuries have, once again, left traces well visible that go beyond the history of Rome: here lived pre-roman populations of the Italic peninsula such as the Faliscans and the Capenates and it is where the Etruscans dwelled, the most visible testimony of which is the archaeological sight of Vejo. There is another archaeological sight of great interest, *Lucus Feroniae*, the wood sacred to the Sabine goddess Feronia, not far from which there is a splendid villa of the Roman period. History continues in the relentless flow of centuries showing us the mighty castles where the fierce battles between noble families often related to the Pope were fought and those places of peace where still today, in the silence of a hermitage with ruined walls or in front of the hieratic beauty of a sanctuary, the soul seems to forget the woes of the world. And everywhere... green. If the Tiber is the ancient waterway which cuts across this area, since many centuries ago two ways, created by man, connect Rome to the North of the country: the consular roads Cassia and Flaminia, unquestionably more attractive than the nearby motorway. As in this area nature and history are inextricably connected, the former often prevailing upon the latter, we will propose a single naturalistic itinerary which, for greater ease, is divided into two distinct routes: the first along the Cassia and the Flaminia, the second along the Via Tiberina and the motorway. For the lovers of traditional flavours we instead suggest an itinerary in search of olive oil, the excellent quality production known as Soratte oil, from the name of the mount which with its 691 metres dominates an area which is mostly flat.

How to get there
by car:
Via Cassia bis, Via Flaminia, and Via Tiberina, Rome - Florence A1 Motorway.
by bus:
CO.TRA.L. (tel. 800/431784) leaving from Saxa Rubra (tel. 06/3328333, Tiburtina F.S. railway (tel. 06/44242419) and Lepanto-Metro tube line A (tel. 06/3214827 - 3244724)
by train:
tel. 147/888088, for locations connected by the Roma Nord - Piazzale Flaminio railway.

From Vejo Park to Soratte Natural Reserve, following the Via Cassia and the Via Flaminia

The naturalistic itinerary

The itinerary starts on the Via Cassia, built between 171 and 124 B.C. which takes us to the *Parco di Vejo* (Rome Municipality), founded in 1997. Its 15.000 hectares, covering the territory of several municipalities, include agricultural and wooded areas and other areas prevalently of tufa stone where there are treasures which are still for the most to be explored: the archaeological sight of the ancient Etruscan city which rivalled Rome, destroyed in 396 B.C. by Furius Camillus. Amongst the objects found the most important is the statue of the god Apollo now at the museum of Villa Giulia, whilst the most interesting archaeological sights are the extra-urban sanctuary of Portonaccio, part of the walls of the acropolis, the temple of Apollo and the necropolis along the Via Formellese, as well as that of mount San Michele known for the tomb called Campana, a chamber inside which are preserved important frescos. Our destination is the *Natural Reserve of the Valle del Treja*, but we will be stopping off to visit some attractive citadels such as **Formello**, the place-name of which would seem to connect it to Vejo as it would appear to derive from *"formae"*, the name of the ducts which brought water to the city in the VI and V centuries B.C. Formello was to follow the fate of the powerful neighbouring Etruscan city: reduced to the status of residential area during the imperial era, it vanished completely at the fall of the empire only to reappear in the eighth century with the birth of the *domus cultae*, a cross between farms and forts instituted by the popes in order to protect the countryside around Rome. The *Domus Culta of Capracorum*, which included the territories of many other citadels in the area, was born in the eighth century thanks to Pope Hadrian I and disappeared between the X and XI centuries.

Vestiges of the past are everywhere, but the most remarkable of finds was that of the *Olpe Chigi*, a protocorinthian vase which is now at the museum of Villa Giulia in Rome, found in one of the three tombs in a tumulus on mount Aguzzo. A little further on there are the ruins of a more recent past: the abandoned Villa Chigi (1664) built by Cardinal Flavio Chigi on the model of Versailles. In the medieval village we find the Municipal Palace and the **Church of San Lorenzo**. Palazzo Chigi, which dates back to the sixteen hundreds, is built where there once was the Palazzo of the Orsini, local lords between the thirteenth and seventeenth centuries, which had in turn been built upon an ancient *castrum*. It is here that we find the seat of the *Museo dell'Agro Veientano*, where amongst others we can admire a rare natural size statue of Priapus, god of fertility. Just by it, the *Church of San Lorenzo* with

Formello: the romanesque steeple of the church of San Lorenzo

View of Sacrofano

its beautiful romanesque bell tower and XVI Century fresco attributed to a local painter showing an Emperor carrying a gigantic cross and surrounded by a group of saints. A short distance away is the **Church of San Michele Arcangelo**, it too with a romanesque bell tower and portal in peperino stone dating back to 1500. Farther North is **Sacrofano**, till 1928 known as Scrofano, probably from "scrofa" the Italian term for sow, such a common animal in our countryside that it has the honour of appearing on the coat of arms of the municipality. Situated upon the volcanic Mount Musino (376 mts.), the town is certainly of Etruscan origin, as the many tombs found in the area demonstrate. However, from an historic point of view, we can only trace it back to medieval times as part of the properties of the Prefects of Vico and, later, of the Orsini family who took it for its strategic position at the cross-roads between the Cassia and the Flaminia. Once again we find a vaulted arch surmounted by the municipal emblem which gives access to the typical medieval "borgo" dominated by the imposing presence of the **Church of San Giovanni Battista** (XII-XIII C.), restructured during the Renaissance, inside which there are contemporary paintings and a beautiful wooden ceiling. Also dating back to the 1500's is the baptismal font with the coats of arms of the Orsini and della Rovere families. The bell tower dated 1100 is given a very special touch by the presence of a weights and pendulum clock dated end XVII Century made by a craftsman from Magonza. Outside the "borgo" we find the **Church of San Biagio** and the **Palazzo**, once the seat of the municipality. The church, first built during the Renaissance, was extensively modified during the XVII Century, as is evidenced by the baroque style of the decorations which are also dominant in the Palace of the 1700's. Finally, Sacrofano is the only place in the Province of Rome where the memory of a Jewish Ghetto, which one reaches from the ancient "borgo", survives. For those who love to be in contact with nature we recommend a walk or a ride on horseback in the **Parco Naturale di Monte Musino** so as to be able to admire that Roman countryside which has so miraculously survived the onset of cement from the top of the little conical mount. On horseback one can also

Visits on horseback

Those wishing to discover this area on horseback can enquire at several centres: at Campagnano at the C.E.C. Valle del Sorbo (tel: 06/934 2539), at Riano at the Centro Ippico Benny (tel: 0330/389082), and at Sacrofano at the following centres: Trekking Horse Club (tel: 06/9382199) - Circolo Ippico Pallino (tel: 06/9039193) - Associazione Cavalcanti dell'Agro di Vejo (c/o Cardariello - Via Sacrofanese-Cassia) - Centro Ippico Fattoria Nuova.

Il Santuario della Madonna del Sorbo

Legend relates that the Madonna appeared amongst the branches of a sorb tree before a shepherd with only one hand, asking him to have a sanctuary built in that place. The shepherd, healed through miracle by the Virgin who had given him back his hand, ran off to tell everyone what had happened and it was thus that, thanks to the commitment of the two villages, the sanctuary came to be. Inside there is a painting of the XI Century representing a Madonna with Child in Byzantine style and nearby there are the remains of the alas totally abandoned Carmelite monastery. Those interested in spiritual itinerary can continue as far as Sant'Oreste in order to visit the ancient hermitages at Mount Soratte and then at Ponzano Romano, in the area of which we can find one of the most ancient Benedictine monasteries in our country, the Abbey of Sant'Andrea in Flumine.

reach the *Sanctuary of the Madonna della Grotta* with the charming effigy of the Madonna painted on a block of tufa stone or the better known *Sanctuary of the Madonna del Sorbo*, half way between Sacrofano and Campagnano, an object of contestation, all be it within a common spirit of devotion, between the people of Formello and Campagnano, and which has also been the object of pilgrimages since it was built in 1487.

Just a few kilometres farther on we reach **Campagnano di Roma** which looks upon the valley of the Baccano, once occupied by a lake, from the

Campagnano: the main square of the village

heights of Mount Razzano. The name Baccano probably has its origins in the name of the Roman god of wine, Bacco. Hence the term Baccanale, the good local red wine which marries so well with other typical local products. Villanovian necropolis, Etruscan findings, the remains of Septimius Severus' villa on the Cassia, as well as remains of thermal baths and one of the very few Roman postal stations (perhaps first Century A.D.), tell of the ancient history of the area where now stands the village, which however only dates back to medieval times. Soon to become a castle, Campagnano followed the fortunes of many like it, passing from one noble family to the other, and of that period the historic centre is typical with its medieval structure here and

Typical products

Since ancient times Roman gastronomy has been based on simplicity and the use of products from vegetable gardens and pastures. Thus many are the recipes based on the meat of sheep, goat and pork as well as entrails, as well as excellent cheeses and vegetables. It will hence not be difficult to find tasty cheese "caciotte", excellent Roman "pecorino" cheese or the typical "ricotta" cheese and, in the local "trattorie", try the local sausages and savoury meats. Amongst the most famous vegetables are the artichokes of Campagnano. Many are the "sagre" or village feasts: at Morlupo on the last Sunday of October the "sagra" of the sausage has been celebrated for the last thirty years, whilst at Rignano Flaminio there is that of the "porchetta" (a whole roast pork with crackling) on Pentecost Sunday. At Magliano Romano, not by chance once known as Magliano Pecoreccio for the importance of its sheep, there is the "sagra" of the sheep in mid-April, during which the shepherds make cheese in the piazza. Lastly, at Filacciano, on 1 May there is the "sagra" of the "fava" (broad bean) with local "pecorino" cheese.

there modified by Renaissance and more recent changes. Many of the houses belong to the XI and XII Centuries, together with the pretty *Church of the Pietà*, in the apse of which there is a beautiful fresco of the *Pietà* dated 1518, and the *Church of Santa Maria del Prato* alongside which there is a convent. The *Church of the Gonfalone* and the Fontana dei Delfini (fountain of the Dolphins), the dry fountain, a shrine with the emblems of the village and of the Orsini family who owned it for about three-hundred years, and *Palazzo Galli* with its portico and lodge in peperino stone all date back to the Renaissance. Of the period of the 1600's is the bell tower of the *Collegiata di San Giovanni Battista* which however overall keeps its medieval appearance. Inside, of particular interest are the chorus and the ceiling of the presbiterium (1582) by Giacomo del Duca and a painting representing the *Madonna col Bambino* (Madonna with Child) of the Lombard school (XVI C.). A curiosity: the inhabitants of Campagnano are particularly tied to the "Tifo", a figure in prayer painted in a niche in the Vicolo del Tifo (VII-IX C.) which, like the Roman Pasquino, uncovers the misdeeds of the authorities. The next stop is **Mazzano Romano**, in the territory of the Faliscans, a

Mazzano Romano: view of the "borgo"

Mazzano Romano: the park of the Valle del Treja

pre-roman people who spoke an indo-european language who have left several well and chamber tombs in the area together with the remains of the city of *Narce* (IX-VIII Century B.C.) tied to Vejo. Also **Mazzano** was one of those centres born in the IX and XI centuries of the need of the population to flee the maraudings of the Saracens by escaping to inaccessible places. The ancient medieval "borgo", characterized by its houses in tufa stone, the lanes and arches which adorn it, is in fact built upon a precipice dug by the River Treja, in a particularly wild landscape. The castle, already mentioned as far back as 945 A.D., is tied to one of the most resounding names of the time: Prince Alberico, Lord of the City of Rome and father of Pope John XII, whom he had nominated to the papal seat at the youthful age of seventeen. In the "borgo" there are the remains of the *Church of San Nicola*, against the castle walls, which was demolished in 1940 after the collapse of the bell tower, and the *Palazzo Baronale*, for the most recently rebuilt, surrounded by houses built in the Renaissance period. But the real attraction is the *Parco Suburbano della Valle del Treja*, 1000 hectares of land governed by the municipalities of Mazzano and Calcata, in the region of Viterbo, characterized by volcanic tufaceous stone which has been dug by the flow of water to form gorges and the narrow bottom of the river valley rich in vegetation. Woods of oak, maple and hazel trees hide in their midst foxes, weasels, badgers, porcupines and boars, and also birds of prey, owls and reptiles, amongst which the *vipera aspis*. Elsewhere, on the cliffs of tufa which plug into the valley, one sees holm-oaks, heather and strawberry trees whilst in spring, in the undergrowth, it is not uncommon to find wild orchids. In crossing the park it is possible to see several tombs, underground passages and fortifications built by the Faliscans who had the rather rare custom of burying their dead in the hollows of tree trunks. One of the most charming places, which one can reach taking a right turn just before reaching Mazzano, is the waterfalls and the *mola di monte Gelato*, often used as a film set for westerns and historic films such as *Francesco, Giullare di Dio* by Rober-

Mazzano Romano: the waterfalls of monte Gelato in the parco della Treja valley

to Rossellini (1950), *Per qualche dollaro in più* by Sergio Leone (1965), the cold waters of the Treja have even seen *Zorro* duel with his sword. It is enough to cross the bridge over the river in order to find oneself in an atmosphere which belongs to the past: the waterfalls, the mill and the tower which defended it, built in the XII Century. We now go back to the Cassia and, passing again through Campagnano, we go towards the Flaminia in search of another area of considerable naturalistic and historic interest: the **Riserva naturale di monte Soratte**, but first we will take a diversion to **Magliano Romano**, known as Magliano Pecoreccio up until 1907, sheep (pecora, in Italian) being the major local occupation. In the middle of what was once Faliscan territory, standing where once there was the first Roman *statio* (guard station) on the Flaminia, we first find mention of the place in the XI Century and, as for many places like it, it was contended for by different noble

The 'rocca' of Magliano Romano

families such as the Anguillara and the Chigi. Interesting is the *Rocca* (XIV-XV C.), which today belongs to the Arnaldi family, which has in time been considerably restructured and, next to it, the **Church of San Giovanni Battista** (XIV C.) with its romanesque façade. Inside there is a statue of Saint Pudenziana and some interesting paintings. Certainly more taking is the **Grotta degli Angeli**, outside the village, perhaps once an Etruscan tomb turned into a church by hermit monks of oriental origin (VI-VII C.). Finally, on the road which connects the Cassia to the Flaminia, there is a chapel built in the XVIII Century and dedicated to the Madonna delle Grazie. By now in sight of Monte Soratte, it is worth stopping off at **Rignano Flaminio** where, in very distant times there must have been the sea, given the many findings of fossils of sea life. More recent is the origin of the village which would seem to be connected to a *Castrum Ara Jani*, a Roman camp erected near an altar dedicated to the two faced god Janus, as remains dating back to Roman times testify: marble reliefs set into the walls of the houses such as the famous female bust known as the "Senini di Rignano", fragments of columns which appear here and there in the piazza and a splendid sarcophagus with a bas-relief which represents marital scenes. The imposing Rocca Savelli in tufa and travertine and much changed in time was originally built in the XIV Century, near it stands a more recent Spanish cannon, a rare piece of artillery also known as the "cannon of Cesare" Borgia, probably left there by the Lansquenets and used for folkloristic purposes up until the early 1900's. Worthy of mention is the **Church of Santi Vincenzo e Anastasio** with its Renaissance altars and XV and XVI Century paintings; the third chapel on the left – commissioned by Francesco and Giovan Battista Borghese, brothers of Pope Paul V (1605-21) – is instead frescoed with the *Storie della Croce* (1607-14) attributed to Anastasio Fontebuoni and framed by rich decoration in gilded stucco. Outside the village there is the **Church of the Santi Abbondio and Abbondanzio**, simple in its romanesque structure set in the greenery, it is believed to have been erected on the sight of the altar to Janus in honour of the two saints martyred in the II Century A.D. In the basements one can see, together with other alas badly kept frescos of the X Century, that known as *dell'Angelo* (of the Angel) which, according to popular tradition, instead represents Saint Theodora as she cries for the transfer to Rome of her body and that of the two martyrs

Rignano Flaminio: the church of Santi Vincenzo e Anastasio

Monte Soratte

Situated on the border between the lands of the Faliscans and the Capenates, a sacred place for the presence of a temple dedicated to a Faliscan divinity and then later to the sun god Apollo, very soon this mountain which has geological characteristics so different to the area which surrounds it (to the extent of generating the hypothesis that it might be a meteorite fallen from the skies in the dim and distant past) ended up by becoming part of the territory of Rome as an ideal place for residential villas and farms, such as the villa in the locality of Giardino. In effect the Soratte is a truly a terrace overlooking the province: from its heights one can admire the Tolfa mountains and the Treja, the Tiber and the Sabatine mountains, the Lucretili and the Terminillo and in the background the thousand lights of Rome and the sea. It is not then surprising that over and above trekking and riding on horses or mountain bikes one can also go paragliding, hang-gliding and free climbing. It is also an interesting place for speleologists due to the presence of many karst caves, the so called "meri", on the northern side of the mountain along the way to the abandoned church of Santa Romana.

found in the same place. In fact, not far off are the catacombs of the two martyred saints within the church dedicated to this Roman matron who initiated their construction which took place in a period of time which went from the persecutions of Emperor Diocletian to 424 A.D. But here is imposing, in the middle of the countryside, the "candid *Soratte*" sung by the latin poet Horace and by Virgil (XI canto of the *Aeneid*). The mountain and the recently constituted natural reserve (guided tours, only on foot, and the possibility of passing the weekend at the hermitage of Santa Maria delle Grazie) are in the territory of the Municipality of **Sant'Oreste**. The naturalistic and historico-monumental patrimony that the reserve intends preserving is of great value: woods of oak of various types, of white and of black hornbeam, poplar, but also pastures and olive groves grow upon the sides of the Soratte, where various species of birds and mammals are also to be found. There are many clearly indicated itineraries to be followed amongst which of particular interest is that of the *Percorso degli Eremi*.

The name Sant'Oreste takes its origin from Edisto, later Eristo and then Oreste, a young martyr of the period of Nero who was later sanctified, to

The May Torch-Light Procession

If the Soratte is in itself magical because of its natural qualities and for the history it evokes, this magical atmosphere has its culmination on the last Sunday in May with the torch-light procession dedicated to the Madonna, which has been held every year since 1859. In the dark the mountain is illuminated by the light of fires set upon its slopes and down as far as the hermitage of San Silvestro, whilst the procession wends its way down the streets of Sant'Oreste.

La via degli Eremi del Soratte

The silence, the caves, the vicinity of the sun and the stars have made of the Soratte a place of cult since its beginnings and thus it has remained through to more recent times when in the place of the destroyed temple of Apollo churches and hermitages were built. The best known is San Silvestro, one of the first Benedictine coenobiums, first mentioned by Gregorio Magno (590-604) in relation to the miracles performed by Saint Nonnosio, prior of that

the large valley at the foot of the mountain

monastery. Legend has it that it was founded by Pope Sylvester who fled there during the persecutions of Emperor Constantine who, later, cured of leprosy by the same pope, had himself baptised by him. A few verses of Dante engraved on the main doors seem to give credit to this legend. Another illustrious name connected to this place is that of Carlomanno, father of Charlemagne, king of the Franks who, having had restored in 747, would seem to have retired there.

Sant'Oreste: the hermitage of San Silvestro on Monte Soratte

Today the church, built of irregular calcaric blocks, appears imposing and grave, having had to combine in the course of centuries both defensive and spiritual functions. Of interest are the frescoes on the walls, and the pillars some of which date back to the XIII Century but with numerous superimpositions. The itinerary continues with the ruins of San Sebastiano and Sant'Antonio, with the church of Santa Lucia, restructured in 1970, and of Santa Maria delle Grazie, built upon a chapel of the 1500's dedicated to the Virgin thanks to it being donated by Cardinal Alessandro Farnese to the Cistercians. Inside, one can admire a fresco removed from the apse of the hermitage of Sant'Antonio, now totally abandoned. A different itinerary takes one to Santa Romana and the "meri". Built inside a cave, the hermitage is now no more than a group of ruins where one can still see the remains of a fresco representing Pope Sylvester baptising the saint and a large marble basin considered to be miraculous for women without milk.

whom the Roman lady Galla wished to dedicate places of cult within her land. The origins of Sant'Oreste go back to the X Century, but the ancient "borgo", despite much medieval testimony, has a markedly Renaissance appearance. Dating back to that period are *Palazzo Canali*, attributed to Vignola and decorated with frescoes probably by the Zuccaris; the *Monastero Agostiniano di Santa Croce* which includes the ancient *Palazzo Abbaziale*, and the *Collegiata di San Lorenzo Martire* which keeps an ancient treasure: an organ built by Ennio Bonifazi in 1638 and still used for baroque music concerts. Outside the village is the *Church of Santa Maria Hospitalis*, dating back to the year 1000, later restructured, decorated with frescoes and

Morlupo: a view of the "borgo"

marble reliefs of the Carolingian period. Coming back into Rome along the Flaminia and deviating just a few kilometres, we can visit **Morlupo**, Castelnuovo di Porto and Riano. Legend has it that, contaminated by pestilential humours during the feasts dedicated to Apollo on the Soratte, the inhabitants of Morlupo were forced to live roaming like wolves (in Latin: *more luporum*), animals which, in fact, have infested the area up until the 1800's. Perched upon a tufa rock, the village is situated near where there once was an ancient *statium*, the most conspicuous remains of which is *the ad vigesimum* catacomb, created in the tunnels of a Roman cistern. The plan of the "borgo", called "Mazzocca" or "village of the artists", typical of fortified mounts, dates back to the XIII Century and was restructured in the XIV and XV Century, period to which the old "borgo" of Santa Maria dates back.

View of Castelnuovo di Porto

The *Castello* was rebuilt at the end of the 1500's by the Orsini family in place of the Benedictine fort (XI C.) destroyed during the siege of Pope Martin V (1425) and the same fate beset the *Church of San Giovanni Battista* which was rebuilt at the end of the XVI Century and in which one can admire a painting of the 1500's of the Dürer school. Also of interest is the *Church of Santa Maria Assunta* dating back to the Trecento with frescoes dating back to the XVII and XVIII Century, and the *Cappella della Madonna di Costantinopoli* built inside a XIII Century house. Also **Castelnuovo di Porto** was a fortified village, *Castrum Novum*, and here took hiding the inhabitants of the nearby Porto destroyed by the Saracens. In a dominating position is the *Palazzo Colonna*, built in the XIII Century and then remodelled in the middle of the 1500's, period to which date back frescos stylistically near to the art of Federico Zuccari and his school. More recent than the fortifications is the *Church of Santa Maria Assunta*, remodelled in the XVIII Century, the bell tower of which has had its spire struck down by lightning. Inside there is a painting of the *Deposizione* of the school of the Carracci and a triptych attributed to Antoniazzo Romano. Just outside the village one finds the *Church of the Madonna della Virtù* (XVII C.), the little *Church of San Sebastiano* with a beautiful fresco of the 1500's, as well as many archaeological remains, amongst which a piece of ancient Roman road visible in the vicinity of a medieval postal station.

Riano: the gates to the "borgo"

Finally, the area is full of water springs low in mineral content that gush out of Mount Sant'Antonio, from the name of the saint who, on his pilgrimage to Rome, probably stopped there. The last stop along the Flaminia is **Riano**, a name said to derive from the Latin *rivus*, thanks to its numerous streams. In 1151 there is a first mention of a castle which defended the citadel the origins of which are lost in time and which, as for many others, passed from one lord to another until in the XVIII Century the Ruspoli family, whose family coat of arms stands over the main gates, gave it its present appearance. The *Castello* has a quadrangular tower, perhaps once part of the ancient fortifications, and three round towers; in front of it is the *Church of the Immacolata Concezione* with a beautiful portal of the XV Century.

Following the meanderings of the River Tiber along the Via Tiberina

This second itinerary follows the meanderings of the Tiber in the opposite direction. The final objective is the *Riserva Naturale Tevere-Farfa*. The first stop is **Capena**, known as Leprignano up until 1933 when, nearby, the remains of the ancient Capena were found, one of the most important cities before the birth of Rome, inhabited by the italic people known as Capenates and allied to Vejo in its fight against the Romans. The centre of the citadel is medieval. Worthy of note is the *Palazzo dei Monaci*, so called because it was inhabited by monks up until the XIX Century, the *Torre dell'Orologio* dating back to the XVI Century and the *Parrocchiale di San Michele Arcangelo* built in the last Century, inside which there is the triptych *Il Salvatore e i santi Pietro e Paolo* by Antonio da Viterbo (1452). In the old cemetery there is the **Church of San Leone**, probably built upon an ancient Roman temple some time before 1218, date in which we first find mention of it. Of special interest is the structure of the church itself and some frescos dating back to the X and XVI Century. Finally coming back from Capena towards Fiano Romano, we meet an important archaeological sight: Lucus Feroniae. Perhaps in origin linked to the ancient Roman *Flavia* family, the village of **Fiano Romano** in all probability developed due to the need of the people of Capena to flee to a safer

The Torre dell'Orologio at Capena

Capena White Wine

In the area a D.O.C. white wine (a wine subject to controlled origin and denomination) is produced which takes its name from the citadel of Capena and which comes from the vineyards in the areas of Capena, Fiano Romano, Morlupo and Castelnuovo di Porto.
A wine which is suited to any type of meal, it is particularly good with artichokes and cheeses, and is celebrated on the last weekend of October with a feast of ancient Roman origins, the **Vendemmiale**.
For the occasion the stairs of the Church of Sant'Antonio, closed to prayer, are adorned with laurel and bunches of grapes and, in the best of Roman traditions, wine gushes from the marble head of a lion set between two staircases.

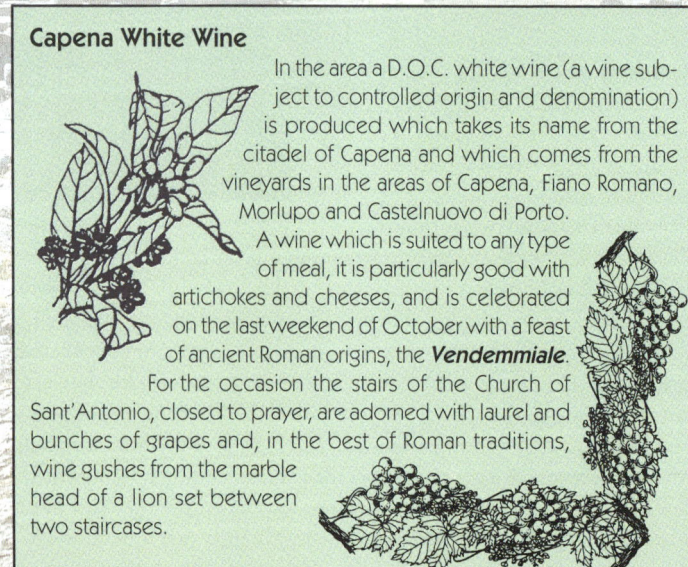

Lucus Feroniae

The archaeological site of **Lucus Feroniae**, sign posted along the motorway in the vicinity of the Fiano exit, was in origin a small centre which grew up around a sanctuary dedicated to the goddess Feronia who here had a sacred wood (*lucus*), a place of worship, but also of commerce thanks to its position. We here find remains of great interest dating back to the IV-III Century B.C. and, nearby, a villa amongst the most interesting ever found in the vicinity of Rome: the **Villa of the Volusii Saturnini** – a powerful senatorial family of the I Century B.C. – which bears evidence of various stages of transformation from sumptuous villa with splendid mosaics to farm.

Fiano Romano: the archeological area of Lucus Feroniae

Lucus Feroniae: female figure in marble

Lucus Feroniae: floor mosaic

place, but it is only in the year 1000 that it appears as a fortified castle of the monks of Saint Paul, later to become the property of the Orsini family. Surrounded by the walls of the castle, the medieval "borgo" looks down upon the Tiber and one enters it through the monumental gates of **Porta Capena**. The **Castello Ducale** of the Orsini is of the 1400's and very much remade, whilst on the Piazza there is the more recent **Parrocchiale di Santo Stefano Nuovo**, built upon the ruins of two churches, where we can admire a fresco by Pastura: the *Madonna con Bambino* surrounded by four saints and with the altar-piece *Il Salvatore e due angeli* attributed to Pinturicchio, but more probably of the Lazio school. Outside the village there is the **Church of Santo Stefano Vecchio** built in the 1200's, decorated with marble and granite. Another village which would seem to derive from the needs of the people of Cape-

The castello Ducale of Fiano Romano

Civitella San Paolo: view of the battlements of the Castello and the square tower

na is **Civitella San Paolo**, of which however no mention until the XIII Century. Here too the fulcrum of the village is the *Castello* (XI-XII C.), with a hexagonal tower and a square one, in front of which there is the *Parrocchiale di San Giacomo* designed by Francesco Vespignani and enriched by a beautiful boxed ceiling. And finally we arrive at the *Riserva Naturale Tevere-Farfa* which includes the municipalities of **Nazzano** and **Torrita Tiberina**. Situated between the Tiber and the Cimini and Volsini mountains, it is reasonable to presume that Nazzano was built upon the ruins of Seperno the more so because pre-roman and Roman necropolis have been found there together with the remains of residential villas. The oldest part is the *Rocca* (XII C.) whilst the borgo, which winds round it like a spiral, is of a later date. The *Castello*, built between the XIII and XIV Century upon a jutting piece of tufa rock South of the "rocca" and almost one with the rock face behind it, is imposing. Outside the village there is the

The imposing Castello of Nazzano

Church of Sant'Antimo built before 952 and subsequently rebuilt to the extent that it is normally dated between the XII and XIII Century. The columns inside probably date back to a previous temple dedicated to the goddess Feronia. Onto a wide bend in the Tiber which for its shape is called "fiasco" (the traditional bulb shaped Chianti bottle) faces **Torrita Tiberina**, already inhabited in the late republican period of early ancient Rome and born as a military tower on the river in the VIII Century. In the "borgo", over and above Medieval and Renaissance buildings, one can see the ***Church of Santa Maria del Monte*** or ***dell'Assunta*** with a painting of the 1200's called Il *Martirio di San Sebastiano* and a bell which Saint Carlo Borromeo donated to the village in 1500. Something of a mixture between a place of worship and a fortress is the ***Church of San Tommaso Apostolo*** with a white marble tabernacle dated 1400 and some paintings.

Torrita Tiberina: a building in the "borgo"

The Tevere Farfa Natural Reserve

It is situated in the area in which the Tiber forms a large basin into which the River Farfa flows. The reserve, which covers an area of 700 hectares, has many different types of natural environment: cane groves, the ideal habitat for birds such as the coot, moorhen, mallard, kingfisher and mammals such as the coypu; marshland woods, dominated by alder and weeping willows, which one can enter thanks to special raised pathways. Elsewhere there are forests of oak, turkey oak, maples, elm, with splashes of red from Judas trees and, along the water's edge, bull-rushes and marshland irises. In the undergrowth there are broom, various types of berries and cyclamens and orchids. In the reserve the Didactic Park of Nazzano has been created, an area of 24 hectares of pasture land and woods for the purpose of environmental documentation and education. The information centre is available for enquiries on the services offered: excursions on foot, by bicycle and on horse back, canoe trips, 'green weeks' and school camps.

*Filacciano:
the façade of the
Castello del Drago*

*The parrocchiale of
San Nicola di Bari
at Ponzano Romano*

Filacciano and Ponzano Romano are the last two stops on the itinerary. Like other villages situated in a panoramic position on the Tiber, **Filacciano** probably owes its name to the Faliscans but as is uncertain the origin of the name so is the period of construction of the castle which the Del Drago family transformed into the palace we can today admire, which blends so well with the "borgo" of the 1600's designed to the canons of scenographic effect of the time. Not far from the palace there is the romanesque *Church of Sant'Egidio Abate* (X C.) with XIII Century frescos restored just a few years ago. And finally **Ponzano Romano**, a name which probably derives from that of a Roman family, *Pontia*, which in the XI Century belonged to the Monastery of San Silvestro on the Soratte but was also under the influence of the powerful abbey of Farfa. The "borgo", fortified at the end of the 1200's, still preserves its medieval appearance, even though the **Parrocchia di San Nicola di Bari** is of the XVIII Century. Inside it there are some interesting works which come from the Abbey of Sant'Andrea in Flumine such as a medieval silver reliquary a fresco of *Santa Maria delle Grazie* and a tryptich of the XV Century. Outside the village there are the **Church of Santa Maria ad Nives**, with sepulcral functions, and the imposing **Abbey of Sant'Andrea in Flumine**.

The Abbey of Sant'Andrea in Flumine

It is set in a strategic position upon heights from which it dominates the valley set between the Tiber and Mount Soratte. In fact, the abbey for many years also had the function of controlling the traffic along the river to Rome. A first written record, even if unconfirmed, is the *Chronicon* by a certain Benedetto, a monk who lived there in the X Century, who attributes the foundation of the church to a noble Roman lady called Galla (VI C.), and of the monastery to Charlemagne, who had retired there. And this would indeed explain the close links between the abbey and Saint Sylvester. What is certain is that it was founded by Benedictine monks and that Charlemagne, King of the Franks, visited the place several times. Badly damaged during the Saracen invasions (IX-X C.), Sant'Andrea in Flumine saw the onset of its decline at the beginning of the XII Century; in the IX Century it had been completely abandoned by the monks. Restored in 1959, the church, once protected by fortified walls of which there is only a tower left which now serves as a steeple, still has a certain charm despite the wear and tear of time which, it has to be said, has been a lot less clement with the monastery which now reduced to ruins. The church is composed of three naives with granite columns topped by Corinthian capitals, whilst the floor is in Cosmatesque marble. The walls are decorated with frescos of which the most interesting is that which represents the *Resurection*. To be noted is the presence of a very rare structure of the end of the XII Century known as *Jubè*, situated in a position which separates the presbytery, reserved to the clergy, and the naive, which was for the public, and which served the function of pulpit. The name derives from the fact that from there, before reading the Gospel, the priest used to recite the *Jube Domine Benedicere*.

The olive oil way of the Soratte

The whole of the area of the valley of the Tiber is also of gastronomic interest, not only is the area renowned for its cheeses and preserved meats, artichokes and wine, but it is also and above all known, and has been for centuries, for its excellent olive oil. Indeed, the inhabitants of Sant'Oreste are proud of the letter received from the famous architect Jacopo Barozzi, better known as the Vignola, in which he sings the praise of the local olive oil. And it is superfluous to remember that the benedictine monks, who lived in a self-sufficient way, worked hard to keep up the production of oil even in the darkest of centuries. Thus, following the recommended itineraries, one will end up by following a true and proper way of olive oil, along which, whilst visiting a castle or a natural reserve, it will be possible to take a gastronomically rewarding stop in a local "trattoria" or at one of the producers of this precious condiment which gets its typical flavour from the type of olives, called "sirole" or "sierala", grown on the slopes of the Soratte. Used as a condiment for other local products, olive oil made from "sirole" olives is of a yellow gold colour with reflections of green and has a special flavour which gives local dishes that extra touch which makes them special. Naturally there are also the "sagre" or feasts for olive oil, first and foremost that known as "Il tempo delle Olive" (time for olives), held at Sant'Oreste on the second Sunday of December with meetings on olive oil and the distribution of "bruschetta". "Bruschetta" is the simplest and perhaps most typical dish of Roman cuisine, it is wholesome country bread toasted on wood fires and flavoured with olive oil, salt and garlic.

From the Tiber to the Aniene

The Aniene in the vicinity of Jenne

- "Roccas" and castles
- Archaeological sites
- Places of worship
- Parks and natural reserves
- Cheese
- Wine
- Olive Oil
- Mushrooms
- Chestnuts

From the Tiber to the Aniene following saints and hermits

The Tiburtino-Sublacense area, the largest tourist area of the Province, stretches from the Tiber to the boarders of the Abruzzo and includes two natural parks, the valley of the River Aniene and about fifty municipalities where lovers of archeology and art will have lots to choose from out of a vast range of sights to be visited: roman ruins, medieval and renaissance castles, pretty "borgos" set in time but, above all, hermitages, churches and monasteries, to the extent that the Valley of the Aniene is known as "valle Santa". The gullies, recesses, the natural caves, where the river is at times placid and at times torrential in its flow, were for the early hermits the ideal place in which to go into retreat from the world and to be closer to God. It was here that St. Benedict founded his first coenobiums, here stopped St. Francis and everywhere, be it in oral tradition as in the frescos in churches, their tale and their miracles are recounted. We recommend visiting this area so vast and rich in art treasures by dividing it into itineraries based on different interests: the lovers of olive oil can follow the way of the Sabina, combining the tasting of local olive oil and wine with a visit to a castle or some trekking in the park of the Monti Lucretili. One can also go South, towards the boundary with Frosinone, in order to enjoy the smooth and slightly bitter flavour of Cesanese di Olevano Romano, the excellent red wine produced at Olevano and Genazzano. Those who prefer art can follow an archeologico-monumental itinerary, visiting famous ancient Roman villas and stately homes, whilst those who seek the peace and quiet of solitary places rich in history can choose the religious itinerary which goes from the Monastery of San Cosimato at Vicovaro to the Sanctuary of the Trinità at Vallepietra.

How to get there

By car:
for the Sabina area take the Via Salaria, the Via Tiburtina, the A1 Rome-Florence Motorway to the Fiano Romano or the Magliano Sabina exits; for the remaining areas take the Via Tiburtina, the A24 Rome-L'Aquila Motorway to the Vicovaro-Mandela or Castel Madama exits, or the A1 Motorway to the Anagni exit

By bus:
CO.TRA.L. bus lines (tel. 800-431784) with departures from Ponte Mammolo-Rebibbia (last station on Metro Line B), from Lepanto, from Tiburtina Railway Station (on Metro Line B) and from the Anagnina.

By train: (tel. 147-888088 and 06-47303050) the Rome-Pescara line to Arsoli, Roviano, Mandela, Sambuci, and the Rome-Tivoli line to Tivoli, Palombara, Marcellina, Castel Madama, Guidonia Montecelio and Sant'Angelo Romano

The way of olive oil of the Sabina

The itinerary of olive oil and wine

The Sabina is that part of the Province that is East of Rome and the history of which dates back to well before the birth of the famous city, as the utensils and fossils of the lower paleolitic found at Cretone testify. An ancient Italic people, the Sabines were soon to come into contact with the Romans. Everyone knows of the legend of the rape of the Sabine women, thanks to which, it would seem, the Romans were able to ensure their descent. It is however certain that the first kings of Rome were Sabines and that they were conquered by the Romans in 290 B.C. As we follow the way of olive oil we will come across cultivated areas of olive trees, vines and fruit, and pastures, and also mountainous areas which have peeks which rise to more than 1300 mts. Everywhere we will see ancient olive trees, in Autumn loaded with fruit and the rest of the year with their silver fronds of leaves. The olive tree is one of the distinguishing features of the Sabine countryside and the oil is healthy and tasty, without it local cuisine would not be the same. Oil presses and producers of the prized "gold of the Sabines" are disseminated everywhere, so it will not be difficult to taste and maybe buy some olive oil and other local products during an excursion or a visit to a medieval "borgo".

The olive oil of the Sabina

It is a D.O.C. extra virgin olive oil of a bright golden yellow colour and with a fruity back flavour, the history of which goes back to the origins of our civilization. Vinyards and olive groves have always been part of the Mediterranean landscape. It is not however known when the Sabines started cultivating olives. Some ancient Roman writers mention the production of olive oil in the Sabina as long ago as the I Century B.C., but it was only a century later that it took on such a degree of importance that every Roman villa in the area had a warehouse for stocking wine and oil. The area includes both the part of the Sabina in the province of Rome and that in the province of Rieti, it covers about 18,000 hectares and produces 4,600 tons of oil a year. The oil producing municipalities along this itinerary are: Montelibretti, Mentana and Monterotondo, on the left bank of the Tiber, Palombara Sabina, Moricone, Monteflavio, Marcellina and San Polo dei Cavalieri within the Monti Lucretili Park and, finally, Nerola, Montorio Romano, Sant'Angelo Romano and Guidonia-Montecelio.

The olive oil "Sagre"

There are many "sagre" or feasts dedicated to olive oil where one can taste, produce and enjoy processions and traditional games. At San Polo dei Cavalieri the *Sagra dell'olio d'oliva e della bruschetta* is held in January on the feast day of Sant'Antonio Abate, in March there are the *Rassegna Nazionale dell'Olio d'Oliva* at Marcellina and the *Sagra dell'Olio* at Moricone and Nerola, whilst in August at Palombara Sabina there is the *Rassegna dell'olio extravergine della Sabina* with a torchlight procession in honour of Saint John the Baptist. At Mentana the day dedicated to oil is instead between the end of September and the beginning of October, whilst the last "sagra" is at Monteflavio on the third Sunday of December.

An olive grove and, in the background, the village of Nerola

We will start our itinerary from the municipalities of Monterotondo, Mentana and Montelibretti which can be easily reached from the Via Salaria, the ancient way of salt. Defined as the "Paris of the Sabina" in a XIX Century book, Monterotondo is at the doors of the city of Rome. The discovery, a few years ago, of a *cippus miliarum* (an ancient roman mile stone) with the inscription "XVIII mile" (from Rome) gives credit to the hypothsis that the this town was built on the sight of ancient *Eretum*, one of the most important Sabine cities which, according to the latin historian Strabone, was at the crossroads of the Salaria with the Nomentana. The older part is medieval, originally a fortified citadel, and the most important buildings are the **Palazzo Ducale** and the **Church of Santa Maria Maddalena.** The XII Century palace was restored after the 1915 earthquake and after the German and Allied occupations. It has a fine well, circa 1500, and frescos which decorate its halls, amongst which *Scene della Storia di Adone* attributed to Girolamo Siciolante (1521-1580) better known as il Sermoneta. The church, inaugurated in 1640, is baroque and is the work of Domenico Castelli, probably on a design by Bernini, as the richness of the stucco-work decorations, especially in the apse, would indicate. The alter is made from a sarcophagus cut from a piece

The flavours of the Sabina

Renowned for the fertility of its soil, the area of the Sabina also produces a D.O.C. wine, the *Colli della Sabina*, both white and red, and a wide variety of fruit including the famed Ravenna cherries to which the *Sagra delle Cerase*, which is held in Palombara Sabina on the first or second Sunday of June depending on how the cherries ripen, is dedicated. During the festivities floats decorated with the strangest and most amusing composition of cherries are paraded in the streets. Sant'Angelo Romano also has its *Sagra delle Cerase* in the last but one or last week of May in concomitance with the feast of Saints Michael and Liberata, whilst at Marcellina the date is decided year by year.

of cipolin marble of the late Roman period containing the remains of St. Sixtus and St. Boniface, and brought here from the Via Appia. Lastly, the **Church of Santa Maria delle Grazie**, inside which there is one of the most interesting sepulcral monuments in Lazio. Dedicated to Girolamo Orsini who died in 1484, it has a marble niche with a high relief of the nobleman's profile, as was required by the rigid equestrian tradition. The more important period of history is that connected to Garibaldi's epos. In 1849, after the futile defence of the Roman Republic, Garibaldi lodged here together with Anita in the Cappucine Monastery. Later, in 1867, having fled from Caprera, he took Monterotondo, where the papal troups had barricaded themselves, entering the town through Porta Romana, since then called Porta Garibaldi. But, only a few days later, the french and papal troups beat Garibaldi's volunteers at **Mentana**. Here, in memory of the hapless event, we find the *Ara Ossario* of the fallen, inaugurated by Benedetto Cairoli in 1877 and which became a national monument in 1899, in which there is a sarcophagus containing the remains of those soldiers of Garibaldi who died there in 1867, and also the *Museo Garibaldino*. By one of those strange quirks of fate it was in this place, where Garibaldi tried to put an end to papal secular power, that, many centuries earlier (800), Pope Leo III had met Charlemagne and the Holy Roman Empire was born. Mentana derives from the Latin *Nomentanum*, a place mentioned by Virgil in the *Aeneid*, conquered by Tarquin Prisco and upon the territory of which the ancient Romans built many villas because of the pleasant climate and the excellent local wine. Still today around the end of September there is a *Sagra dell'Uva* with floats decorated with bunches of grapes.

Amongst the buildings of that period, to be mentioned are the *Horrea Agrippinae*, warehouses the property of Agrippina minor, mother of

Monterotondo: The palazzo ducale

G. Siciolante da Sermoneta, Birth of Adonis *(detail) Monterotondo, Palazzo Ducale*

Monterotondo: Chiesa delle Grazie, Giordano Orsini's funeral monument

> **The Museo Nazionale Garibaldino della Campagna dell'Agro Romano per la Liberazione di Roma**
> Built alongside the Ara Ossario, this museum is divided into sections based on themes: uniforms of Garibaldi's army from 1859 to 1870-71, weapons such as chassepots, rear loaded French rifles, and documents amongst which some original and rare period photographs of the XIX Century. Part of these heirlooms have been donated by members of the families of the fallen or by those who fought in the area in 1867.

A view of palazzo Borghese at Mentana

Montelibretti: one of the bastions of the Rocca and, in the background, the gates to the "borgo"

Nero, of which one can still see gigantic ruins. There are also many ancient roman findings in the medieval 'borgo', such as the sepulcral monument of the Apuleians walled into the side of a house, or the fragments of sarcophaguses set in the walls of the **Church of San Nicola** (XIII C.), which in turn has an impressive portal surmounted by a beautiful fresco of St. Sebastian. The "borgo" is dominated by the **Palazzo Borghese** (XVI C.), seat of the municipality, a short distance from the ruins of the castle destroyed in 1486. Also worthy of note are the **Palazzetto Santucci** which can be easily identified thanks to the marble bust with toga set in one of its corners and, like most other findings, from the archeological sight of *Nomentanum*, and **Palazzo Crescenzio** (IX C.). Both are on the Via Castello. Travelling North, we reach the boarders of the Province of Rieti and **Montelibretti**, for centuries closely linked to the Abbey of Farfa and it too connected to Garibaldi's adventures. Indeed, after 1860 the city became a fortress on the boundary between the Ponticial State and the Kingdom of Italy and, in 1867, just a few days before the battle of Mentana, in the area there were skermishes between Garibaldi's volonteers and papal troups. The old part of the town is dominated by the Castello, destroyed in 1058-59 and rebuilt by the Barberini family in the XVII Century. Two floors out of three and only two of the cylindrical towers, as well as some of the original furnishings, inside survive. The **Church of san Nicola di Bari** was first built in the XVI Century but was then completely rebuilt in the XVIII Century, it contains frescoes and paintings of the Seicento. A short way further North-East is the quiet "borgo" of **Nerola**, perched upon a spur of rock of the Lucretili Mountains and wrapped in a spiral around the **Castello**, built before 972 for the purpose of defending the surrounding territory. In the XIV Century the Orsini added four towers and a keep which made it truely impregnable. And it is indeed to the Sabine word for strength, "neri" or "neriene", that one owes the name of this citadel rather than to Nero who is said to have taken refuge there after the fire in Rome. The castle is privately owned and has recently become a hotel. Shortly on reach **Montorio Romano** set between the valley of the Tiber and the valley which runs along the base of Mount Terminillo. It too was fortified against barbarian incursions (XI C.), but today only the portal is left and it is the gateway to the citadel. In the XVI Century, Montorio was under Cardinal Flavio Orsini, lord of Montelibretti and founder of Monteflavio. Given the type of ornaments, the **Palazzo Baronale**, also Palazzo Corte, would seem to date back to the XVIII Century, whilst the older

The Castello at Nerola

nucleus dates back to the XVI Century, period in which it probably substituted the castle. A fine example of romanesque architecture, the **Church of San Lorenzo di Noblat** – named after a VI Century french saint – cannot be dated exactly even though the architectural style and a few frescos inside would seem to place it in the XIII Century. During works in 1966 two frescos by an unknown author were found: *L'Annunciazione*

View of Montorio Romano

Bartolomeo di Cristoforo and Lorenzo Torresani, detail of the frescoes in the apse of the church of San Leonardo di Noblat at Montorio Romano representing the Archangel Michael, Saint Barbara and Saint Catherine of Alexandria, XIV Century

and *Due Santi* (XV-XVI C.), whilst in 1988 two of the original frescos of the apse were discovered and attributed to two painters from Verona: the Torresani brothers. The **Chiesetta di Santa Barbara**, mid XVII Century, is tied to legend in that it is said to stand where the saint was martyred. Inside it one can see a water spring which is said to have come gushing forth from the ground when the martyr's head fell to the floor. Those who like a bit of a walk can go up to the top of the Monte delle Macchie to the **Church of the Santissimo Crocifisso di Monte Calvario** which contains a wooden crucifix which is still today the object pilgimages. A few kilometres farther on we enter into the **Parco Natuarale dei Monti Lucretili** which protects the natural, historical and cultural resources of the area. Always on environment, another interest-

> ### The Feast of the Holy Cross
> This ancient and moving feast is held in Montorio from 1 to 4 May. On the first evening there is a torch-light procession during which a wooden crucifix is carried from the top of the mountain down to the village where it is put on show in the church for the whole of the duration of the celebrations. On the last day it returns to the "parrocchiale" church where it has always been kept.

ing is the **Riserva Naturale del Monte Catillo**, born in 1997 and run by the Province of Rome, 1000 hectares of land which dominate the centre of Tivoli.

Here are Montefavio and Moricone. Founded in the mid 1500's by Cardinal Flavio Orsini, **Montefavio** is at the foot of Mount Pellecchia, the

The Monti Lucretili Natural Park
The park extends over 18,000 hectares in the provinces of Rome and Rieti. The history of this area began 200 million years ago when, in the sea water which covered it, deposits of limestone began to form. It is thus that today's limestone Mount Gennaro and Mount Morra were formed, whilst the "lagustelli", Pericles's lakelets, are a typical example of how lakes form due to the deposit of debris. The local landscape is thus mountainous and, in parts, particularly barren, with deep valleys and high plateaus. The nature of the soil and the climate, harsher in the interior and milder to the West because of the effect of the sea, allow for a variety of vegetation which goes from Mediterranean "macchia" to the cultivation of olives and fruit, oak woods and, between 400 and 1,000 metres above sea level, holm-oaks, beech and maple trees. Nor is the flora less varied with examples of rare plants such as holly, wild orchids and Sabine irises. Thanks to such a sparsely populated environment, the local fauna is also very varied and includes wild cats, foxes, martens, weasels, dormice, boar and occasionally wolves. The area is also populated by a variety of both nocturnal and daytime birds of prey such as buzzards, sparrow hawks and owls of various types. In the mountain heights there are golden eagles of which there are only three hundred in the whole of Italy, and we here find one of the few couples in the Apennines. To see it fly with its two metre wide wing span is an amazing sight which one can have the good fortune of enjoying during one of the excursions on foot or on horse back organized by the Ente Parco/Park Administration. Of particular interest is Mount Morra (1,036 m.) the limestone cliffs of which are an excellent climbing ground with various degrees of difficulty for those who like free climbing. Upon its slopes, almost one with its surroundings, there is also the convent of Sant'Angelo sulla Morra (XII-XIII C.).

Moricone: view of the "borgo"

highest of the Lucretili Mountains. But its origins are perhaps not so recent in that they could be connected to the presence of a castle called Montefalco which stands at a 1000 mts above sea level and just 1 klm. from the citadel. It is now reduced to ruins but these are so imposing that they give an idea of what a mighty castle this must have been in times gone by. Of interest there is also the *Parrocchia di Santa Maria Assunta*, circa 1600 but rebuilt in 1961 to the extent that of the exterior there are only the doar posts and emblem of the Orsini and one of the side doors left. Inside there is a remarkable XIV Century tabernacle in stone which comes from the Basilica of Santa Maria Maggiore in Rome and, amongst others, a painting by Vincenzo Morani (1809-1870) called *Madonna della Pietà*. The **Chiesa Cimiteriale di San Martino**, the oldest here, dates back to the XIII-XIV Century and has been recently restored. The origins of **Moricone** are remote, given the discovery of tombs dating back to 2000 B.C. There are two hypothesis on the origins of this citadel: according to some it is situated where there once was *Orvinium*, but the more credited possibility, put forward by Nibby, sees it as the heir of the Sabine city of *Regillum* which disappeared as a result of barbarian invasions. Mentioned for the first time as a castle on Mount Morrecone, it underwent considerable change during the domain of the Borghese family (1619-1871), to whom we owe the construction of the sober and imposing *Palazzo Baronale*, the acqueduct and a number of oil mills which underline the importance of olive oil even in those days. The medieval appearance of the older part of the village has remained almost intact. The imposing *Rocca*, probably XII Century, was turned into a convent in the XVIII Century, and next to it there is the *Parrocchiale dell'Assunta*, XVIII-XIX Century, built upon a smaller and older building of which one can still see a white marble tabernacle for holy ointment dated circa 1400 and a tomb stone of the end of the 1600's. The interior is markedly Settecento, with various paintings amongst which *Il Salvatore* (XV-XVI C.)

View of Palombara Sabina

by a member of the school of Antoniazzo Romano and an alter-piece representing the *Assunta* by Corrado Giaquinto (1703-1765). Outside the "borgo" we find the **Villa Aureli**, Settecento, where the painter and engraver Ludovico Prosseda once lived and which is now the Municipality. Going South, amidst olive and cherry groves, we come to **Palombara Sabina** set at the foot of Monte Gennaro and where the presence of man probably goes back to remote times, as the discovery of the so called "Cretone Man", today at the Pigorini museum in Rome, would seem to indicate. The name derives from Columbaria and first appears in a papal edict of 1029 which designated the posessions of Duke Alberico, a descendant King Desirio. During the XIII Century it was under the Savelli family to whom is tied the name of the Castello, already mentioned in in records in 1064 and subsequently amplified and changed until it became the imposing building it is today. Of interest are the halls with their rich decorations and frescoes, particularly the appartments of Troilo Savelli, and the so called Appartment of the Cardinal. During the course of the centuries the edifice has hosted both popes and anti-popes, emperors such as Frederick Barbarossa, famous men such as Benvenuto Cellini, and even a court for the judgement of some Templar knights (1310). Around the castle there is a medieval "borgo" where there is the **Collegiata** dedicated to San Biagio, the martyr who according to legend used to appear to the population in their sleep in order to warn them of iminent invasions. The original nucleus of the church dates back to the VIII Century, but its main structure, refurbished in the 1200's, 1800's and the last century, is circa 1100. Amongst the paintings and frescos which adorn the interior, the most interesting is a XV Century tempra, the *Madonna delle Nevi*, attributed to Antonio da Viterbo the Elder and probably brought there by the Savellis from Rome. On our way up Monte Gennaro we reach the **Convent of San Nicola di Bari** built upon the remains of an ancient roman building – some parts in *opus reticulatum* are still visible – and decorated with frescoes of the XIV Century. Also of interest is the **Castello di Castiglione**, abandoned in the XV

The Olivone and the Madonna della Neve

On one's way from Palombara to Marcellina along the Via Maremmana, one can see the most ancient olive tree in Lazio (12.5 m. in circumference) in the trunk of which there is a large cleft where, during the pilgrimage to the Madonna della Neve/Madonna of the Snow (5 August), the faithful used to put wine in order to keep it cool. The traditional veneration of the Madonna della Neve is one of the most ancient in the area and is linked to the fact that in these parts snow used to be collected and taken to Rome in blocks on special two wheeled carts drawn by oxen where it was used for the purpose of conserving foods. Next to the Convent of San Nicola di Bari and elsewhere on Mount Gennaro and Mount Pellecchia one can still see the wells which were used for the conservation of snow.

Century because of a plague, or perhaps due to bloody feuds between families, but to this day so well preserved as to appear to be inhabited by ghosts.

The Abbey of San Giovanni in Argentella

The abbey was founded in the IV Century, probably by Basilian monks from Greece, in the place where there once was one of the many ancient Roman farm-villas of the area and from which were taken many of the Roman remains we can today see built into its structure. Situated in a well fortified and powerful looking building, the abbey owned much of the surrounding land, above all in the X and XI Century, thanks also to its strategic position along one of the principle itineraries of transhumance.  It was modified across the centuries to the extent that little is left of the original building. The church we can today admire, thanks to its restoration in 1984, is an edifice which is clearly archaic romanesque in style with a beautiful and austere exterior made of irregular yellow tufa stone blocks which give it a severe and solid appearance only slightly softened by the presence of pilasters and arches. Similarly, in the interior the slim ionic columns, certainly once part of ancient Roman buildings, lend a lighter touch to the rather severe mysticism of the whole. The chapel dedicated to the Virgin and decorated with mosaics is probably XII Century, whilst the splendid tabernacle at the main altar dates back to the VIII Century. It is decorated in white stucco work and supported by small marble columns which are certainly of ancient Roman provenance. What are of great interest are what is left of the frescoes, which date back to the XIV Century and probably covered the whole of the inside of the church, depicting historic events connected to the Cistercian monks, and the ornaments in polychrome mosaics which are probably the work of the famous XII Century Roman marble craftsmen known as the "Cosmati". The steeple, which towers over the surrounding vegetation, is also romanesque in style. The medieval convent nearby is instead in dreadful conditions.

The castle aside, the most important and richest in history of the monuments of Palombara is the ***Abbey of San Giovanni in Argentella***, the name of which would seem to derive from the silvery waters which ran down from the surrounding hills. A national monument since 1895 and visible thanks to the service provided by the Fraternità Ecumenica Laica who live in the nearby convent, it preserves a unique charm.

A few kilometres from Palombara there are the thermal baths known as ***Terme di Cretone***, with two pools of hot sulphureous waters and open from May to September. Further South we should stop off in another important olive oil producing centre, **Marcellina**, the ideal place from whence to start an excursion to Mount Gennaro and Mount Morra, which rises upon a sight in which there once was a vaste complex of ancient roman villas the remains of which were extensively used in the

The Abbey of Santa Maria in Monte Dominici
It is on the road to San Polo dei Cavalieri and was built in the XI Century on the remains of an ancient Roman villa. In subsequent centuries it underwent modification and restoration which was unfortunately not always appropriate. However the XIII Century frescoes constitute a particularly interesting example of medieval art in Lazio, worthy of special attention are the scenes of the *Antico Testamento* and the *Nuovo Testamento* (Old and New Testament) which are of the Roman school but of Byzantine inspiration, as the rigidly frontal figure of *Santa Maria delle Grazie* (XII C.) on the main altar indicates.

construction of many of its buildings. Also Marcellina is tied to the story of an abbey, *Santa Maria in Monte Dominici*, built in a strategically important place, it being the point of access to the mountain, and constantly in conflict with the Marcellini family who, since 1153, owned a nearby fortified castle. What is today Marcellina dates back to the XI-II Century when, the castle having been destroyed by the abbey, the population took refuge around this powerful place of worship.

The nearby abbey of **San Polo dei Cavalieri** was also the property of the monks of the order of Saint Paul, after which it is named. The appellative "dei Cavalieri" was infact only added in the 1700's and its ori-

San Polo dei Cavalieri: view of the village

gin has given rise to every manner of congecture. In the XI Century it was a fortress upon the ruins of which the Orsini family (XV C.) built their **Castello** which today has been turned into a noble residence. It was Cardinal Federico Cesi (XVI C.) who adorned the interior with decorations in a style close to that of the roman mannerist school of the Zuccari. To him we also owe the construction of the steeple of the **Church of San Nicola**, said to be built in the XIV Century by crusaders who wished to thank the saint for their safe return. There are also the **Church of Santa Lucia** (XV C.), near the "Rocca", and the churches of **San Rocco** and of **Santa Liberata**. The first was built in the XVIII Century, the second, also a cemetery, was built upon a more ancient edifice of which we can still see the apse with its beautiful fresco of the Cinquecento representing the *Madonna della Misericordia, il Giudizio Universale e la Gloria dei Santi*. The last two centres to be visited on our "way of sabine oil" are outside the park of the Lucretili Mountains. They are Sant'Angelo Romano and Guidonia-Montecelio, both on the Cornicolani mountains. **Sant'Angelo Romano** perhaps rises in the place where there once was the ancient Sabine city of *Medullia* later conquered by Rome. In the area, in the locality of Poggio Cesi, one can see the remains of a large ancient roman farm villa and, close to it, the ruins of a medieval hamlet abandoned in the XV Century. Born as a fortress for defense against the barbarian and saracen invasions (XII C.), it was first called Monte Patulo, the hill upon which it stands, and later Sant'Angelo. Here too the influence of the Cesi family (1594-1668) was to be important, it is to them that we owe the transformation of the fortress into a stately home with marbles, frescos and decorations, recently renovated. In the ancient part of the citadel there are the **Church of Santa Maria e San Biagio** (1748) which contains a triptych by Antoniazzo Romano and the **Church of Santa Liberata** which, according to a legend re-evoqued by the painter in one of his works, was built for votive reasons. During the plague of the end of the 1300's the people promised to build a church should the terrible plite spare them, and the place where it should be built was chosen by following three children. The church and its convent, rebuilt in the XVIII Century, contain some interesting paintings. Lastly there are the churches of **San Michele Arcangelo** and **Sant'Elena**. The first, consacrated in the middle of the XII Century and serving also as a cemety, is today only opened together with that of Santa Liberata in one of the last two weeks of May for its patron saint's feast and the more profane "sagra" of

Sant'Angelo Romano: a view of the Rocca

> **The Grotta Cerqueta Forest**
> From Sant'Angelo, an interesting excursion is that to the **Grotta Cerqueta Forest**. This park, which is the property of the municipality, is of particular environmental importance. It covers an area of 30-35 hectares of typical limestone conformation, known for three dolinas called the "Fossi" and a cave. But the real treasures of this botanic park are its vegetation, with many protected species amongst which as many as 24 different types of wild orchids, and the numerous species of birds that live there.

cherries. The second is a rural church of the last century which is worthy of mention for two reasons: its splendid position looking onto the forest of Castigliano, or of Mars as the famous ancient roman historian Titus Livius called it; the fact that inside it, behind the alter, there is an olive tree to which an artful craftsman has given the shape of the Cross. An interesting excursion is that to the forest called **Bosco di Grotte Cerqueta**, a park of considerable environmental importance.

Guidonia Montecelio was born in 1937 from the unfication of two municipalities: Guidonia, built two years before for the purpose of serving the nearby airport and named after General A.Guidoni who died in 1928 whilst testing a parachute; Montecelio which, instead, has behind it centuries of history. Already inhabited in the protohistoric era, a castle was built there in the X Century of which we can still see the remains which tower over the village which was founded when the population of the plains were forced to flee from the invasions of the Normans. It was once again the Cesi family, lords of Monticello from the mid 1500's to the end of the 1600's, who were to realize important architectural works, amongst which the **Palazzo dei Principi** which substituted the fortress. Opposite, the **Church of San Giovanni Evangelista** contains an olive wood sculpture of the *Immacolata Concezione*

Guidonia Montecelio

(1627) venerated by the local population. The virtually intact medieval "borgo", with its houses in stone and the lanes with their pretty views merits being visited. Here we find the **Church of San Lorenzo Martire**, probably built in the XIV Century, as it contains frescos of that period. Outside the citadel, on Mount Albano, is the **Church of San Michele Arcangelo** (1724), built where maybe there once was a small XIV Century church, in turn been built upon the ruins of a temple. All the frescos, decorations and paintings, damaged by humidity, are by minor franciscan friars – who lived in the adjacent convent until 1873, when the complex became property of the State – and in particular of father Michelangelo Cianti.

The way of Cesanese di Olevano

Our itinerary based on local flavours takes us South, near the Province of Frosinone where, from the small black grapes of the vines grown everywhere in the municipalities of Olevano Romano, Affile, Genazzano, Roiate and Arcinazzo is made one of the few red wines of the Province: the "Cesanese di Olevano Romano".

The Olevano Romano Cesanese Wine

There is also a Cesanese di Affile which has become almost impossible to find. Cesanese is a D.O.C. wine which takes its name from the vine used, called "Cesanese". It is a ruby red tending to burgundy with a violet centred perfume and a soft but slightly bitter flavour, and is well capable of competing with other more famous wines. And it would seem to be the perfect wine to combine with the typical products of the area. What could be better than a good dry red with home-made fresh pasta with a sauce made from the mushrooms picked fresh in the woods of Olevano or the plateaus of the Altipiani di Arcinazzo, or with a plate of "abbacchio", the typical Roman grilled or roast lamb which at Roite is celebrated at the end of September with a "sagra". But there is also a sweet sparkling white Cesanese which is perfect with typical local sweets such as "tozzetti" and "pangiallo" or chestnuts, which the area produces in great quantity. In all of the Tiburtino-Sublacense area there are "sagras" dedicated to this delicious autumn fruit which can be cooked in several ways: roast ("caldarroste"), boiled, turned into a typical cake made from chestnut flour and called "castagnaccio". At Bellegra and Roccagiovine the "sagre" are held in October, at Arcinazzo Romano, Riofreddo, Pisoniano and Vivaro they are held in November. Lastly, at Capranica Prenestina, on 8 December there is the *Sagra delle Mosciarelle*, dried chestnuts the ancient method of preparation of which is kept alive through popular song and dance.

We will start with **Olevano Romano** where, together with the production of its excellent wines, olive oil is also produced, probably giving origin to its ancient name. First mentioned in records in 967, *Olibanum* became a fortified citadel owned by the Colonna family in the XIII Century. Today only the ruins of the castle remain to dominate over the medieval "borgo" from the height of the hill. Next to the ruins is the

Olevano Romano: view of the village

The "borgo" of Roiate

small church of **Santa Maria della Corte**. But it was not until the mid 1700's that the first nucleus of houses of what is today Olevano was built around the **Church of San Rocco**. Of interest is the **Church of Santa Margherita**, built on the model of Saint Paul's and dedicated to the saint, a member of the Olibria family said to have beeen killed by one of its members, who lived at the time of Emperor Theodosius. But the true attraction of Olevano is its scenery which has inspired painters from all over Europe – first among them the Tirollean Joseph Koch (1768-1839) – who gave birth to a "school" of landscape painting of strong romantic inspiration and which remained active until the end of the XIX Century, so much so that in 1935 a museum dedicated to the "Pittori del Ottocento" was inaugurated. One of their favourite subjects was the Bosco della Serpentara which covers the whole of Mount sant'Arcangelo, near the village, the wild beauty of which seems to have also inspired Gustave Dorè who must have taken it as a model for his illustration of the "Selva Oscura" (dark forest) for Dante's *Divine Comedy*. Today this wood and "Casa Baldi", a meeting place for italian and foreign painters, are the property of the German Federal Republic. As we proceed to the East the landscape becomes ever more mountainous: first the Ernici Mountains, then the Affiliani and, finally, the high plateau of Arcinazzo. We first meet **Roiate**, the name of which probably comes from one of the mineral water springs in the area, the Roia. In the IV Century B.C. it was inhabited by the Equians, but we first find trace of it in documents of 313 A.D. The buildings of interest are churches, such as the *Parrocchiale di San Tommaso Apostolo* which, in the mid 1500's, was in part rebuilt and extended at the cost of the frescoes inside it, the *Church of San Rocco*, built after the plague of 1350 and abandoned at the end of the XIX Century, and the *Church of San Benedetto*, built because of a miracle. Indeed, here people venerate a limestone rock upon which St. Benedict would seem to have left his imprint. There are those who swear that on 21st March, day of the saint's feast, one can see it transpiring droplets of swet. The nearby **Affile** also has its miracle. It is said that it was here that

Affile

St. Benedict performed his first miracle returning to new a vase broken by his nanny. Situated on the Affilani Mountains, the citadel is certain to have been inhabited by pre-roman peoples and subsequently by the Equians, who were then subjugated by the Romans who turned it into a colony and who gave it its prevalently agricultural character. From that period remain a roman cistern today known as the "cicerara", upon which was built the church of Sant'Angelo now disappeared, and a nearby wall in *opus reticulatum*. Subject to invasion first by the Longobards and then by the Saracens, Affile was fortified circa 1000 and, amongst other events, was under the domain of the Abbey of Subiaco until the middle of the XV Century. Of considerable interest are its churches: *San Pietro*, mentioned by Gregorius Major, upon the primitive edifice of which was built the current one, which contains frescos of considerable value, such as *Il Primo Miracolo di San Benedetto*; the X Century *Church of Santa Maria*, with fescos of the Duecento; the *Chapel of the Madonna del Giglio*, built after the 1759 earthquake when, the local people having taken refuge in the presence of an image of the Madonna, she stopped the earthquake; lastly, the *Parrocchiale di Santa Felicità* and the *Church of Santi Rocco e Sebastiano*. The first, which dates back to the early XIV Century, was extended in the XIX Century and contains some frescos by local painters dated 1538. The second, which has a fine XII Century bell tower, contains a fresco of the Cinquecento. The last municipality on this itinerary is **Arcinazzo Romano**, set in the rocks of Mount Pianezze. It is 850 mts above sea level, and the view it offers is truely enchanting: woods, chestnut groves and, farther down the valley, the green of vineyards and olive trees, whilst in the distance we can see the Monti Tiburtini and Prenestini. It will come as no surprise to learn that since ancient roman times this was a popular holiday resort. Up until 1892 it was called Ponza and was certainly a fortified citadel in the period around 923. Its history was, for a long time, tied to that of Affile as both were owned by one Ildemondo (XI C.) who was the founder of the family to which Pope Alexander IV belonged, well known for his perennial contrasts with the Abbot of Subiaco. The historic centre has a markedly medieval character. One should visit the *Church of Santa Maria Assunta* (XI C.), once gothic in style but extensively modified in the XVI and XIX Century to the point of completely changing its structure and, alas, at the expense of the frescos it once contained. Parts of it, such as the main doarway, added in the the XVII Century, the marble for the alter and the holy water fonts made from capitals, come from Trajan's villa. Also worthy of interest are the churches of *San Giorgio* and *of Santa Lucia*. The first, a rural church, was built at the end of the 1500's but extensively modified during the last century. The second, built in the same period, contains interesting frescos representing Saint Lucia, Saint Catherine and Saint Francis.

Arcinazzo Romano: the gates to the "borgo"

Excursions on the Altipiani di Arcinazzo

For those who like to go walking in a natural environment Arcinazzo is a perfect point of departure. From here one can reach the Affilani Mountains and the Colle della Croce (1,158 m.), the peeks of Monte Pianezze (1,332 m.), of Mount Altuino (1,158 m.), and of Monte Scalambra (1,420 m.) from whence there is a beautiful view of the Sacco Valley. But the most interesting place to visit in the area is the so called *Villa di Traiano* (Trajan's Villa) the construction of which, thanks to the finding of some I Century A.D. ancient Roman brick seals during excavations in the Eighties, has been back-dated by about fifty years to the period of Nero, who must have loved the area a great deal seeing that he also had himself a villa built on the Aniene River just under what is today Subiaco. The villa is near the ruins of "Piè di Campo" tower which dates back to the period of Ildemond, and is a vast complex of buildings which covers four square kilometres with terracings in *opus incertum* which give it three different levels. The thermal baths, with marble decorations, mosaics, columns and remains of the water pipes in lead are visible, whilst the rest of the buildings are still under ground.

Excursions on horse back

The horse riding centres in the area are: at Altipiani di Arcinazzo, the *Centro Ippico San Giorgio*, Via Sublacense Km 30.300 tel. 0775/599751; at Licenza, the *Associazione C.I. Rangers* Via Licinese, Km 34.200 tel. 0347/271292

A view of Tivoli

The Archaeological monumental itinerary

This itinerary, which runs along the valley of the River Aniene, takes us back in history to admire the remains of ancient roman villas, both rural and those of emperors, and visit castles and fortified citadels perched on rocks, fruit of that phenomenon of fortification which took place circa 1000 as a consequence of invasions. The starting point is **Tivoli**, the ancient *Tibur* on the origin of which there are many legends, situated in a militarily strategic position at the entrance to the valley of the River Aniene. It was soon to fall under the influence of Rome and became an important centre for the quarrying of travertine (the stone which has dressed so many monuments in Rome, both ancient and new). It was also to become a sought after holiday resort as of the II Century B.C., a favourite with famous names such as the poet Catullus, Julius Caesar, Anthony, Brutus and, later, Hadrian. There are many remains from that period, among the most interesting are the *Tempietti di Tiburnus* and the *Sibilla Albunea*, both of which once adorned the acropolis and today dominate the narrow gully in which cascade the waters of the falls. In the vicinity there is the imposing *Temple of Ercole Vincitore*, which probably dates back to about 100 B.C. and which, in time, has been transformed from sanctuary to convent and even used as a foundry for cannons and as a paper mill. The *Ponte Lucano* crosses the Aniene and, a short distance away, there is the *Sepolcro dei Plauti* (I Century A.D.). Near the imposing *Rocca Pia*, built by Pope Pius II (1458) and today still virtually intact, part of the ancient *am-

Tivoli: the Bleso amphitheatre at the foot of the Rocca Pia

> ### The Inchinata
> It is one of the most moving of religious festivals which would seem to date back to the 1300's and is held every year on 14 and 15 August. It is told that the apostles, having found themselves miraculously in Jerusalem at the death bed of the dying Virgin, saw Jesus take his mother's soul and "assume" it in heaven. The feast hinges upon this idea of encounter between mother and son. Two processions of faithfuls, one coming from the Church of Santa Maria Maggiore with the painting of the *Madonna delile Grazie* and the other from the Cathedral with the *Trittico del Salvatore,'* meet in Piazza Santa Maria Maggiore where the two effigies bow three times respectively, one in front of the other, and are then taken into the church where they remain all night. The following day, after a parting bow, they are taken to where they came from. In the procession, also the wooden statues of the patron saints of crafts are carried. The "Festa dell'Inchinata" is held in many other villages in the area.

phitheatre has been brought to light. Outside the city there is the **Villa Adriana**. After the fall of the Roman Empire, Tivoli was to live through a very difficult period due to invasions, the feuds between Popes and Emperors (during the reign of Federico Barbarossa (1153) the city walls were restored and extended) and between noble families, above all the Orsini versus the Colonna family, which continued up until the end of the 1400's. Despite this city managed to keep its municipal autonomy up until 1522 when it passed under the domain of the Apostolic Chamber. It was thus that Cardinal Ippolito D'Este, second of Lucrezia children and governor of Tivoli from 1550, was to build one of the most impressive monuments in the area, the famous **Villa d'Este**.

Tivoli has several churches of the medieval period: the **Church of San Pietro alla Carità**, built in the XII Century (probably by Pope Simmacus, 468-483). It has a romanesque façade and the remains of a cosmatesque pavement and frescoes; contemporary to it, the **Church of Santo Stefano**; **the Church of Santa Maria Maggiore** or **San Francesco**, built in the IX Century and in part rebuilt in the XIII and XIX Century. This last contains some valuable works of art, such as a painting of *Sant'Antonio da Padova* (XV C.) by some attributed to Antoniazzo Romano, and a wooden crucifix by Baccio da Montelupo (1469-1535). The **Cathedral of San Lorenzo** is of the Seicento and was built upon a VI Century church, it contains a wooden sculpture known as the *Deposizione* which is a splendid example of art of the Duecento, a XII Century triptych in tempra on wood known as the *Trittico del Salvatore*, and a marble statue called the *Immacolata Concezione* (XVII C.) which counts many devotees amongst the locals as it is said to have saved them from being stricken by the plague. Outside the city, in the shade of an olive grove, there is the **Sanctuary of Santa Maria di Quintiliolo** (in the

Tivoli: the frescos in the apse of the church of San Silvestro

vicinity of the villa known as Quintilio Varo) built by the Benedictines in the XI Century and which contains an image of the Madonna known as *Madonna in Trono con Bambino* (XIII C.) which is linked to a miracle very

The Villas of Tivoli

A visit to the three villas, all of which are extremely beautiful, is a must. Imposing and fascinating both from a historical and an artistic point of view, the *Villa Adriana* is the biggest ancient Roman villa ever discovered (tel. 0774-371007/8, visits from 9 a.m. until one and a half hours before sunset). A lover of travelling and of Hellenistic culture, Emperor Hadrian (117-138 A.D.) chose

Tivoli: a view of villa Adriana

this area at the foot of the Tiburtini Mountains as the sight for a splendid villa composed of numerous edifices which he named after the places he had visited during his travels and which it would seem he personally contributed to the design of. Built at the beginning of his reign upon the remains of a republican building, the complex covers an area of 120 hectares with housing and service buildings set amongst gardens and walks so as to blend nature and architecture in-

P. Ligorio, Fountain of the hydraulic organ, villa d'Este

to a harmonious whole, according to a principle already used at Nero's villa at Subiaco. The museum is also worth visiting, where one can see a model of the villa as it was and artifacts found during excavations. Returned to its original splendour thanks to restoration works on the building and the fountains, **Villa D'Este** (1551-1565) is the result of the transformation of a convent called the Convento di Santa Maria Maggiore. The design is by the architect Pirro Ligorio (1510-83), whilst the contemporary decorations in the interior, which celebrate the d'Este family, are by Federico Zuccari and his school as well as by Livio Agresti and Girolamo Muziano. But there is no doubt that one's attention is drawn by the scenographic effect of the gardens articulated in parallel terraces, quite clearly inspired by Bramante's Belvedere at the Vatican as well as by the imposing Sanctuary of Palestrina. Water, gushing from more

than a hundred fountains, is here the dominating element. In a manner typical of the XVI Century, all is marvel, with water jets of every type imaginable which contrast with the static mythological figures which decorate the fountains and, once again, eulogise the d'Este dynasty. **Villa Gregoriana** is in the gully dug by the river right under the acropolis. In the park, nature, untouched by man, explodes with all its fascinating power, with cascades of green and tree lined avenues, amongst which there are archaeological remains, including the walls of the so called villa of Manlio Vopisco.

G. Muziano, Banqueting Hall, villa d'Este

The Acque Albule Thermal Baths
In the locality called Bagni di Tivoli there are the thermal baths which in ancient times were known as *Fons Albunea*, because they were sacred to the nymph by the same name. They were later renamed Acque Albule for the whitish colour of the mineral waters which contain bicarbonate, sulphate, alcalines, soils and sulphur (23° C.), and which are excellent for the treatment of rheumatism, respiratory diseases and dermatitis. These thermal baths, which cover an area of approximately six hectares, are fed by the waters of two lakes and, in turn, feed five pools immersed in greenery, and where one can see the remains of the thermal baths which Agrippa built for Emperor Augustus.

similar to that of the Sanctuary of Vallepietra. Legend has it that it was found in an olive grove by St. Isidorus, patron saint of farmers, thanks to the oxen who were pulling the plough which stopped and knelt down infront of the image when they saw it on the ground. The Madonna is taken from the sanctuary to the cathedral in Tivoli on the first Sunday of May and stays there for three months.

At this point, wanting to follow a purely archeological itinerary, our objectives should be Horace's villa at Licenza and Villa Manni at Ciciliano. We must take the A24 motorway to Vicovaro-Mandela and follow the signs for **Licenza**, in the Lucretili park right in the centre of the long and narrow Valle Ustica, still peaceful and fertile as it was in the days of Horace. It was this latin poet who first called the rocks of the peek upon which the village now stands Ustica, name which in time was extended to the whole valley. Here is the villa that Maecenas, man of culture and lover of the arts, gave to his friend Horatio Flaccus (34/32 B.C.). Of interest is a visit to the ruins of the villa (in the locality of San Pietro) and the Horat-

Horace's Villa
"A shaded valley hidden amongst the mountains, though not to the extent that the sun does not illuminate its right side at dawn and, at sunset, tinges its left side with red ... There is a spring which gushes into a stream" wrote the poet describing the place where his villa was. A land he loves and where, as soon as he can, he goes to in order to meditate and compose verses in the serene peace of the countryside in a dimension so different to Rome, where he could enjoy the simple pleasures of life such as genuine food, cheese made by the local shepherds, fruit taken from the trees and the excellent local oil. The villa, which covered an area of forty hectares, included a wood, pastures, fruit and olive groves, a house, a portico and thermal baths. One can still see the external walls, part of the floors with mosaics and the thermal baths. The **Museo Oraziano** is instead in the Palazzo Orsini and contains findings from the classical and the medieval period.

ian Museum. The citadel of Licenza, named after the torrent that here joins the Aniene, became the property of the Orsini family in 1275 who gave their name to the *Palazzo Baronale* (XI C.). Around where it stands, on top of a hill and surrounded by olive groves, from whence it dominates the valley, is the old medieval part of the village with its lanes, small stone houses and staircases. Of interest is the *Church of the Beata Vergine Immacolata* built upon the old oratorium of San Giovanni. On the highest part of the hill is Civitella di Licenza.

View of Licenza

Situated on a rock spur, typical place on which to build defensive structures, we reach **Roccagiovine**, another dwelling place inside the Lucretili Park. This place too is tied to the memory of Horace, there is indeed a place called "il poetollo" (the suffix "ollo" is diminutive in Italian, an evident allusion to the all but remarkable height of the latin poet) where it is said he used to go together with one of the women who inspired his verses, the "rustic Fidilia". We have little knowledge of the history of the "borgo" up until the

Roccagiovine

An Excursion on Mount Follettoso

The name would seem like one given it by a child but its origin is linked to the legend that would have this mountain populated by "folletti" or elves. What is certain is that the place is tied to both Christian and pagan spirituality. In the days of the Sabines it was here that the temple to the goddess Vacuna, protector of crops, was and which Emperor Vespasian had destroyed and then rebuilt. Later the **Santuario della Madonna dei Ronci** (XIII-XIV C.) was built there, the ruins of which we can reach at a height of about 600 m. From the peek (1,004 m.) we can enjoy a beautiful view of the Gran Sasso. The name Madonna dei Ronci comes from the name of the place where it is said that the miracle took place. It is indeed told that one of the Orsini, after having used blasphemous language, had a monstrous apparition from which he freed himself by invoking the Virgin. Out of gratitude he commissioned the painting which we can today see in the Church of San Nicola di Bari and to which homage is rendered every 8 March.

> **Spelt**
>
> "Farro" or spelt is a cereal only recently rediscovered by gastronomy but which dates back thousands of years. Not having bread, the ancient Romans used it a great deal, all the more so because it was very resistant to decay, to the extent that every legionnaire always carried sufficient rations for a military campaign. At Licenza pasta made from spelt can be found everywhere and there is even a "sagra" called the *Sagra delle Sagne 'e Farre*, home made pasta made with spelt flour and dressed with a simple peperoncino sauce.

Percile: a view of the "borgo"

middle of the XVII Century when it is recorded as being the property of the Orsini family and, after various viscisitudes, of the Del Gallo family who still own the very much remodelled Rocca which cannot be visited. The **Church of San Nicola di Bari** is of particular interest with its valuable XVII Century paintings and an alter-piece with the *Madonna di Ronci* of the school of Perugino (XVI C.). Outside the village there is the **Church of Santa Maria delle Case**, said to have been built exactly in the place in which Horace had chosen to compose his verses. Always in the same valley we will also find the villages of Percile and Mandela. Already inhabited in ancient roman times, **Percile** appears to us in isolation in the midst of woods and fields and in a truely enviable position. Its appearance seems locked in medieval times. The XVII Century, and many times restored, **Parrocchiale di Santa Lucia** which dominates the village. Inside it we can see a fresco dated 1583 called the *Madonna del Rosario con San Domenico e Santa Caterina*. The **Church of Sant'Anatolia** is of a slightly later period, whilst the **Church of Santa Maria della Vittoria**, which was restored last century, is older and based on a temple dedicated to a pagan divinity, parts of which are still visible in the gardens, and a romanesque edifice. However, Percile's major attraction are the famous "Lagustelli", two little lakes situated at the the foot of Colle Faieta, particularly attractive for their caves and dolinas where rare birds nest. Returning South we come to **Mandela**, mentioned by Horace in a verse of his (*XVIII Epistola* - book 1) in which he describes it as " 'borgo' shrivelled by the cold". The village, which maintains its medieval appearance despite having in part been remanaged during the XVII Century and later, has its strong point in **the Castello dei Del Gallo**, which became palazzo baronale in the XV Century, and next to which is the **Church of San Vincenzo** now closed. In the centre of the village there is the **Parrocchiale di San Nicola Vescovo**, patron saint of the village. On the saint's feast day, the first Sunday in December, there is also the "sagra" of

The church of San Vincenzo at Mandela

polenta (savoury maize porridge). In order to visit the last archeological sight, Villa Manni, we must move on South to the midst of that group of mountains known as the Ruffi, Tiburtini and Prenestini. As we go down the Empiglione Valley (which takes its name from a X Century castle built upon a roman villa, the remains of the external walls of which are still visible) we come into sight of **Ciciliano** perched upon a double hill and near which there is the ancient centre of *Trebula Suffenas*. Of the ancient citadel destroyed by the Saracens in the X Century only the poligonal walls are left. In its place the benedictine monks of Subiaco later built a "borgo". The *Castello Theodoli*, which dominates the surrounding houses, was built in the XII Century but was considerably changed, especially by the Theodoli family in the XVI Century. Near it there is the ***Chiesa Parrocchiale di Santa Maria Assunta***, restored in 1795 but still containing frescoes of the XVI Century. Lastly, the churches of *Santa Liberata* and *della Palla*, the name of which derives from a miracle. It is said that the Madonna appeared before two boys who were playing ball (palla, in Italian) on the edge of a precipice and that she stopped them from falling over the edge. In Santa Liberata (built in the XV Century but changed in parts during the XVII Century) there are some interesting frescos. Before reaching Ciciliano, we turn right in order to reach *Villa Manni* where there are the remains of *Trebula Suffenas*.

If one prefers visiting the "rocche", it will never the less be possible to see medieval buildings and Renaissance castles whilst moving rapidly from impervious areas to more amenable ones, and having the added

The Excavations of Trebula Suffenas

They are in the grounds of a private villa, but can be visited by appointment. One should commence the visit with the forum with its paving of rectangular travertine stones and a funeral altar in the centre, some taverns, thermal baths with mosaics (II C.), the remains of what was probably a house and other buildings. Everywhere one turns one sees fragments of buildings, statues and epigraphs, as if one were in an open air museum but which is probably a mere fraction of what further excavations could bring to light.

opportunity of establishing closer contact with local tradition and cuisine. We will therefore depart once more from Tivoli in the direction of three villages set in the mountains known as Tiburtini and Prenestini: San Gregorio da Sassola, Casape and Poli. As we reach the vicinity of **San Gregorio da Sassola**, which owes its name to Gregorius Major, owner of the whole

> **Typical products of the Tiburtino-Sublacense area**
>
> The "sagre" give us a good indication of the typical products linked to the local economy so strongly conditioned by the presence of the mountains. Local gastronomy is based on simple and genuine products from sheep and herd animals in general, as well as those from the woods, and home made pasta. Whether it is called *ramiccia* or *strengozzo*, *sagne*, *gnoccacci* or *cecamariti*, it is always a tasty home made pasta dressed with in a whole variety of different ways: with baccalà (stockfish) at Pisoniano, with a sauce made from garlic, tomatoes and peppers at Rocca Canterano, with mushrooms at Rocca Santo Stefano, and with a sauce with wether meat at Percile. There is also "polenta", a sort of corn porridge, and fresh ricotta cheese which are celebrated with a "sagra" at Guadagnolo (Capranica Prenestina) on the first Sunday of June – a good occasion in which to see how this delicious product, and also pecorino cheese, is made and, obviously, ... to taste it.

area, we immediately catch sight of the imposing **Castello Brancaccio**. The original X Century building was modified in the XVI, XVII and XIX Century without however loosing its charm thanks to elements such as the draw-bridge, the battlements and the great walls. In the wing built by Cardinal Prospero Publicola Santacroce (XVI C.) there are some rooms with frescos by Zuccari. Cardinal Carlo Pio di Savoia, who was lord there during the period of the terrible plague of 1656, also carried out important works. It was he who had the old medieval "borgo" refurbished and who built **Borgo Pio**, which is a road, flanked by five rows of houses, which ends in an eliptic square divided into four "quarters" dedicated to saints and significantly called "teatro" (theatre). Here we find the churches of **San Sebastiano**, built in the XV Century and rebuilt in the XVII and XVIII Century, and of the **Madonna della Cavata**, also XV Century and many times modified. Also of interest are the **Church of San Gregorio Magno** (XV C.) in the medieval part, and, ouside the village, the **Convent of Santa Maria Nova** and the **Church of San Giovanni Evangelista** of the XV Century. The area is also full of remains of acqueducts and villas, signs lef by the an-

San Gregorio da Sassola

> **Olive oil and olives at San Gregorio**
> The whole of the area of the Tiburtina produces good olive oil, less famous than that of the Sabina but nevertheless excellent. The ancient Romans appreciated the *oleum Tiburtinum*, and still today where ever one looks one sees olive groves. Hadrian's Villa, for example, is set between two splendid olive groves and, at Roviano, there is an edifice known as the Montano (the ancient name for olive press) where there is today the **Museo della Civiltà Contadina della Alta Valle dell'Aniene**, which contains objects connected to agriculture and the cultivation of olives. San Gregorio da Sassola is famous for its olive oil and for its tasty olives in brine which are celebrated with a "sagra" on the last Sunday in August and on the first Sunday in September, in concomitance with the feast of the Madonna della Cavata. The tradition in production of preserved olives, of which some 400 tons a year are produced, is over a century old. Also to be remembered, between the end of October and the beginning of November at San Gregorio, and in December at Casape (where excellent olive oil is produced as well), is the *Sagra della Bruschetta*.

cient roman people since the times of the Republic. Just a few kilometres from San Gregorio we come to **Casape**, in the Monti Prenestini, at the origin of which there is yet again a roman villa I (Century A.D.) and which, during the XVII Century, was also under the dominion of the Pio di Savoia family. The fulcrum to the village is the Palazzo Baronale around which the medieval "borgo" is clustered. The palace was built in the X Century and was originally a defense tower, it was later turned into a castle and finally into the noble residence of today. We can get an idea of the modifications it has undergone through the ages by looking at the fresco painted in the 1700's in the **Church of San Simone**, outside the village and situated on private property, in which the castle is portrayed with elements that today no longer exist. Inside the **Chiesa Parrocchiale di San Pietro Apostolo** there are an anonymous wooden crucifix of the XII Century and a byzantine style painting known as the *Cristo Benedicente* (X-XI C.). Lastly, climbing to the top of a tufa rock promontory, we reach **Poli**. Already a fortified citadel in the XI Century, in the XVI Century the fortress was transformed into the *Palazzo Baronale* by the Counts of Segni. The back part still has walls and windows which date back to the medieval period whilst the front was only completed in the XVII Century. The two parts of the edifice however give the appearance of being one unit, and access to the palace is through a fine late renaissance style gate, probably built in 1592. Inside the palace, most of which is decorated with grotesques which are not all in a good state of conservation, there is the seat of the

Poli

municipality. Amongst the frescoes, one would appear to portray *Villa Catena*, a villa of the 1500's situated outside the village the construction of which was overseen by the poet Annibal Caro. In the *Cappella Conti*, inside the palace, there are rich decorations composed of frescoes and stucco works, amongst which *San Francesco in Estasi* by Cavalier D'Arpino (1568-1640), the late mannerist painter to whom some attribute the whole of the chapel. One ought also to visit: the *Palazzo Pellicioni* of the Settecento, with frescoes of the XVII and XVIII Century, and the *Church of San Pietro* (1603) with a fine XVIII Century organ with silver pipes and engraved gilded wood work as well as a towering baroque steeple; the XIV Century *Church of Sant'Antonio Abbate* which was considerably changed in the XV and XVI Century and contains frescos of the XVI Century; its contemporary, the *Church of San Giovanni Battista*, in part resting upon naked rock and full of sunshine and vegetation as it no longer has a roof, but with frescos still in part visible, offers a truely interesting sight. A tour of the castles cannot but include, a few kilometres from Tivoli but North of the places just visited, a visit to the beautiful castle of **Castel Madama**. The remains of villas and of an acqueduct tell of the presence of ancient romans in this area in times gone by. In the XIV Century, when the area was under the domain of the Orsini family, there was a *Castrum Sancti Angeli* the history of which is closely linked to that of the *Castrum Appoloni*, founded in the VIII Century by the Benedictine monks of Subiaco. The castle would however appear to date back to the X Century, even if it was extensively modified in the XIV, XVI and XVIII Century. Its "borgo" was called Castel Sant'Angelo until 1635 when it was renamed Castel Madama in honour of Margaret of Austria, widow of Alessandro Medici, who, charmed by the castle, decided to establish herself there and improve it by turning it into a stately home, building a new "borgo" round the external walls almost as if to have a second ring of walls around the castle. The castle, restored and now property of the municipality, has a lovely cloister with portico and open arcade with an attractive well in its centre. In the upper part of the citadel there is the *Church of San Michele Arcangelo* (1775), built upon a chapel of the XV Century, and the little *Church of San Sebastiano* with frescos attributed to the school of Zuccari, which should be seen. Another castle is the **Castello Massimo** at Arsoli, recently restored, which dominates the village and the valley of the Bagnatore. In order to get there from Castel Madama we can choose to carry on along the Tiburtina Valeria or take the motorway. If we choose

Castel Madama: church of San Michele Arcangelo

the former we will be able to visit a number of small centres on the way, all of which are situated in a mountainous area once inhabited by the Equians, a people of tusco-umbrian origin soon to be subjugated by the romans who, in the area of Riofreddo, have left some necropolis datable VII-VI Century B.C. We will start from **Cineto Romano**, which has as many as three castles, two of which, the *Castello di Camminata* and *Castello del Lago*, are totally in ruins and one of which, transformed into the *Palazzo Baronale*, still dominates the citadel. Built towards the end of the year 1000, the castle, then known as "Scarpa feudale", was soon to become the property of the Orsini family, during which time the "borgo" started to form around its walls. To be visited are the **Church of San Giovanni Battista** (1650) – built upon a church of the XIII Century – where we can admire a painting of great value known as *San Giovanni Battista nel Deserto* (XVI C.) and, outside the village, **Santa Maria delle Grazie**. The history of this church is marked by a series of destructions and reconstructions. It was first built by St. Gregorius Major but then destroyed by the Saracens to be then rebuilt in 1217, with the exceptional patronage of St. Francis who layed the first stone and there established a franciscan convent, which existed until the middle of the XVII Century. The church we see today is of the 1700's. Just outside the village, along the road to Riofreddo, there is a place with a rather special charm to it: the *Pozzo della Morge*, a chasm about three metres wide and fivehundred deep which is surrounded by olive groves and upon the origins of which one can only speculate. At the bottom of the chasm there is the entrance to a tunnel 1,700 mts. long, of which we have records from the XVI Century when it was used as a jail for those who had committed capital crimes. Carrying on along our itinerary we reach **Roviano**, perched up on the side of Mount Sant'Elia (990m), and the **Castello** of which dominates the Tiburtina and thus the traffic between Lazio and Abruzzo. Founded by the benedictine monks of Subiaco sometime before the XI Century and today property of the municipality, the castle has undergone

Cineto Romano

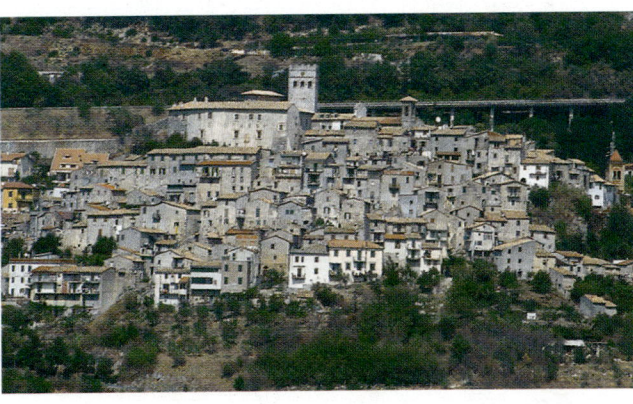

View of Roviano

Roviano: the Castello

frequent changes. Of the baroque period, but much changed since it was built, is the **church of San Giovanni Battista** which, in 1984, became the *Santuario di San Fortunato* after the martyr saint who is buried there. Lastly, Porta Scaramuccia, is so called after the conflict which broke out in 1570 between the Colonna family, feudal lords of the village, and the Zambeccari family of Arsoli. On a height of karst origin which runs from 600 to 1000 mts. is Riofreddo, the name of which ("freddo" means cold) makes obvious reference to the cold waters of the Bagnatore which cross the area and across which the bridge known as **Ponte della Nerva**, still today visible, was built. Those who might think of it as a faraway lost village that is difficult to reach should know that it was here that the wedding of the famous musician Gaetano Doninzetti was celebrated, the house he lived in and in which he composed some of his works still exists, and that Garibaldi's son Ricciotti was the one who built the **Castello** now in part property of the municipality. Also thanks to the restoration work done, the medieval historic centre and the **Castello Colonna** with its two cylindrical towers have kept all of their charm. Built in the XIII Century, the typically medieval **Oratorio dell'Annunziata** is decorated with fine frescoes (1422) by Arcangelo di Cola da Camerino, a pupil of Gentile da Fabriano, whose refined and elegant style is typical of the international gothic of the end of the XIV and beginning of the XV Century. Next to it is the ancient *"Ospitale"* where the local municipality has its seat. Farther along our itiner-

Vallinfreda

> **The Sagra of the Fagiolina Arsolana**
> It is a rather unique "sagra" which is held in the third week of August or the first of September and has been in vogue since the Sixties. It is dedicated to a typical local product: a white dried bean which is easily digested and which is gathered in mid August and dried on the "pannuni" or cloths laid streets and lanes. Vallinfreda also has a "sagra" dedicated to beans, the *Fagiolata*, celebrated on 15 August and dedicated to a local dish made with the excellent local beans, flavoured with pork rind, olive oil and aromatic herbs.

ary we reach **Vallinfreda**, situated on the heights of Monte della Croce. Probably born between the end of the 1400's and the beginning of the 1500's, in connection with the passing of St. Benedict and the foundation of his coenobiums, the citadel was repeatedly invaded, from the Normans, to the Saracens, to the Longobards who remained there until the arrival in Italy of Charlemagne. There are two monuments worthy of note: the *Church of San Michele Arcangelo* built in the 1500's and greatly modified during the century after, which contains restored frescos and paintings of good quality; the *Oratorium of the Santissimo Crocifisso* (XV C.) with decorations and frescos of the same period. Our itinerary now takes us to **Vivaro Romano**, situated on the offshoots of the Monte della Croce such that its height above sea level ranges from 500 to 1081 mts. Its origins go back to the ancient Equian *Vivarium* which became roman in 90 B.C. and later became part of the Longobard domain. First records of it, under the name "Vivaro", date back to the beginning of the year 1000 when it was already a fortified citadel under the domain of the Abbey of Farfa. It later became part fo the lands of the Orsini family who, apart from the "Castello Baronale", decided to further fortify it with walls and towers which were alas destroyed during the french siege of 1799. Today all that is left is some large ruins and part of the tower that dominated the gates to the castle. The *Parrocchiale di San Biagio* is neogothic and contains the fresco known as *Madonna Illuminata* (XII C.) of oriental origin, whilst the *Church of the Madonna Illuminta* is probably XIII Century. On the fifth and the sixth of August the feast of the Madonna is celebrated with a beautiful torch-light procession during which the sacred image is taken from the Sanctuary to the Parrocchiale. Our final stop is in **Arsoli** where there are many roman ruins such as the remains of farm villas and poligonal walls, the

Arsoli: the castello Massimo

Claudius and Marcius acqueducts (circa 200 B.C - circa 100 B.C.), the Scutonico and the San Giorgio bridge, and the columns of the XXXVI and XXXVIII mile of the Via Valeria. St. Benedict here founded one of his 13 coenobiums, Sant'Andrea, from whence the monks began to reclaim the valley and to fortify it for defense purposes. Built in the IX Century, the castle first belonged to the benedictine monks and then to various noble families until, in 1574, it became property of the Massimo family. Restored many times over, and modified extensively by Vignola and Giacomo della Porta, the *Castello* has hosted popes and princes and even the great sicilian writer Luigi Pirandello, who gave the citadel the the nickname "little Paris". Inside the castle, in the halls with frescos by the Zuccari brothers and by Marco Benefial (1684-1764) we can see period collections of arms, instruments and furniture, and a XIII Century chapel. Finally, in the italian style garden, there is the **Chapel of Santa Maria di Belmonte**, tomb of the Massimo family, with a statue of the goddess Rome found during the excavations of Constantine's thermal baths at the Quirinale. Next to it is the **Parrocchia del Santissimo Salvatore**, built in 1580

Sambuci: view including the castello Theodoli

on a design by Giacomo della Porta as a replacement for an earlier ruined church. Of interest are a gilt wooden tabernacle, a painting known as the *Trasfigurazione*, attributed to Domenichino, and a processional shoulder-frame with a painting of the Settecento which portrays *Nostra Signora di Guadalupe*, an image which has always been the object of great veneration. Also of interest is the small **Church of San Rocco** with frescoes of the XVI Century.

The last castle we shall visit is that at Sambuci, the history of which is tied to the Benedicitnes of Subiaco and to Frederick of Antiochia. The name **Sambuci** probably derives from the presence of the many elder-berry trees (sambuco in Italian) which there are in the area. It began life as a farm sometime before the VII Century A.D., was later fortified by monks, subsequently to become, together with Saracinesco and Anticoli, part of the domain of Frederick of Antiochia, natural son of Emperor Frederick II, whose son Corrado in turn gave his name to Anticoli Corrado. Later to become part of the Orsini and then the Theodoli family property, the *Castello* was extensively modified during the XIII and XVII Century. It has splendid italian style gardens which are today property of the Municipality. Inside the castle there are halls with frescos with, amongst others, scenes drawn from *Gerusalemme Liberated* by Tasso, by Giovan Angelo Canini who was a pupil of Domenichino. The frescoes on walls and ceilings of the *Salone del Carro del Sole* were instead painted by the roman painter Mario De' Fiori. They were brought here from the now destroyed Palazzo Theodoli in Rome. Also worthy of note are: the **Church of San Michele Arcangelo**; the **Church of San Pietro Apostolo**, of benedictine origin and joined to the castle, the ceiling of which is perhaps attributable to Mario De' Fiori and which contains a fine painting of the Seicento known as *Consegna delle Chiavi a San Pietro*; the baroque style **Church of Santa Maria delle Grazie**.

The name **Saracinesco** instead calls to mind the legendary victory of the King of the Franks against the Saracens, some of which, perhaps tired of warring and charmed by the beauty of those impervious places, decided to stop there (916) and set up a village, the inhabitants of which in part still today have names which recall those of their ancestors. In the year 1000, benedictine monks built a fortress which was soon to become a fortified citadel. Even though there are no monuments worthy of note it is well worth visiting this citadel situated with the wooded Monte Macchia behind it and the ancient "borgo" which seems to have bridled the past in order to jealously preserve it. We end our itinerary with **Anticoli Corrado** of which we first find mention in records in 997. The village is in part

Piero Gaudenzi, La Vecchia Lolli, charcoal and oil on wood, 1916-'25, Civico Museo d'Arte Moderna, Anticoli Corrado

The models of Saracinesco and of Anticoli

Famous and much sought after in the XIX Century and the beginning of the XX Century were the youths of Saracinesco whose oriental appearance was the source of inspiration for both Italian and foreign artists and painters, as where the beautiful young women of Anticoli, some of which became famous models. Anticoli was also to become a famous centre for artists, who were inspired by the beauty of its landscapes. Amongst the most famous Sartorio, De Carolis, Carena, Martini and Capogrossi. Many of the local stables have been transformed into artists' studios where artists still today live and paint.

Anticoli Corrado: the fountain by Arturo Martini (1924-1927) in the piazza delle Ville

medieval and in part baroque. In truth not much is left of the former as the remains of the **Church of Santa Vittoria** are hardly visible due to the fact that it was thoroughly restructured in the 1700's, whilst the **Palazzo Baronale**, built in the 1600's, with its fine roof-garden, encompasses the "Rocca" which dates back to approximately the year 1000. The **Palazzetto Brancaccio** contains the **Museo Civico**, where there is a collection of paintings by italian and foreign artists for the most inspired by the village and its surroundings. In the typical Piazza delle Ville, which has buildings dating back to all the periods of history the village has lived through, there are the *Fontana dell'Arca di Noè* which is attributed to Arturo Martini (1924-1927), and the XI Century **Church of San Pietro** with frescos ranging from the XIII to the XVII Century, much ruined despite restoration. Outside the village there is the **Church of the Madonna del Giglio**, celebrated every second Sunday of September with a rather unusual "festa" known as the "Ballo della Marmotta", when a large puppet is paraded across the streets of the village to the sound of bagpipes, flutes and tamburines. This feast, also called "Mammocchia" or "Mammoccia" and linked to ancient rituals, is typical of the area.

Detail of the tempietto di san Giacomo at Vicovaro

The religious itinerary

The last of these itineraries in this area runs the length of the Aniene valley following the foot steps of the benedictine and franciscan monks as well as those of the thousands of pilgrims who every year visit the many sanctuaries in the area. We start with the Monastery of San Cosimato at Vicovaro and then proceed to the Santuary of the Santissima Trinità at Vallepietra, crossing the valley, which broadens after Arsoli to become rocky and wild to the extent that it should not be a surprise to know that it is said to have been a land of saints and brigands. The area is full of little villages, still intact and set in the silence of forests, where local traditions, still very much alive, are an integral part of the local culture. It is supposed that **Vicovaro** was built on the remains of the ancient Equian city of *Varia*, situated in a strategic position along the Via Valeria where, in the XIII Century, the Orsini built a quadrilateral fortified "Rocca" of which one can today see only the base of the lookout tower together with a part of the outside walls, the gothic entrance gates and some frescos of the Trecento and Quattrocento. At the start of the 1700's the new owners, the Bolognetti family, began transforming it into a 'palazzo baronale' (stately home) designed by Sebastiano Cipriani. Next to it is the late baroque style **Church of San Pietro** (1755) with two belltowers in the style of Borromini. The "borgo", where there are the **Church of San Salvatore** and the **Church of San Sabino**, is typically medieval. A true masterpiece is the **Tempietto Ottagonale di San Giacomo** which shows the fact that it was built in stages, construction was infact started by the Orsini in the mid 1400's as a family tomb and was finished about 1474. The lower part, the work of Domenico Capodistria, is late gothic in style, whilst the upper part, by Giovanni Dalmata, shows renaissance characteristics. This blend of styles is so harmoniously executed as to make the monument unique. Outside the village there is the XV Century **Church of Sant'Antonio Abate al Borgo** which was modified in the XVIII Century but leaving intact the steeple and the portico, the columns of which come from ancient roman villas. The **Church of Santa Maria delle Grazie**, already served by friars in 1223 and probably by wish of St. Francis, who had died the year before and who had stopped here on his pilgrimage to Subiaco. On the alter there is an appreciable byzantine icon painted on lebanese cedar wood and portraying the Virgin, donated by the humanist Marcantonio Sabellico. In Vicovaro, on the 15 August of every year, there is the feast of the 'Inchinata' during which the confraternities carry this image and that of the Saviour in procession to the Tempietto. But our most important destination is the ***Complesso Conventuale di San Cosimato***, near Vicovaro, in the narrowest point of the valley of the Aniene which, as long ago as the V Century, was an area already frequented by hermits who followed rules of oriental inspiration.

Leaving Vicovaro, we can choose one of two possible routes: towards the Sanctuary of Sant'Anatolia a Gerano, or that of the Mentorella on mount Guadagnolo. We will start with the latter but, before reaching it, we could also stop at Pisoniano and San Vito Romano which, together with Capranica Prenestina, are in an area once inhabited by the Equians. **Pisoniano** owes its name and origins to an ancient Roman

San Cosimato

A visit to it really takes one back in time. Here, in a place of such mystic atmosphere, amongst cliffs and cyprus trees, in about the year 500 an oratory dedicated to Saints Cosma and Damian was built upon the ruins of an ancient Roman villa, which was to be the nucleus of the church built later. Next to it was built the monastery which suffered destruction at the hands of the Longobards and the Saracens, but which was always rebuilt and which had periods of great power and splendour. In 1680 the convent was passed from the Benedictines to the Franciscans. At about the same time all the frescoes which decorated the portico and the chapel were lost and, in 1727, the convent itself was completely rebuilt. Today we can there admire frescos of the XV Century and a gothic style chapel with a cross vault. Two of the three lunettes of the portico painted by Antonio Rosati (1670) illustrate a legend according to which the church was constructed in the place were Charlemagne defeated the Saracens. Another legend, which concerns Saint Benedict from Norcia (480-circa 547) tells that, the fame of the saint having spread, the monks of San Cosimato invited him to put order into the life of their hermitage after the death of their abbot. The saint accepted, but the rules he imposed were too heavy for some to the point that they decided to poison his drink. When Saint Benedict placed a benediction upon it, the chalice miraculously broke spilling the wine on the floor and staining a stone which was put in the caves where the monks carried on their monastic life and which can still today be seen. The caves of San Benedetto and the saints look out from a rock face which drops down to the River Aniene and are linked to the monastery above and to the river below via a complicated system of tunnels and stairs cut out of the rock which form a truly special sight.

The entrance to the cave at the convent

family, Pisonia, who in all probability owned the villa the remains of which are still to be seen near the valley of the Giovenzano. The houses which grew up around it are of today's village, sometime destroyed and later rebuilt. In the XIII Century it was a fortified citadel and belonged to the monks of Subiaco, then, after having changed hands several times, it became part of the domains of the Theodoli family in the second half of the XVI Century. The *Parrocchiale di San Paolo Apostolo*, in the old part of the village, rebuilt in the 1900's contains a painting of the *Madonna del Rosario* (XVIII Century) by Francesco Ferrari, whilst the *Chiesa Rurale di Santa Vittoria Vergine e Martire*, which was probably first built in the VI Century, was much modified in the XVIII and subsequent Centuries. Of particular beauty is a painting on wallnut wood of the saint in which she is depicted from a rigidly frontal perspective typical of the byzantine style. Legend has it that it was found by a peasant in 1014 in the place where the church now stands. Shortly after having left Pisoniano we come upon **San Vito Romano**, the ancient Vitellia, in a dominant position on the valley of the Sacco. Once a fortified citadel dedicated to Saint Vito by the Benedectines, it was occupied by the Longobards and later destroyed by the Saracens (IX C.), but the inhabitants who managed to survive founded, with the help of the monks, a new village around a fortress set on the peek of a rock. The "borgo" we see today is of the XIV Century and is almost intact, whilst the *Castello*, founded in the XII Century but subsequently greatly modified in the XVI Century by new owners, can clearly be seen to be composed of parts which belong to different periods. It is to the Theodoli that one owes the rather strange structure shaped like a ship and the frescos in some of the halls, as well as the surrounding "Borgo" Mario. Tradition has it that it was here that Oddone Colonna, later to become Pope Martin V, was born (1365). Worthy of a visit are the baroque *Church of Santi Sebastiano e Rocco*, the XV Century *Church of Santa Maria de Arce*, next to the castle, that of *San Vito* (XVIII C.) situated on a rise, and the *Church of San Biagio*, rebuilt in the XVII Century upon the ruins of an oratorium of the XII Century. Outside the village there is the *Church of the Madonna di Compigliano*, which dominates it. It was founded in the XVI Century, when a young boy recovered the power of speech after having seen the Virgin, and completed in the XVII Century. As the apparition had taken place in the branches of a cherry tree, the image of the Madonna kept in the church and restored in the last century is painted on cherry wood. And now we move on to **Capranica Prenestina**, a pretty medieval 'borgo' the origins of which date back to the IX Century. To be seen are: the XVI Century *Palazzo Capranica*, built on the remains of medieval ruins part of which were included into the structure; the *Church of San-*

San Vito Romano: the Castello

Capranica Prenestina: Palazzo Capranica

ta Maria Maddalena which dates back to the early 1500's and was restructured in the XVIII Century, according to some to a design by Giuliano Pantigati, a pupil of Michelangelo, and according to others by Bramante. The very plain façade is flanked by a square based romanesque bell tower, whilst the cupola, or "cupolino" as it is called, is shaped like a sort of giant lantern and is XVI Century in style. The inside is neoclassic and it is worth seeing a marble lion and a bas-relief head of Aeolus, which some rather dubiously attribute to Michelangelo. The Church of the Madonna delle Fratte probably dates back to the XVI Century. It is told that a shepherd found an image of the Madonna with Child in the "fratte" (bushes) near Capranica which he took back to his village, Castel San Pietro. But the day after the image had miraculously returned to Capranica and was found in the place where the church was subsequently built. Near Capranica there is a hamlet called Guadagnolo where there is the *Sanctuary of Santa Maria della Mentorella*.

We can now take the road to Bellegra and then head on up to Gerano. Near **Bellegra**, we reach the *Convent of San Francesco* the origins of which are not known but which was certainly a Benedictine hermitage in the XIII Century. Extended in the XIX Century, the convent (perhaps founded during the saint's pilgrimage to Subiaco) has a small *Fran-*

The Sanctuary of the Mentorella

There is a miracle at the origin of this church as well. The story goes that, after having seen a stag with a luminous cross between its horns, the Roman general Placidus changed his name to Eustace and was martyred during the reign of Hadrian. To him Constantine decided to dedicate the church founded in the first half of the IV Century A.D., and which was modified in the course of the centuries. It is known that in 594 it was part of the properties of the monks of Subiaco and that, after a period of abandonment, it was completely restored thanks to Father Atanasius Kircher (late XVIII C.) who collected funds all over Europe. Both inside and out, the church is purely medieval despite the many restorations. Of interest are a series of frescoes of the XV Century and a wooden statue of the Madonna with Child of the XIII Century, one of the most important examples of this type of sculpture. Every year there are many pilgrimages to the sanctuary.

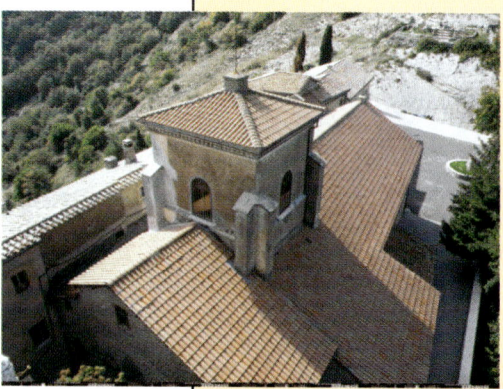

ciscan Museum situated in the friar's cells where we can see relics and other objects of various kinds pertaining to the world of franciscans. In the chapel which flanks the convent is a *Crocifisso* (XVII C.) made in wood by Father Vincenzo da Bassiano and famous for its realism. On a rise in front of the convent there is the **Church of Monte Calvario** (XVIII C.) to which, during Lent, goes a *via crucis* which sets out from the convent. Known in the X Century as Civitella, the village changed name in 1880 and the presence of inhabitants in ancient times is tetified to by the fact that there are ancient cyclopean and roman walls. Between Bellegra and Gerano there is the village of **Rocca Santo Stefano**, already present in the X Century and the "borgo" of which, gathered round the *Parocchiale of Santo Stefano Protomartire*, has kept its medieval appearance with its houses with arched doars and roads in stone. The fortress which gave its name to the place has instead disappeared. From on high the late baroque style *Parrocchiale della Beata Vergine Assunta* dominates the village, inside it there is an umbrian school painting called the *Martirio di Santa Barbara (XVI C.)*. The

One of the streets in the centre of Bellegra

Church of Santo Stefano, which contains frescos of the XVI Century, is older but has undergone several changes in time. The **Sanctuary of Santa Anatolia**, about 11/2 klms. from **Gerano**, originally a *curtis dominica* (VI C.) and known to have been a sanctuary as far back as 936, underwent many changes until the XVI Century when it took on the appearance it now has. The origins of this citadel is connected to that phenomenon of encastlement typical of the IX and X Century. The inhabitants of *Vico Trellanum*, a citadel born after the fall of the Roman Empire, when threatened by barbarian and saracen invasions, repaired to the nearby mountain of *Geranum* where there was a fortress which was at the time the object of contetion between the abbey of Subiaco and the bishop of Tivoli. Here one can see: Abbot Giovanni V's *Torre*, a control tower built in defence of the "Palazzo" by the same name; the *Palazzo di Corte* (XIV C.); the **Church of Santa Maria Assunta**; the **Church of San Lorenzo Martire**. Of these two churches, the first, which we today see in its XIX Century form but which was originally built in 1077 by Abott Giovanni, contains a representation of the Madonna known as the *Madonna del Cuore* which is attributed to Sebastiano Conca (1680-1764), whilst the second, born where there once was a votive alter, was rebuilt in 1786.

View of the Rocca di Santo Stefano

The church of Santa Anatolia at Gerano

Another famous representation of the Madonna is to be found in the church of Marano Equo, it is known as the *Madonna della Quercia* and in order to go and see it we must return towards the Tiburtina Valeria or, more accu-

The Feast of Santa Anatolia and the Madonna del Cuore

At the feast of Saint Anatolia, the village's patron saint, lay and religious aspects blend together. In the wide and open space in front of the church, only a short distance from a medieval "borgo" and ancient Roman tombs of the II Century B.C., there is a fair for agricultural products and, often rare, craft works. The gipsies set camp here and liven the evenings with song and dance. In the evening there is the procession to the sanctuary in honour of the young Roman girl martyred in 250 A.D., whose full size statue is kept in a niche on the back wall of the church. Another traditional feast is the *infiorata*, dedicated to the Madonna del Cuore and the most ancient in Italy. It was started in 1770 and is held on the first Sunday after 25 April. The night before, artists prepare theme based pictures (250 m^2) made from petals of fresh flowers, and on this rather unique carpet the procession passes the day after, carrying with it on a float with the picture of the Madonna del Cuore which is kept in a niche in the back wall of the Church of Santa Maria Assunta, and which is linked to a miracle. It is told that the picture was brought to Gerano by two Jesuits whose task it was to spread the word of God. Having successfully accomplished there mission, the two could not take the picture away with them because every time they took it out of the church it started to rain violently. It was thus that, believing this to be divine will, they left the picture there.

rately, the Sublacense which takes us through three attractive villages immersed in the peaceful greenery of woods: Cerreto Laziale, Canterano and Rocca Canterano. **Cerreto**, takes its name from the local woods of Turkey oak (cerreto, in Italian). It was inhabited in remote times and during the roman period, but the first mention traced is of 1005 when it is recorded as being a fortified "borgo" under the domain of the Benedictine monks of Subiaco, and thus it remained until the middle of the XV Century. The *Rocca,* built at the end of the XIV Century, is in the upper part of the village. The **Church of Santa Maria Assunta** was built between the XII and XIII Century but subsequently underwent extensive transformation, it contains some interesting works of art amongst which the XVI Century paintings the *Madonna delle Grazie* and the *Salvatore* as well as a wooden crucifix. The **Church of San Sebastiano** is probably of the XVI Century and is open only on certain occasions. **Rocca Canterano** would seem to have been founded in the X Century as a fortress for the defence of **Canterano** below it and has remained unchanged in the course of time, unlike Canterano which, after World War II, was extensively renovated – even the cyclopean walls in the locality of Croce were re-assembled. At Rocca Canterano is the **Parrocchiale di Santa Maria Assunta** built in the XVII Century in place of a smaller church of which only the oratorium is left. Inside there are a fresco of the *Ascensione della Vergine* and a XVII Century organ.

Returning North we reach **Agosta**, perched on the side of a cliff. The name derives from a nearby spring called *Augusta* in honour of Emperor Augustus who had it fed into the Marcius Acqueduct (144 B.C.).

The countryside in the area of Canterano and, in the background, the village

The Festa dei Cornuti

Amongst the various feasts and "sagre", the one held at Rocca Canterano around 11 November, feast of Saint Martin, is unquestionably the most bizarre. It is the feast of the cuckold, during which the locals carry enormous sets of horns, the symbol for cuckolds (who in Italian are called "cornuti", that is "horned") down the zigzag lanes of the village in a burlesque procession. Those who like this kind of rather ribald event are welcome and will also be able to taste the excellent local chestnuts known as "role".

Its history is much the same as for other X/XI Century castles in the area, contended by the Abbey of Subiaco and local lords. Today the castle and the old 'borgo' are ruined. Architecturally fine is the *Parrocchiale di Santa Maria* built in the 1700's upon a preceding church. Much venerated, in the locality of Fonte, is the small *Church of the Madonna del Passo*, this since 1615 when the representation of the Madonna regave a peasant women the possibility of walking. Perhaps originally founded by the Equians, hence the name **Marano Equo**, this village rests upon a hill surrounded by woods, but also vineyards and olive groves and, as afore mentioned, the area is also rich in mineral water springs the therapeutic qualities of which were sung as long ago as ancient roman times by Plinius the Elder. The area is particularly suitable for those who wish to find a place where to enjoy nature in peace. Records dating back to 864 indicate that Marano was at the time a fortified citadel under the control of the abbots of Subiaco. All that is left from those times is a circular corner tower, and part of the escarpment, which after transformations in the XVIII and XIX Century has become the seat of the local municipality. Of interest are the *Parrocchiale di San Biagio*, which contains an alter-piece datable in the middle of the Seicento attributed to Vincenzo Manenti (1600-74), a pupil of Cesari and of Domenichino, and the *Church of Santa Maria*

Agosta

View of Marano Equo

della Pietà built in the early 1700's upon the ruins of an earlier chapel of which practically nothing is known. Unique in its kind for the elegance of its façade, this church has the vault of the nave decorated with frescos representing the *Assunzione di Maria in Cielo*. However, the most frequented place of worship in the area is the ***Sanctuary of the Madonna della Quercia***, just outside the village.

From Marano we can now head for Subiaco and the sanctuary at Vallepietra, thus following the road many pilgrims take on the first Sunday of Pentecost and on 26 July for the feast of the Santissima Trinità. Reaching Cervara di Roma we enter the ***Parco Naturale dei Monti Simbruini***, the administrative offices of which are at **Jenne**, and where the writer Antonio Fogazzaro, charmed by the place, set his novel *Il santo*. Little is known of the origins of this citadel, the first

The Sanctuary of the Madonna della Quercia

This sanctuary is tied to a miracle recounted in chronicles of the XVII Century, where it is told that the Madonna appeared to a shepherd called Fausto in the vicinity of an oak tree. The year in which the miracle occurred is not known, but it was probably between the end of the XV and the beginning of the XVI Century, and, in memory of it, the miraculous oak tree was placed under the alter of the church. It is impossible to establish the date of foundation of the sanctuary, all one can do is presume that it can be dated at more or less the same time as the frescos on the counter façade which are of the XV Century. The miracle is remembered in a fresco by Francesco Cozza (1605-1682) in the presbytery. Opinions vary as to whether the sanctuary was built before or after the miracle. What is certain is that the church was dedicated to the Madonna della Quercia before the date in which the miracle was reported in the chronicles. The church and the convent were in Franciscan hands from 1570 to 1653, when they were passed over to the Abbey of Subiaco. The feast of the Madonna della Quercia is held on 5 August and, as always, is both a lay and a religious celebration with the procession which carries the picture of the Madonna followed by song, dance and fireworks.

recorded traces of which date back to the IX Century, and it too with a castle built by the Abbot of Subiaco Giovanni of which there are today only ruins. The most important edifices are the ***Parrocchiale of Sant'Andrea Apostolo*** (1874) which contains an anonymous wooden crucifix of the XVI Century, and the ***Church of the Madonna della Rocca*** with XIV Century frescoes.

Jenne

The Natural park of the Monti Simbruini

It covers an area of 35,000 hectares and takes its name from the limestone mountains between Lazio and the Abruzzo, so called for the abundance of rain fall in the area, *sub imbrinus* in Latin means "under the rain". Rocky peeks such as that of Mount Autore (1,853 m.), plateaus of pasture land and, lower down, gullies and caves dug out by the waters such as that of the Inferniglio, near Jenne, and the Simbrivio, near Vallepietra, make of the park a true paradise for those who like excursions in all seasons. Reaching this area by car along the roads, or by bicycle, on horse back or on foot along the special paths, one can enjoy peace and the natural beauties of the place as well as admire the major part of plants and animals typical of the Apennine Mountains. At the upper altitudes there are beech trees, maples, yew and red fir and, further down, woods of durmast, holm-oak, hazelnut and chestnut trees, whilst in summer in the fields there are lilies, narcissus and orchids. In will not be easy to meet wolves, wild cats and foxes but one will certainly run into porcupines, squirrels and boar or see peregrine falcons vaulting in the sky together with sparrow hawks and perhaps eagles. Finally, the Aniene and the Simbrivio are still populated by trout, barb and fresh water prawns. Inside the park, in that part which is in the Province of Rome, there are the municipalities of Cervara di Roma, Camerata Nuova, Subiaco, Jenne and Vallepietra. Amongst the sports one can do here there is skiing and free climbing on Mount Livata, the only skiing resort in the province, and 15 klms from Subiaco. Lovers of skiing will be able to climb to 1,800 m. and ski on 16 tracks of varying difficulty, there are also four tracks for cross-country skiing and eight ski-lifts. There is also a branch of the national school of ski instructors.

"Cervara di Roma / lives alone, sculpted into the top / of a mountain of rock. / It is a sculpture in the sky, / which to the sky would fly / if the wind could sustain it ...", thus wrote Gabriel Alberti, and his verses aptly describe **Cervara di Roma**, which is perched on Monte Pilione (1053 m), and dates back to around the IX-X Century. Some in fact sustain that it is recorded as being part of the properties of the Abbey of Subiaco as long ago as 867 and that the monks built a fortified citadel there. Others instead maintain that it was founded by a group of Saracens who escaped after defeat at the battle of Vicovaro in 916. What is certain is that *Cervaria*, name which derives from the fact that a deer's lair ("cervo" means deer, in Italian) was found in such an impervious place, was in the XI Century a Bene-

View of Cervara di Roma

> **The Open-air Museum of Cervara**
>
> Given the beauty of the local landscape, Cervara has attracted, since the beginning of the 1800's, numerous Italian and foreign artists (amongst whom Koch and Pinelli). During the XX Century it was frequented by famous painters such as Sante Monachesi, Domenico Purificato, Aldo Riso as well as many others, and some of these began to paint frescoes on the walls of the local buildings. At the end of the Eighties Vincenzo Bianchi, together with pupils from the Accademia delle Belle Arti of Florence and with the collaboration of the local population, made a series of monumental sculptures, amongst which the *Scalinata degli Artisti*. As a result of this it was deemed necessary to create a museum of contemporary art based on the theme of peace. The first artists to donate works to this museum of the "Arte per la Pace" were Treccani, Mastroianni, Fazzini, Tamburi, Biasion, D'Ariego and Garofalo. But the main characteristic of the museum is that it is situated in the open air, regenerating itself continuously and freely together with the elements of nature.

dictine fortress and that it remained such up until the second half of the XVIII Century. The remains of the *Rocca*, known as the Corte, still today dominate the village which grew up around it and still maintains its medieval characteristics. Below the Corte there is the **Collegiata of Santa Elisabetta e San Francesco Martire** (XV C.), set against a rock spur, with Renaissance doars, an ancient steeple and, inside, an alter in polichrome marbles and various paintings amongst which a *Visitazione* and a *Madonna del Carmine* of the XVIII Century as well as the *Assunzione della Vergine in Cielo*, which is certainly older. There is also a prescious tempra on wood dated circa 1400 and portraying the *Santissimo Salvatore*. Also of interest is the **Church of Santa Maria della Porta**, just outside the village, where a Madonna with Child in terracotta is venerated.

Further North, at an altitude of 1220 m., we find **Camerata Nuova**, about the medieval period of which we know little except for the fact that its origins date back to the X Century. Destroyed by fire in 1859, the citadel was rebuilt where it is currently situated thanks also to financial help from Pope Pius IX. Of the old citadel we can still see the remarkable ruins near to which there is the **Sanctuary of the Madonna delle Grazie** (XVI C.), a destination for pilgrimages on Easter Monday. At Camerata Nuova we can instead see the *Parrocchiale di Maria Assunta* which contains a wooden statue of the Madonna which survived the fire. From here we can with ease reach the highlands of Camposecco (1400 m) with its fields and woods, where we can admire wild horses. Here we can also see the Fioio Valley and Mount Autore from whence we can reach the dead citadel of Camerata Vecchia. From here we return to Cervara and follow the Via Sublacense till **Subiaco**, where history has left an extraordinary and heterogeneous testament. Indeed, still today we can see, right under the monasteries, the imposing ruins of the *villa* which Nero had built in the narrow gulley of the Aniene, after having placed a dam in such a way as to create three attractive lakes, the *Simbruina Stagna*, which mirrored this imposing group of buildings which occupied a vast area offering a scenographic effect of symbiosis with nature. During excavations carried out at the end of the XIX Century two important pieces were found: an Efebus and a head of a sleeping girl which are now at the Museo Nazionale Romano. Abandoned in 60 A.D. after lightning had struck where Nero was dining – an event taken to be a bad omen – the villa was probably later restored by Emperor Trajan, but after that it was abandoned definitively. It was exactly in this place linked to an emperor who has been branded by history for his atrocities that St. Benedict founded his first coenobium, **San Clemente**, in the VI Century, using materials from the ancient villa for the construction of the monasteries of Subiaco. But it is medieval times which have left an indelible mark: at the end of the V Century the still young Benedetto da Norcia retired to a cave which had already been frequented by other hermits on Mount Taleo where he stayed three years and where he wrote his *Regola* which he then diffused and made operative through the foundation of thirteen coenobiums. All but two of them, the Sacro Speco and the monastery of San Silvestro which was the most important and was later dedicated to the saint's twin sister Saint Scolastica, went destroyed during Saracen incursions. A few centuries later, in the footsteps of St. Benedict, St. Francis of Assisi reached the area on a pilgrimage and it is to him that we owe the **Ponte** (bridge) called after him (1358), one of the few humpbacked bridges still intact, and the nearby **Convent of San Francesco** (1327) which was built on an ancient hermitage donated to the saint in 1224. The church, of extremely simple design, contains a triptych by Antoniazzo Romano (1467), called the *Madonna col Bambino Affiancata dai Santi Francesco e Antonio da Padova*, in its lower section, and one called *Santissima Trinità con Angeli* in the upper. There are also works by Pinturicchio, Giulio Romano and others. The cloysters and refectory are also decorated with frescos respectively of the XIX and XVII Century. The historic centre of the citadel, dominated by the **Rocca Abbaziale** which was founded by Abbot Giovanni V in the XI Century for the purpose of defending the village and where Cesare and Lucrezia Borgia were later born, is medieval. In part destroyed during the feuds with the Colonna family, it was rebuilt in the mid 1400's by Rodrigo Borgia – later to become Pope Alexander

Subiaco: Sacro Speco di San Benedetto

Subiaco: the medieval bridge of san Francesco

VI – who added a tower which still today exists. It was then amplified in 1778 by Pietro Campores who joined the pre-existing buildings together and turned the fortress into a stately home. Of interest are: the apartment on the ground floor, renovated by Francesco Colonna (1557-1559) with its frescoed halls attributed to the Zuccari brothers but more probably linked to Perin del Vaga and the the group that worked at Castel Sant'Angelo; Pius VI's apartment on the first floor with frescos by Liborio Cocetti (XVIII C.) which portray the castles of the upper valley of the Aniene. Below the Rocca there are the churches of the **Madonna della Croce** with XIV Century frescos, of **San Pietro** with an XI Century steeple, and of the neo-classical style

The Monastery of Santa Scolastica

One reaches it by following the Via dei Monasteri shaded by ancient holm-oaks all the way to the Sacro Speco, the same ones, it is told, that stooped at the sight of Saint Benedict and which have ever since remained in this oblique position. As we climb to the abbey going round a few final hair-pin bends we reach the complex of buildings of different periods which is Santa Scolastica, founded by Saint Benedict. The remains of the previous Carolingian edifice are visible in the basements of the church, whilst from outside we see three separate constructions: the most ancient is built around a Cosmatesque cloister (XIII C.), the second, the church, which has a gothic atrium (XIV C.), and the last in chronological order but the first we come to built around a cloister of the XVI Century. There is also a 30 m. steeple with a preromanesque base, XI Century tower and the top two floors of the XIII Century. The atrium, which underwent many transformations until its gothic transformation which is the one we can see today, was once the main entrance to the hermitage. The cloister, also built over a long period of time, has an elegant *flamboyant* arch, pieces from Nero's Villa and frescos with scenes from the life of Saint Benedict which are contemporary to the building. In the VI Century a simple oratory, the church has undergone several transformations and is today in neo-classical style as designed by Giacomo Quarenghi at the end of the 1700's. The Biblioteca or library is also of great interest, it is one of the most ancient in Lazio and has become a national monument. It contains over 100,000 volumes, amongst which manuscripts of the IX and X Century and precious incunabula, as it was here that the first typographical printing press in Italy was established (1465).

The façade and steeple (XI-XIII) of the monastery

The Sacro Speco or Monastery of San Benedetto

As we go up the road to Jenne we reach this impressive complex of buildings which almost looks as if it is one with the surrounding rock, as it includes two caves: the upper cave where the saint retired in prayer for three years, and the lower one where he used to receive shepherds, connected to each other by the Scala Santa or Holy Staircase. Apart from the very faded frescoes in the Grotta dei Pastori (IX C.), in which the oldest image of the Madonna in the whole area is kept (VII C.), the monastery can be dated around the XIII Century. The two superimposed churches are worthy of special attention: the upper church has frescoes painted by XIV and XV Century by artists from Siena which, amongst other things, depict episodes in the life of Jesus and Saint Benedict (*Il Miracolo del Calice di Vicovaro*). From here we can enter the lower church which is on various floors and also has beautiful frescoes of the Roman school, some of which signed by one *Conxulus*. In the cave of Saint Benedict there is the statue of the saint by Antonio Raggi, a pupil of Bernini, whilst in the *Cappella di San Gregorio*, dedicated to Pope Gregorius who wrote the saint's biography, one cannot but notice the powerfully expressive figure of Saint Francis without stigmata and painted almost natural size. On a different level there is the *Cappella della Madonna* with frescoes depicting the story of the Virgin by painters of the Sienese school.

Above: the Grotta dei Pastori, Madonna with Child and saints, VII Century
Centre: Sienese school, Adoration of the Magi, XIV Century
Below: detail of the fresco with Saint Francis, XIII Century

Santa Maria della Valle which contains a fine XVI Century painting, the *Madonna dell'Assunta*, and a XII Century polichrome wooden statue, the *Vergine*. There are also the small **Church of San Lorenzo** which was rebuilt upon the preceding IV Century building, and the **Concattedrale di Sant'Andrea** which dates back to the second half of the XVIII Century but was partly rebuilt after the bombings of World War II. Here are the two bronze doors sculpted by the con-

Fresco in the Santuario della Santissima Trinità at Vallepietra

temporary artists Giammei and Canevari.

The last destination on our itinerary is the ***Sanctuary of the Santissima Trinità*** at **Vallepietra**. Its origins date back to the VI Century when, during barbarian incursions, the inhabitants took refuge in this highly impervious place. The ruins of the ***Castello***, the ***Torre Caetani*** (XIV C.) and the ***Parrocchiale*** are still visible but the main attraction of the village is the Sanctuary, which rises at a height of 1.300 mts on the slopes of Mount Autore and is the destination for over 500,000 pilgrims a year. The Sanctuary is

The Festa della Santissima Trinità

The feast and the connected pilgrimage are held twice a year: the first Sunday after Pentecost and 26 July, Saint Anne. What one sees in these occasions, apart from the cultural, religious and traditional values it portrays, is truly moving. People of all ages come to the mountain from afar and often on foot, singing prayers, and camp there for the night so as to enter the Sanctuary in the morning. The climax of the feast is the *Pianto delle Zitelle* (the weeping of the spinsters), a chanted sacred laudat which represents the passion of Christ sung by girls from Vallepietra, which takes one back through the centuries.

Home-made cheeses from the Pastures

The cuisine of Lazio is in great part based on the products from its pastures. Rearing pasture animals has been the major activity for all the peoples which inhabited the area, from the times of the Sabines, the Etruscans and the Romans. Milk and cheese have always been part of the local staple diet, and still today excellent quality cheeses are produced in the whole of the province and thus also in the Parco dei Simbruini so rich in pastures. One can thus here try tasty "caciotte", the round squashed cheeses, usually served fresh and made with uncooked milk from sheep or cows. They are truly excellent served with local vegetables and Vicovaro's famous "pane casereccio" (local bread baked in a wood fired oven). But there is also the classical "pecorino romano" (a seasoned cheese made with sheep's milk) with its much sharper flavour, the production of which is protected by laws which determine the area in which it can be produced, its characteristics and how it should be made. Without this D.O.C. cheese many pasta dishes, such as "spaghetti cacio e pepe", "rigatoni all'amatriciana" and "spaghetti alla carbonara", would loose their particular flavour. And one must also remember that "pecorino" is traditionally eaten with raw broad beans, the typical local way of celebrating 1 May. And lastly, although there are also many other cheeses worthy of note, one must mention "ricotta", the fresh cheese made with whey from sheep's or cow's milk. Its delicious flavour makes of it a much sought after cheese which is excellent as a second course as well as one of the basic ingredients for cakes and ravioli.

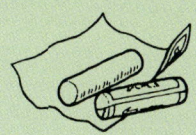

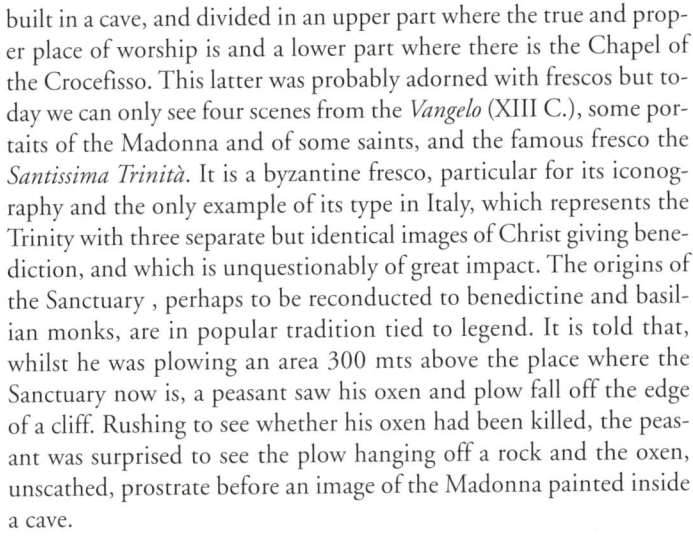

built in a cave, and divided in an upper part where the true and proper place of worship is and a lower part where there is the Chapel of the Crocefisso. This latter was probably adorned with frescos but today we can only see four scenes from the *Vangelo* (XIII C.), some portaits of the Madonna and of some saints, and the famous fresco the *Santissima Trinità*. It is a byzantine fresco, particular for its iconography and the only example of its type in Italy, which represents the Trinity with three separate but identical images of Christ giving benediction, and which is unquestionably of great impact. The origins of the Sanctuary, perhaps to be reconducted to benedictine and basilian monks, are in popular tradition tied to legend. It is told that, whilst he was plowing an area 300 mts above the place where the Sanctuary now is, a peasant saw his oxen and plow fall off the edge of a cliff. Rushing to see whether his oxen had been killed, the peasant was surprised to see the plow hanging off a rock and the oxen, unscathed, prostrate before an image of the Madonna painted inside a cave.

Castelli Romani - monti Lepini

View of Monte Cavo from Tuscolo

From the vineyards of the Castelli Romani to the woods of the Monti Lepini

How to get there
By car: for the Castelli, the Via Appia, Via Tuscolana, Via Anagnina, Via Casilina, and Via dei Laghi or the A1 Rome-Naples Motorway; for the area of the Prenestina-Monti Lepini, the Via Prenestina and the Via Casilina or A1 Motorway
By bus: CO.TRA.L. (tel. 800-431784) for the Castelli, from the EUR-Fermi (tel. 06-5920402) or the Anagnina (tel. 06-7222153) bus stations; for the area of the Prenestina-Monti Lepini, from the Anagnina and Ponte Mammolo-Rebibbia (tel. 06/4181501) bus stations
By train: for the Castelli, departures from Termini or Tiburtina (tel. 147-888088) stations; for the area of the Prenestina-Monti Lepini, trains that take the Rome-Caserta or the Rome-Colleferro (tel. 147-888088) lines.

The Castelli, that group of citadels on the hills South-East of Rome, have always been a favourite holiday resort for both romans and foreigners, be it for the unquestionable beauty of the landscapes and of the works of art one can see there, be it for the typical local cuisine to the success of which the excellent local wines contribute in a determining way. The area of the Prenestina-Monti Lepini, where villages become sparse and give place to big green valleys and at times rather wild looking mountainous areas where there are still vestiges of pre-roman populations, is instead less known. Woods dominate the landscape, but there are also many places of historical-artistic interest. Despite the fact that the two areas are fundamentally by different from the point of view of what they offer in terms of tourism we have decided to unify them in order to be able to offer itineraries which can satisfy everyone's interests: from the pleasure of admiring an enchanting landscape modelled by the presence of man to the wish to isolate oneself in nature; from the search for good food to the discovery of ancient traditions. We will thus follow a naturalistic monumental itinerary and a religious one for both areas, as gastronomy and wines in particular are a key attraction in these parts. We will also propose a transversal enological itinerary for those who love "delving in cellars".

The naturalistic-monumental itinerary

Despite the fact that its nearness to Rome has determined intense urbanization in the area of the Castelli, the views are nevertheless fascinating. In order to protect this inestimable heritage, in 1984 the *Parco Regionale dei Castelli Romani* was constituted. It covers an area of 9.500 hectares which include all the municipalities of the area (excluding Ciampino), woods, pastures, farm land, two lakes and monuments ranging from ancient Roman times to the medieval period, and from the Renaissance to the Baroque. But, if we go East the landscape changes significantly. We here meet the Monti Prenestini with villages perched on strategic hilltops and the Monti Lepini where nature is uncontrasted.

> **The Parco Regionale dei Castelli Romani**
> Geologically speaking, the area of this park took shape about 700,000 years ago with the eruption of a great volcano which also formed the lakes of Albano and Nemi. Over the course of centuries the chestnut tree became the dominant tree, substituting the typical woods with a mixture of varieties of trees such as beech, maples, durmast, holm-oak, hazelnut and ash. Furthermore, the soil, because of its volcanic origin, is particularly suited to the cultivation of vines. As to the fauna in the area, there are foxes, badgers, porcupines and squirrels. The park is an ideal place for sports such as mountain bike, trekking and horse riding, as well as sailing, canoeing and windsurfing on the lakes. For those who love going on excursions, there are several recommended itineraries be it on foot, by bike or on horse back. One can also go on excursion up one of two mountains, the Maschio delle Faete, the tallest in the park (956 m.), and the Maschio d'Ariano (891 m.). The park administration organizes excursions, usually on Sundays, to be booked by the previous Friday.

Departing from Rome, the first town we meet is **Ciampino**, which takes its name from that of a prelate called Giovanni Giustino Ciampini who had a villa in the area. The birth of the town itself is however strictly linked to the construction of the airport in 1916. Having been almost completely destroyed in the bombings in 1943, the town is modern in appearance, but for a few buildings such as the *Church of San Luigi Gonzaga*, situated on the Via dei Laghi, which dates back to the mid 1600's. Carrying on along the Appian way, *regina viarum* for the ancient romans and built in 312 B.C. by the consul Appius Claudius, we will be able to follow an interesting archeological itinerary given the fact that the Castelli (which literally means castles) was a favourite resort for the ancient Romans. Men of culture as well as nobles built sumptuous villas there. Indeed, the first archeological sight we shall visit is that of *Emperor Domitian's Villa* (81-96 A.D.) which is in the grounds of the Propaganda Fide Palace at **Castel Gandolfo**, the Popes' summer residence. The villa, built on three terracings, spans from the lake to the Appian Way and also occupies the area where there is the citadel of Albano. Thus, going down from the citadel to the lake we can admire its ruins. Remains found in the course of excavations and in particular from the area of the theatre, as well as sculptures found in the area of the *Begantino Nymphaeum*, are to be found in the *Antiquarium* at Villa Barberini (vists should be requested by fax: 066988 3437 and addressed to the Direzione delle Ville Pontificie). But the origins of Castel Gandolfo are much more ancient than those of Rome. It in fact seems certain that this is where *Alba Longa* was (XII Centu-

Castel Gandolfo: Doric nymphaeum

The Bergantino Nymphaeum and other Ancient Roman Remains

The nymphaeum, also known as "Bagni di Diana" (Diana's Baths), which is near the shores of the lake in the locality of Orziero, was built for Domitian's villa in an ancient quarry. What we can see of it today is a frontal part with a circular basin decorated with what little is left of polychrome mosaics, and a posterior one, it too with a basin and several niches in the walls in which there used to be statues. In the XVII Century, Pope Alexander VII used it for a place where to repair the brigantine he used to go sailing on the lake with. Quite close by there is also the older (I Century B.C.) *Ninfeo Dorico* (Doric Nymphaeum), which is built into the rock and was probably part of a villa. A truly extraordinary piece of hydraulic engineering is the *Emissario del Lago di Albano*, a water duct about two thousand metres long built by the Romans between 398 and 397 B.C. and which serves to keep the waters of the lake at a stable level. Amongst the remains of other ancient Roman villas those of the *Villa di Clodio* (Clodius's Villa) should be mentioned, they date back to the republican period and are inside the gardens of Villa Santa Caterina.

ry B.C.). This ancient city was founded by Aeneas's descendents and was one of the cities which led the Latin League, whose representatives were wont to meet once a year on Monte Calvo (949 m.) at the temple of Jove, of which we can today see only some enormous blocks of tufa stone. The rivalry between Alba Longa and Rome ended in the

VII Century B.C. with the destruction of the former at the hand of King Tullus Ostilius. But the more recent history of this citadel, the ancient nucleus of which dates back to the XII Century, is closely linked to that of the Papacy, starting with Pope Clement VII (1523-1534).
And its major attraction is undoubtedly the presence of the complex of pontifical villas which are connected to one another by bridges and a loggia. These are ***Villa Cybo, Villa Barberini*** and ***the Palazzo dei Papi***, designed by Carlo Maderno for Pope Urban VIII (1623). The palace, built on the ruins of the old Savelli castle, was completed by Gian Lorenzo Bernini who, commissioned by Pope Alexander VII (1655-1667), designed the whole of the ***Piazza della Libertà***

Castel Gandolfo: palace of the Popes

The Lakes of Albano and Nemi

Immersed in greenery and enriched by the presence of ancient Roman archaeological remains, the two lakes, which formed many millions of years ago on the slopes of a volcano, are one of the major tourist attractions in the area, be it for those who love nature and archaeology, be it for those who love open air sports. Indeed, on the shores of the lakes there are centres which offer water skiing and canoeing, but one can also go trekking, cycling and horse riding along peaceful paths amongst yew, holm-oaks, oak trees, beech trees and plane trees. From Albano it is possible to reach the lake taking two roads built by Pope Urban VII, still today called "Galleria di Sopra" (Upper Tunnel) and "Galleria di Sotto" (Lower Tunnel), as the ancient trees which line them form a true and proper vault of leaves over these roads. An interesting itinerary is that which takes to the *Convento dei Cappuccini* at the *Romitorio di Sant'Angelo in Lacu* (XI C.) and then to the ex-*Convento Francescano di Santa Maria in Palazzolo* (XIII C.) built at the top of a cliff overlooking the lake, upon the ruins of an ancient Roman villa and restructured in the XVIII Century in such a way as to alter the original structure considerably. At the beginning of the 1900's, when the building was bought by the Venerable English College for the purpose of turning it into a summer residence for seminarists, work began in order to restore the church to its original gothic-Cistercian style. In the *Church of San Francesco e San Bonaventura*, next to the Capucine Convent, there is, apart from a caravagesque painting by Gherardo delle Notti (Gerrit van Honthorst) known as the *Madonna in Gloria con i Santi Francesco e Bonaventura e la Principessa Flaminia* (1618), commissioned by Princess Flaminia, a very special Presepio with figures of almost natural size sculpted out of marble and travertine by two pupils of Bernini, Andrea Bolgi and Stefano Speranza (1635). Lastly the small wood which surrounds the convent is one of the few examples left of the vegetation there used to be before the mass introduction of the chestnut tree. Lake Nemi is smaller, surrounded by cane groves, farm land and green-houses where, amongst other things, excellent strawberries are cultivated. Its waters too have seen events the memory of which is contended between history and myth, from Caligula's enormous and luxurious ships which sank there, to the bloody but fascinating rights in Diana's woods, offered in honour of the deity. Also of great charm is the *Romitorio di San Michele Arcangelo* for which records have been traced back to 1183. Dug out of rock, this sacred hermitage has been abandoned since the last century, but it is still possible to see an altar shaped like a small temple and some frescoes (XV C.), amongst which the one called the *Crocifissione* is of considerable historic importance in that in the background the ancient city of Nemi is depicted.

Albano: Baths of Cellomaio

The steeple of the church of San Pietro at Albano

from which one can enjoy an enchanting view of the lake. Of particular interest are Throne room of Pope Innocent XIII with two prescious Gobelins tapestries which portray the *Flight from Egypt*, and the papal chapel of Pope Urban VIII with frescoes by the Zuccaris. The fountain in the centre of the piazza is also by Bernini as is the **Church of San Tommaso da Villanova** (1658-1662), with a very plain exterior but very richly decorated inside, especially the ceiling of the dome decorated in gold and white stucco work by Antonio Raggi, a pupil of Bernini. On the main altar there is the *Crocifissione*, by Pietro da Cortona together with Bernini, sustained by angels and dominated by the figure of God (always in stucco work). On the right hand alter there is the *Assunzione della Vergine* by Guglielmo Cortese, and on the left hand one there is the *Estasi di San Tommaso da Villnova* by Giacinto Gimignani. All of these three works are dated 1661. Also of interest is the **Villa Torlonia**, which is now a national monument and contains works by the neoclassical sculptor Bertel Thorvaldsen and paintings by Coghetti and Seitz, and where the german writer Wolfgang Goethe also stayed.

Near Gandolfo there is **Albano**, which is also tied to the ancient city of Alba Longa, from which it gets its name, and to Domitian's villa. The origin of this citadel is linked to the presence in ancient times of the *Castra Albana* (III Century A.D.), fortified camps which Emperor Septimius Severus had built at mile XV of the Appian Way for the legionnaires who had fought against the Parthians in Mesopotamia (information on visits is available from the Museo Civico di Albano). The layout of the soldiers' lodgings in the camp, in part incorporated into the buildings we see today, has had a determining influence on the layout of the city as it is now. Dating back to ancient roman times are the three arched **Porta Pretoria** which used to give access to the ancient Appian Way and, a few kilometres down that same road, the **Mausoleum of the Oratii and Curatii** (I Century B.C.), said to be in memory of the famous duel between Romans and the inhabitants of Alba Longa but more probably a family tomb. Amongst other ruins which date back to ancient Roman times there are many vil-

The Museo Civico di Albano

The Civic Museum of Albano is situated in an elegant neoclassical villa, Villa Ferraroli, which, together with the gardens, is the property of the Municipality. The museum, which has fifteen halls and an archaeological park in which one can go for guided tours, contains findings which go from prehistoric times to the period of the Roman Empire and which all come from excavations conducted in the area.

The neoclassical façade of the museum

The Image of the Madonna della Rotonda

It is told that some greek nuns who had escaped persecution had brought to the Church of Santa Maria della Rotonda a sacred image (VIII C.) to which the people of Albano turned during the terrible cholera epidemic of 1867. The Feast of the Madonna della Rotonda is celebrated on the first Sunday of August, with sacred music in the church and in the square, in memory of the end of the plague.

las, amongst which that of Pompey Major (I Century B.C.) which covers approximately nine hectares and was later used as a christian burial ground, but is now a public park. There are also the ruins of a gigantic *amphitheatre*, and those of the *Thermal Baths of Cellomaius* which date back to the period of Emperor Caracalla. Also of interest is the so called *Cisternone*, a big cistern which still functions thanks to an ancient acqueduct, which was built in order to guarantee water to the military camp. The *Catacombs of San Senatore*, dating back to the II Century A.D., have a central crypt with frescos which range from the V to the IX Century, which shows that they were frequented up until those times. Over the catacombs there is the *Church of Santa Maria della Stella*, built on top of that of San Senatore. Still in the historic centre we can also visit the *Basilica of San Pancrazio*, which stands on an older religious edifice built by Pope Leo III (759-816) and which in turn had replaced the Basilica of San Giovanni Battista which had been built by Emperor Constantine. And then there is the *Church of San Pietro*, inside the thermal baths, restored by Pope Leo III. Despite serious damage caused by bombings, the XI Century steeple still stands. There are also pieces of roman architecture set in the portal and, inside, the remains of an entablature of the imperial period and a III Century sarcophagus. The most significant edifice from a religious

Excursions on Horse Back

There are several horse riding centres in the Castelli, those which belong to "Ante" are at: Genzano, *C. L. Quarto della Mandorla* (tel. 06/9363111) and Rocca di Papa, *Circolo Ippico Funari* (tel. 06/9496917). Lastly, at Rocca Priora in the area of Pratoni di Vivaro there is the Centro Federale di *Equitazione del CONI*. Also some of the "agriturismo" centres (a sort of country bed and breakfast) offer excursions on horse back.

Ariccia: palazzo Chigi and, in the foreground, one of the twin fountains in the piazza

The chiesa dell'Assunta by Bernini at Ariccia

point of view is however the **Church of santa Maria della Rotonda** (1060). It has a romanesque steeple and a portico infront of it, and was built exploiting the nymphaeum of Domitian's villa which had been transformed into thermal baths for his legionnaires by Septimus Severus, some of the mosaics of which can still be seen. Inside it we can see an image of the Madonna with Child which, in the XIX Century, was laminated with gold and silver, altars made of parts of ancient Roman buildings, and a pulpit with polichromatic inlays which is placed on an ancient capital. There are many frescoes, some of great interest such as the *Cristo e la Storia della Vera Croce* and *Sant'Anna con la Madonna e il Bambino tra San Giovanni e Sant'Ambrogio*.

A vibrant example of Bernini's genius is **Ariccia**, which the great architect was invited to redesign completely by Pope Alexander VII Chigi in the second half of the 1600's. Leaving Albano we cross the spectacular three arched viaduct built during the papacy of Pius IX (1846-1878) which was very seriously damaged by the Germans during World War II (then rebuilt in 1948) so as to reach the centre of Ariccia and the scenographic **Piazza di Corte** where there is the recently restored **Palazzo Chigi**. A defense tower in the XII Century, the Savelli built upon its ruins a palace. This building and the surrounding "borgo" reached its greatest moment of splendour during the domain of the Chigi family who transformed it into a fortress-palace built by the architect Carlo Fontana to a design by Bernini. The façade which gives onto the piazza maintains the rigour and simplicity of the original castle, despite the presence of main doars made in the 1700's. The back part, facing the park, is much richer in its design. Inside there are paintings by Cavalier D'Arpino, Salvator Rosa, Giovanni Maria Morandi and others, but also sculptures and ar-

chaeological remains as well as drawings and prints. In the chapel there is the sanguine called *San Giuseppe con il Bambino* by Bernini (signed and dated 1663). In the dining room there are frescos depicting the allegories of the seasons by Mario de' Fiori. Also of interest are some of the original furnishings such as the pharmacy made for Pope Alexan-

The Typical Products of the Castelli Romani

The diaries of illustrious and unknown travellers, prints and paintings of centuries past and, above all, the verses of the famous Roman poet Gioacchino Belli, have not spared words, verses and images in exaltation of the not only artistic attractions of the Castelli. The "Ottobrata", the trip "fuori Porta" (outside the city gates), was a typical excursion for Romans during the period in which the grapes were gathered in autumn, it was indeed a mass phenomenon. The much praised products of those times are the ones of today: wine, olive oil, home made bread, cured meats and the various types of home made pasta. The bread made at Genzano and Lariano has always been renowned, not to mention "porchetta" (roast pork), especially that from Ariccia, cooked in the oven according to simple traditional rules which guarantee its exceptional flavour. One must go to the *Sagra della Porchetta* which takes place at Ariccia and that for bread which is held at Genzano. Also delicious are the berries and the chestnuts from the woods, above all the strawberries from Nemi, to which a "sagra" which started over a century ago is dedicated. Everywhere one looks there are vineyards and olive groves, but the area where olive oil is produced most is that between Velletri, which is also famous for its artichokes, and Lariano. If we happen to stop in one of the local restaurants or trattorias, we must let ourselves be tempted by one of the typical local pasta dishes such as fettuccine with porcini mushrooms, bucatini with amatriciana sauce or the tasty spaghetti with olive oil, garlic and peperoncino sauce. As a second course one must try "abbacchio scottadito" (grilled slices of lamb), devilled chicken and, of course, roast pork. One must also taste the "carciofi alla romana", artichokes cooked with a special local mint, or fried artichokes. And as a sweet one must try the local dry cakes: ciambelle al vino or the typical "Pupazza di Frascati", a biscuit shaped like a woman with three breasts, two for milk and one for ... wine.

der VII and the rare wall coverings in printed "Cordoba" leather. The gardens too are remarkable and were much admired by writers such as Goethe and Stendhal (visits by appointment tel. 06/933 0053, Palazzo Chigi). On the same piazza, in front of the palace, is the **Church of the Assunta**, of circular design and with a large slightly squashed dome and a high lantern. The reference to the Pantheon in Rome is evident, whilst the two lateral porticos re-evoke the solution employed for St. Peter's. In the interior there are many altar-pieces, amongst which the *Riposo nella fuga in Egitto* by Giacinto Gimignani. The ceiling of the apse is frescoed with the *Assunzione della Vergine* by Guglielmo Cortese (known as Il Borgognone, 1664). The great architect in the same period also remodelled the **Sanctuary of Santa Maria di Galloro**, the construction of which, tied to the finding of an image of the Madonna in the nearby woods, had been started in 1624. More hidden away than baroque Ariccia, but none the less interesting, is the ancient roman *Aricia*, the remains of which are visible in the valley. Over and above the legend which would have it founded by Hippolitus, the half-brother of Fedra who, having hidden himself in the wood sacred to the goddess Diana, is said to have fallen in love with the nymph *Aricia*, the

Genzano: Palazzo Sforza Cesarini

city was actually born between the VIII and VII Century B.C. and was part of the Latin League (indeed, in its territory there was the sanctuary dedicated to Diana Nemorensis, one of the three places of worship where the confederates used to gather). Once the League had been beaten, the city entered into the Roman sphere of influence and to this testifies the presence of many **tombs** situated along the Appian way, as well as the grand viaduct known as the **Sostruzione**, built by the Gracchuses (123 B.C.) and about 200m. long. Lastly, we must mention the **Locanda Martorelli**, after the surname of its owner, Antonio, which, in the 1800's, was the inn on the piazza where members of the international *intelighentia* used to gather. Frequented by Goethe, Goya, Gogol, and Massimo D'Azeglio, it is now a place where exhibitions and conferences are held and where we can admire a series of murals by the Polish painter Taddeus Kuntz which illustrate the origins of the birth of the city tied to the myth of Hippolitus.

After Ariccia we reach **Genzano Romano**, which looks upon Lake Ne-

The Infiorata at Genzano

This is a traditional feast held in many villages and towns in the Province, but the one at Genzano is the most famous. It was invented by the brothers Arcangelo and Nicola Leofreddi in 1778 and is held on the first Sunday after *Corpus Domini*. The spectacle is the fruit of real team work. In the preceding days, hundreds of people collect about 5 tons of flowers with which they make 13 different pictures all based on the same theme which together form a carpet of 1,890 m^2 which reaches the doors of the Church of Santa Maria della Cima. Before this the flowers are put in caves dug out of tufa rock under the Municipal Palace, where the temperature guarantees their conservation, then the petals are drawn from the flowers and kept till the morning of the feast day when they are set out on the roads where the designs have previously been outlined.

mi, and the name of which could derive from the presence of an ancient Roman temple dedicated to *Cynthia*, another name for Diana. Its origins probably date back to the XII Century, but it is impossible to establish exactly when the "borgo" became fortified. It was destroyed by fire at the beginning of the 1400's, it was rebuilt by the Cistercian Monks, to whom it then belonged and then, between the XVII and XVIII Century, underwent considerable transformation which changed its appearance radically. As for most of the citadels of the Castelli, Genzano is known for the excellent wine it produces and the Fountain of San Sebastiano (1776), on the main square, would seem to be its celebration. It is a doric column, there in memory of the Colonna family, around which is wound a vine with bunches of grapes. From the piazza depart three avenues lined with elms, known as the "olmate", which lead to the most significant edifices: the **Church of the Cappuccini** and its convent (1637), the **Palazzo Sforza Cesarini** (1643), built upon the old palace of the Colonnas and surrounded by a beautiful English garden built in 1840, and the **Church of Santa Maria della Cima** (1650). Inside it there are paintings such as the *Madonna in Gloria tra i Santi Pietro e Paolo* (1660) by Francesco Cozza, and its contemporary *Crocifissione tra i Santi Antonio Abbate e Antonio da Padova* by Baciccia, whose real name was Giovan Battista Gaulli. There is also a triptych called the *Salvatore e i Quattro Evangelisti*, venerated by the people of Genzano as it is believed to have liberated them from the pest of 1867. Also worthy of note is the **Cathedral of the Santissima Trinità**, neoclassical in style and built between the end of the XVIII and beginning of the XIX Century. As we leave Genzano, between the XVIII and XIX mile of the Appian Way, in the territory of ancient *Lanuvium*, we can see the imposing **remains of a villa,** attributed to the Antoninians. If we leave the Appian Way by turning off to the right, we reach **Lanuvio**, on the southern side of the Colli Albani, situated in a particularly fortunate position dominating the plains of Ardea and Anzio, only a short distance from *Astura* which was its ancient commercial harbour. Until 1914 known as Civita Lavinia and one of the most ancient municipalities of the Province, Lanuvio is situated exactly where myth would have it that the Greek Diomedes founded *Lanuvium*. It is however historically proven that the place was already inhabited in the X Century B.C. and that its fame was tied to the presence of the **Temple of Juno Sospita** (Saviour), protector of marital love, represented with a goat skin drape across her shoulders. And it may be because of this reference to goat's wool (lana, in Italian) that the town took the name Lanuvio. All that is left of the temple and the buildings which sur-

The XIV Century Rocca at Lanuvio

rounded it are a series of arches and a few elements of the temple, whilst the large blocks of peperino stone on San Lorenzo Hill were used for the restructuring carried out between the IV and III Century B.C. and therefore after the war with the Volscians. Lanuvio was however an ally of Rome against the Volscians who's domain had extended to Anzio and Velletri. The Tomb of the Warrior, discovered in 1934 and containing a suit of armour with a beautiful bronze helmet decorated in gold and silver and other apparel, has given many useful indications on that period. These findings are now at the Museo Nazionale Romano in Rome. Other interesting discoveries were the theatre and the terracings of the enormous temple to Hercules (II Century B.C.), which used to stand where there now is the old "borgo". On San Lorenzo hill there is also the late medieval church by the same name, for the construction of which a nympheum of the temple of Juno was used. The medieval "borgo", almost intact, is surrounded by walls in peperino stone and is dominated by the XIII Century **Rocca**. Once a prison, the Rocca is now a wine shop and also contains old agricultural tools and equipment for making wine. Built in the XV Century by the Colonna family and where Marcantonio Colonna (winner of the war against the Turks in 1571) was born, the **Palazzo Baronale** is also of interest. Next to it there is a fountain made from a II Century A.D. sarcophagus, whilst opposite it there is the **Collegiata of Santa Maria Maggiore**, founded in medieval times but completely rebuilt in 1675 by the Cesarini Sforza family, who charged Carlo Fontana with the task. The church has been completely rebuilt since World War II. Inside it there is a *Deposizione dalla Croce* di san Filippo Apostolo attributed to Domenichino. Also of interest are the **Fontana degli Scogli** (1675) by Carlo Fontana and situated in the square which has his name, the XV Century **Curch of the Madonna delle Grazie**, built upon an earlier edifice of the XIII Century and of which there is only a gothic style window left, and **Ponte Loreto**, a peperino stone bridge which dates back to the times of Silla. From Lanuvio we now go to **Velletri**, outpost of the Castelli. Situated on the southernmost side of Mount Artemisio, this the largest city of the area has a centuries long history full of dramatic events. Archaeological findings testify to the fact that ancient *Velitrae* was already inhabited during the bronze age, but it is probable that one should go even further back in time as its name would seem to connect it to the ancient Etruscan civilization. The fortunes of this town were however more closely tied to the Volscians, who occupied it in the V Century B.C. and turned it into one of there most important strong-holds from whence to contrast the

Velletri: Porta Napoletana

power of Rome. History is indeed full of episodes on the war between the Romans and the Volscians, suffice it to remember that one of the most famous of these episodes, that of Coriolanus, even inspired one of Shakespeare's plays. The wars ended in 338 B.C., when Consul Caius Menius put a definitive end to this century long contention. Despite this the Veliternians continued to speak volscian up until at least the III Century as the *Tabula Veliterna*, a 23 cm. bronze tablet from approximately 300 B.C., which was found in the city in the XVIII Century and which is now kept at the Museo Nazionale in Naples, would demonstrate. Having become an ancient Roman municipality, Velletri saw the construction of many villas and farms in the area, but alas little is left of that period even though three temples have been found situated respectively near the Cathedral of San Clemente, near the Piazza del Comune and near the Church of Santa Maria della Neve in the centre of the city. Objects of great interest were found in this last sight at the beginning of the last century, such as the beautiful terracotta dressings for the archaic temple (530 B.C.), now kept in the **Museo Civico**. Almost certainly in origin part of the domains of the *Octavia* family, the one to which Emperor Augustus belonged, Velletri, between the fall of the Roman Empire and World War II, saw important events such as the reconciliation of the Papacy and the Empire with the meeting between Charles V and Pope Paul III in 1536. It has hosted many illustriuous persons such as Boniface VIII, who was its podestà from 1299, King Charles VIII of France, Francesco Garibaldi, and Giuseppe Garibaldi, who was nominated honourary citizen. The city suffered many more invasions and devastations than others in the area. Since the year 1000 it had to transform itself into a fortified citadel in order to fend off Saracen attacks, it suffered the battles between popes and emperors and those between local families, and was violently bombarded in 1944. Despite all this the plan of the city is still medieval and many of its ancient buildings still survive intact: the **Porta Napoletana** which has now been turned into an exhibition area, the gothico-romanesque **Tower of**

The steeple of Santa Maria del Trivio at Velletri

The Museo Civico di Velletri

The Civic Museum of Velletri is in the Palazzo Comunale. It was founded in 1920 and was seriously damaged during the last war, its contents belong to the protohistoric and ancient Roman through to the medieval period and come from the town and its surroundings. Amongst the most important are the clay tablets from an archaic temple found near the Church of Santa Maria della Neve, the marble sarcophagus the bas-reliefs of which represent the labours of Hercules and life in Hades (II Century B.C.), objects from necropolis in the area and the famous copy of the Pallade Veliterna now at the Louvre in Paris.

Trivio (1353) which is 50 m. high and which once rose next to the **Church of Santa Maria del Trivio** which was rebuilt in 1622 by Carlo Maderno and completed over a century later by Carlo Murena. The façade of this last is however of the Ottocento and inside there is an image of the Madonna known as the *Madonna della Salute*. On the Piazza del Comune there are the **Palazzo Comunale** by Giacomo della Porta but designed by Vignola (1572), destroyed during the last war but later rebuilt according to the original plans, the **Palazzo dei Conservatori** (1835), with a beautiful bas-relief in marble which represents the return of Pope Pius IX from exile in Gaeta, and the oratorium of **Santa Maria del Sangue** (XVI C.) which is believed to have been designed by Bramante. One ought also to visit the **Church of San Michele Arcangelo**, destroyed and then rebuilt in the 1800's, and a series of other churches amongst which that of **Sant'Antonio Abate**, and the **Cathedral of San Clemente**, which was probably originally built in the IV Century. It contains fine works of art, amongst which the ancient painting of the *Madonna delle Grazie*, patron saint of the city, a XIII Century cosmatesque reliquiary set upon the tabernacle, some frescoes of the XIII, XIV and XV Century in the crypt, and renaissance doars by Traiano da Palestrina. Next to it is the **Museo Capitolare** where there is a collection of precious paintings, works in gold and religious apparels, amongst which the *Madonna col Bambino* by Gentile di Fabriano and another by Antoniazzo Romano, as well as the *Visitazione* by Bicci di Lorenzo dated 1435.

A few kilometres from Velletri and once part of its municipality there is **Lariano**, the point of departure for an excursion to Mount Artemisio, at the foot of which there is this village which is surmounted by the ruins of its XI Century *Castello* and the remains of a necropolis which probably dates back to pre-roman times. Indeed, even though Lariano is today a modern urban centre due to the heavy bombardments of the last war, it has an ancient history as is testified by the presence of many archaeological sites in the area and to the finding of objects such as the three statues of athletes now at the Musei Capitolini in Rome. Nature, archaeology and the reminiscence of misterious cults are also the attractions of **Nemi**. Also the sight where this village now stands was inhabited in proto-historic times and its name derives from the latin *nemus* which means forest. Indeed, the area was once covered in woods dedicated to the goddess Diana. It is for this reason that the Lake of Nemi was also known as "Mirror of Diana" and was part of ancient *Aricia*, it too voted to the cult of that goddess. Around 1100, when Nemi was already known for its excellent and abundant pro-

Givan Battista Rositi, Trasporto della Santa Casa di Loreto, *oil on canvas carried onto wood, 1500, museo Capitolare, Velletri*

The Sacred Woods

In these parts, where for centuries nature has remained untouched, it was inevitable that the woods – which have always been places of initiation with strong symbolic meaning – should be consecrated to divinities and rights the meaning of which we no longer know. These are woods such as the one mentioned in the *Tabula Veliterna*, the sacred woods dedicated to Diana Nemorense, the *Nemus Aricinum* on lake Nemi and, last but not least, the forest of Ferentano or sacred woods of Marino. The most famous are doubtless the woods of Nemi, the rights of which inspired the Scottish writer James G. Frazer to write the voluminous book entitled the *Golden Bough* in which he describes the bloody rights which accompanied offerings to the three faced and chaste goddess Diana, goddess of hunting and woods, but also infernal divinity, personification of the moon and, as such, protector of births. The priests of her temple, called kings, were neither nominated nor chosen but conquered their 'throne' by killing their predecessor, then to risk being killed in turn at any moment by whoever wished to take their place. Today there is little left of the temple on the shores of the lake, we can see a republican period podium and part of a colonnade and walls, and the remains of other buildings, perhaps the houses in which the priests lived, as well as a theatre. During excavations several objects of interest were found, which are now at Copenhagen museum. The woods of Marino, in the grounds of the Colonna Palace, are what is left of the Lucus Ferentiae which covered the whole of the south western side of the Volcano, sacred to the divinity of earth and forests, and where the pact of the Latin League was signed. It is one of the few places in the area where the original vegetation still survives, and it is thus an excellent habitat for various types of birds and small mammals. The under-growth is full of holly and butcher's broom, which are both protected species, and thus untouchable much as all that was part of a sacred wood was... untouchable.

duction of fruit, it became a fortified citadel which, like many others, changed hands from one noble family to another. Still today the mighty bulk of the **Castello** rises over the medieval "borgo". On the façade there is a plaque with some verses by the English poet Lord Byron who spent some time there, inside there is the *Salone delle Armi* (hall of arms) and four halls frescoed by Liborio Cocetti. Finally, from the garden of the XV Century by the architect Vincenzo Moraldi, one can enjoy a lovely view of the lake. The church of **Santa Maria dell'Assunta** or del Pozzo is instead of the XVII Century. In it there is a fine triptych known as the *Salvatore fra i Santi Giovanni Evangelista e Giovanni Battista*. Lastly, at the entrance to the village we find the **Sanctuary of the Crocefisso** where, since the XVII Century, a wooden Crucifix thought to be miraculous

View of Nemi

> ### The Museum of Ships at Nemi
> This museum was built in the Thirties on the shores of the lake not far from the temple to Diana in order to house those great Roman ships which Emperor Caligula had built and which he used principally during festivities in honour of that goddess. These were two large vessels decorated exactly like an imperial palace, with marble floors, tricliniums, columns and bronzes, and which were moored in front of the villa which was built upon what were probably the remains of one of Caesar's villas, in the vicinity of the temple. One cannot say that fate was too kind to these ships as they sank, probably after Nero's reign. Many attempts to recover them were made, in the XV, XVI and XIX Century, but all that was recovered were various objects which are now in the Vatican Museum and in the Museo Nazionale delle Terme. The ships were only recovered between 1927 and 1932 when, in order to do this, the lake was partially dried out. Alas, in 1944, a fire, perhaps caused by the Germans in retreat, destroyed both the ships and their contents. What we see today are 1:5 scale models and what little of the contents was spared by the fire.

Bronze erma ballustrade representing Silineus (II° nave)

is venerated. It is told, that a lay Franciscan called Father Vincenzo Bassiano made it working only on Fridays after many hours of meditation and penitence, tired and undecided as to how to sculpt the face of Christ, the friar fell asleep and later woke up to find the work finished by divine will.

Still following the Via dei Laghi, we now reach **Marino** which, like that of Frascati, has much closer links than those of other citadels of the Castelli to the production of excellent wine. Situated upon the sight of the fortified citadel of *Castrimoenium*, named after a roman military camp of the I Century B.C., Marino took its present name in the XI Century and, from 1419 to 1912, its history was tied to that of the Colonna family, the illustriuos representative of which Marcantonio Colonna (1535-1548) is still today remembered with a procession during the *Festa dell'Uva* at the beginning of October. Amongst the monuments of the ancient roman period, the Mitreo (II Century A.D.), situated in a cellar in the vicinity of the station and which can be visited by permission of the Pro Loco, is of particular interest. It is a tunnel with a vaulted ceiling about 25 m. long at the end of which there is a fresco depicting the god Mitra as he sacrifices the sacred bull. Of the period of the Frangipane family is the *Castello*, of which only two cylindrical towers and a square one, now part of the *Palazzo Colonna*, still exist. The Palazzo was started in 1532 on a design by Antonio da Sangallo the Younger, construction was carried on twenty years later to drawings inspired by Vignola, and completed in the 1600's, probably by Sergio Venturi. Rebuilt after the war to its original design, the palace is now the seat of the Municipality. Also of interest is the *Casina Colonna* with rooms with frescoes of the XVI Century and the *Fountain of the Quattro Mori* of the Seicento with the statues of four turkish slaves chained to a corinthian column, symbol of the Colonna family and thus a clear reference to the battle of Lepanto (1571). Another beautiful fountain is the Fountain of Nettuno (1899) by Michele Tripisciano, author of the monument to Gioacchino Belli in Trastevere, which is in the piazza where there is the *Collegiata of San Barnaba*, the most important church in Marino. Built in the middle of the XVII Century, the edifice has a dome 36 m. high and, in the apse, a large alter-piece called the *Martirio dell'Apostolo Barnaba* by Bartolomeo Gennari, a pupil of Guercino. Behind the main alter there is a beautiful organ dated 1920. In the church we can also see the only surviving trophy from the battle of Lepanto, a turkish shield. Amongst other churches we must mention: *Santa Lucia*, built in 1180 and restored a century later then to be deconsacrated in the 1700's and put to other uses, it is the oldest and probably one of the most ancient gothic edifices in Lazio; the *Church of the Madonna del Rosario* (with its convent of dominican nuns founded in 1675), by Giovanni Sardi (1712), a capable interpreter of the architectural principles of Borromini, as is evident from the façade which altenates concave and convex elements; the *Church of the Trinità* (XVII C.) with paintings probably by Giovan Francesco Gessi (1588-1649) such as the *Mistero della Santissima Trinità*; the *Church of Santa Maria delle Grazie* which was restored in the 1600's and inside which there is a painting called *San Rocco* attributed to Domenichino, and a marble frame which encases a fresco of the Virgin probably by Benozzo Gozzoli; the *Church of the Trinità* (XVII C.) containing the painting called *Trinità* attributed to Guido Reni, another celebrated bolognese painter of the Seicento; the *Church of Santa Maria dell'Orto* or of the Acquasanta (XV C.), dug out of rock and containing a spring under the alter the waters of which are said to be miraculous. From Marino we now move East in the direction of another main artery of the area, the Tuscolana, which will take us to the area of Tuscolo and Grottaferrata, Frascati, Monteporzio Catone, Montecompatri and Rocca Priora. The origins of Tuscolo are lost in legend. It is said to have been founded by Telegonos, son of Ulysses and the sorceress Circe, but history dates it to the IX Century B.C. and thus it is one of the latin cities, even though an Etruscan period is not to be excluded given the fact that the last king of Rome Tarquin fled there after having been ousted by the romans. It was an extremely powerful member of the Latin League until 338 B.C., when it was defeated and conquered by Rome. Given the pleasant climate, many illustrious ancient romans built villas there, amongst these Lucullus, the famous orator Cato, Cicero and as many as eight emperors. In the X Century A.D. it was under the do-

Marino: the fountain of the Quattro Mori

The Archaeological Itinerary at Tusculum

The remains brought to light by the excavations begun in the XIX Century are of great interest, but a visit here can also be the occasion for a pleasant excursion along paths and lanes or along ancient Roman roads such as the **Via dei Sepolcri** which takes us to the **Cisterna Romana**, and thence to the imposing **Sepolcro** which a plaque attributes to M.C. Viciniano, consul in 53 B.C.. We can then go on to reach an area shaded by "pini d'Aleppo", the large umbrella shaped pines of the Mediterranean, and here admire the ruins of a monument identified as one of the villas of Emperor Tiberius thanks to the finding of a statue of that period, but which is for some more probably a place of worship. Going on we reach the elliptic shaped **Anfiteatro**, an amphitheatre which was probably capable of holding as many as 3,000 people, and which is today covered in vegetation and surrounded by chestnut trees. We can conclude our excursion by visiting an area which is perhaps erroneously said to be the forum, where there is the **Colombario**, a family tomb, and the **Teatro** or theatre (II Century B.C.). This is without doubt the most interesting building, built on the side of the hill and of which we can still see the large cavea, the access ramps and the disposition of the stage. From here we could go on to the top of the hill where there once was the **Acropolis** and from where one can admire a splendid view of the Colli Albani and beyond to the sea.

The theatre and other ruins

Frascati: Villa Aldobrandini

main of the Counts of Tuscolo who, having dared rebel against Rome, were definitively beaten in 1191 when the city was also destroyed. From ancient Roman times we will now go forward to the XVI and XVII Century when cardinals, intellectuals and nobles had splendid villas surrounded by scenographic parks built on the Tuscolo, once again giving life to a perfect blending of architecture with nature. Alas, given that they are private proper-

Tour of the Tuscolane Villas

The tour begins with **Villa Aldobrandini** which dominates Frascati from the top of the Tuscolo Hill. Built by Cardinal Pietro Aldobrandini, nephew of Pope Clement VIII and designed by Giacomo della Porta in 1598, it was constructed in place of a previous building called Belvedere. Its construction was actually only completed at the beginning of the XVII Century by Carlo Maderno and the hydraulic engineer Giovanni Fontana. Inside, the ceilings of five rooms were decorated by Cavalier D'Arpino with scenes from the bible (1602-1603). The Nymphaeum, a point of conjunction between architecture and nature through the dynamic element of water, is of extraordinary beauty. The interior was entirely decorated by Domenichino and his collaborators with scenes depicting the life of Apollo (1616), of which only two are still in situ whilst the rest are at the National Gallery in London. **Villa Torlonia** was alas bombed to the ground during the last war and all that is left today is the public park with the *Teatro delle Acque*, a splendid fountain by Maderno. **Villa Falconieri**, the first of the villas of Frascati and known as "La Rufina", is in its final version exquisitely baroque. It was built upon the sight of an ancient Roman building for Cardinal Alessandro Rufini in the middle of the XVI Century, it was then extended and restructured by Francesco Borromini during the second half of the XVII Century, whilst the interior is decorated by a pupil of Pietro da Cortona, Ciro Ferri, by the Bolognese artist Francesco Grimaldi, and Pier Leone Ghezzi who finished the job during the first half of the XVIII Century and to whom we owe the enchanting scenes which portray the Falconieri family. In the centuries to come the villa had many different owners, amongst whom William II Emperor of Germany, and an exceptional tenant, Gabriele D'Annunzio (1925). Today it is the seat of the European Centre of Education. In a slightly higher position than the others is **Villa Tuscolana** or Rufinella, again after the same cardinal. In 1740 the building was bought by the Jesuits, and the architect Luigi Vanvitelli given the job of restructuring it. Today the villa, which also belonged to Napoleon's brother, has been turned into a hotel from the gardens of which there is a splendid view. There are also **Villa Borghese-Parisi** and **Villa Lancellotti**, both originally country houses later transformed into luxury villas, **Villa Muti**, an example of mannerist architecture and decorated by Passignano and by Pietro da Cortona, the XVI Century **Villa Sora** with frescos by Cavalier D'Arpino and his pupils and, finally, **Villa Grazioli**, in the municipality of Grottaferrata, probably built at the end of the XVI Century by Mascherino and then decorated in three successive phases during the XVII and early XVIII Century. On the boundary between Frascati and Monteporzio Catone there is also **Villa Mondragone**, a classical example of a fortified villa, built in a position with a splendid view, upon the remains of the ancient Roman villa of the Quintilians. Commissioned by Cardinal Altemps at the end of the XVI Century so as to host Pope Gregorius XIII who from here emanated his bull of 1582 with the reform of the Gregorian calendar, this villa, built to a design by Martino Longhi, was modified and extended in 1613 by Carlo Maderno, Giovanni Fontana and Giovanni Vasanzio and is today the property of one of Rome's universities.

Frascati: the park of Villa Torlonia

Frascati: Villa Falconieri, also called La Rufina

Villa Falconieri: one of the halls

Frascati: Villa Borghese-Parisi

I. Buzi, Neptune's Nymphaeum, Villa Aldobrandini, Frascati

ty, it is difficult to visit most of these villas, reason for which the manifestation of the *Giochi d'Acqua e di Verde nei Castelli Romani*, which every year takes place in the first half of June with concerts, conferences and shows set in these splendid places, is of particular importance. Built on the remains of an ancient roman villa, materials from which were used for the construction of the first nucleus of the town, **Frascati** would seem to have taken its name from the thatching (frasche, in Italian) used on the roofs of its houses. In the IX Centuy *Frascata* was a suburb of *Tusculum*, and its population greatly increased when the latter was destroyed at the end of the XIII Century. It was Pope Paul III who in the middle of the XVI Century gave impulse to the expansion of the city when he gave Antonio da Sangallo the task of redesigning it. Since then many have been the popes who have chosen it as a resort and who have changed its appearance. Many are the churches: from the baroque style **Cattedrale** by Girolamo Fontana to the **Church of Gesù** of the end of the 1500's and restrucutred between 1696 and 1700 by the Jesuit architect Gregorio Castrichini. In this last, behind the altar, there is a fresco by Father Andrea Pozzo (1642-1709) which creates the illusion of piercing the wall creating a fictitious quire covered by a dome under which there is a canopy (an evident reference to the one by Bernini in St. Peter's) where Christ is being circumcised. And then the IX Century **Church of Santa Maria in Vivaro**, extended in the 1200's and then rebuilt in the 1400's, it is also known as San Rocco because it contains a XV Century fresco of the saint together with St. Sebastian, these being the patron saints of the town having freed it from the plague. Near the church there is the **Palazzo Episcopale**, ancient rocca of Frascati which was extended and fortified in the 1400's, inside which there are works by Taddeus Kuntz and a painting by Sebastiano Conca. Finally, **Palazzo Micara**, where Pauline Bonaparte stayed and where it is said she received the sculptor Antonio Canova, and the **Palazzo del Municipio** where there are works by Bartolomeo Pinelli (1781-1835). Lastly there is **Rocca Priora** which dominates its surroundings from a height of 768 m. Built to control the Via Latina, only artery for the South of Italy before the construction of the Appian Way, this place was inhabited as early as the bronze age. Of interest are: the ancient "borgo" surrounded by walls with its XIV Century gates over which there is the coat of arms of the Savelli family; the **Castello**, many times destroyed and rebuilt, to the extent that it is today neo-renaissance in style as conferred to it by the restoration conducted by Virginio Vespignani in 1880; the **Parrocchiale di santa Maria Assunta** and the **Church of the Madonna della Neve**, the first built in the XV Century, according to some, on the ruins of a temple dedicated to the goddess Fortuna, today has its original romanesque style thanks to careful works of restoration, whilst the second was built in 1660

Rocca Priora: detail of the castle

Zagarolo: view of the village

in memory of the miraculous snow fall which took place in Rome in August of 352. The citadel is however essentially attactive for its natural beauty given its position between Mount Artemisio and Mount Tuscolo. From here one can indeed depart for many excursions: towards the **Castello della Molara**, which hosted St. Thomas Aquinus in the XI Century, or to the **Pratoni di Vivaro**, where, apart from horse riding and trekking, one can go hang-gliding and parachuting, and also play golf, a sport which has developed in recent years to the extent that there are nine golf courses in the area. Lovers of bird watching should instead go to the **Bosco del Cerquone**, so called because of its many ancient oaks, and station themselves at the Conca della Doganella where one can see falcons, kites, buzzards. We now leave the Castelli Romani and head first for the Casilina, and then on to the area of the Prenestina and the Lepini Mountains. We will stop off in some municipalities which, although they are outside the area of the Castelli, are also famous for the production of excellent wines. These are San Cesareo and Zagarolo which, until 1990 were one municipality. It is believed that the name **San Cesareo** derives from the *villa* which Julius Caesar had in the area and in which he would seem to have written his testament before being killed (45 B.C.). Of the villa some remains were found during excavations in the village. South of the locality of Pallavicina there is the source of the **Felice Acqueduct**, so called after Felice Peretti, better known as Pope Sixtus V (1585-1590), who comissioned Domenico Fontana to do the job. According to tradition, the origins of **Zagarolo** date back further than those of San Cesareo. It is situated on the southern slopes of the Monti Prenestini, and its origins would seem to be linked to the ancient roman colony of *Gabii*, the inhabitants of which, having escaped from its destruction at the hand of Tarquin, created the new citadel. Historic records go back to 970, when it was part of the domains of the Counts of Tuscolo. It later passed into the hands of the Colonna family and then the Rospigliosi family. The small amphitheatre situated on the hill called Colle Pero and known as the *Tondo* dates back to ancient roman times (I Century A.D.) and was part of a villa, it was used by gladiators for practice. We can gain

Zagarolo: detail fo the Porta Rospigliosi

access to the "borgo" through one of two monumental entrances: the gates of **Porta San Martino** with three arches (XVII C.), named in memory of Pope Martin V Colonna (1417-1431) and the winners of the battle of Lepanto, and the gates of **Porta Rospigliosi**, built between 1670 and 1722 – both were built using the remains of ancient buildings taken from nearby archeological sights. In the village there is the **Church of the Santissima Annunziata** (1580). Inside it there is a wooden choir of the Quattrocento and, in the apse, three paintings by Marcantonio del Forno, the *Annunciazione*, the *Flagellazione* and the *Resurrezione* (end XVI C.). The **Collegiata** (1607) is dedicated to the patron saint San Lorenzo, and contains a triptych known as the *Redentore e i Santi Pietro e Paolo* and paintings attributed to Carlo Maratta (1625-1713). Also worth visiting is the **Church of San Pietro** by Niccolò Michetti (1717-1722) inside which there is an alterpiece called *La Consegna delle Chiavi* by Giuseppe Chiari, a pupil of Maratta. Lastly there is the **Church of Santa Maria delle Grazie,** attached to a convent of friars, in which there is an anonymous painting on wood called *Madonna con Bambino* which tradition has it was donated by St. Francis. In the crypt the painter Ludovico Gimignani (XVIII C.) is buried together with some members of the Colonna family. The true jewel of Zagarolo is however **Palazzo Rospigliosi**. Built upon a pre-existing fortress (XII C.), the exterior in part integrates ancient Roman elements, whilst in the interior the decorations of the Cinquecento play upon the exaltation of the past and, at the same time, of the Colonna family who maintained that their ancestors were part of the *Gens Iulia*. Having changed hands and become part of the domains of the Ludovisi family, the palace was extended by Carlo Maderno, who probably also built the Gallery on the first floor, whilst it was the Rospigliosi who had the decorations done. The manifestation known as the *Primavera a Palazzo Respigliosi* is held in the halls of the palace from the 25 April to 1 May, with cultural events, exhibitions of crafts and guided tours of the palace and the sights of interest in the village. If we now head down the Via Prenestina we will reach **Gallicano nel Lazio**, of ancient origins as the many archaeological sites in the area testify. The Castello, which dates back to the year 900, was owned by the Benedictine monks of Subiaco for over two centuries, until it too passed to the Colonna family (XIII C.), and, in the XVI Century, the **Palazzo Baronale**, which is today the seat of the Municipality, was built on its ruins. The ancient part of the citadel is medieval, and here we can visit the **Parrocchiale di Sant'Andrea** built at the end of the XIII Century but then demolished and rebuilt in the XVIII Century. Outside the village there are the **Chapel of Santa Maria Cavamonte**, set between high tufa cliffs, the remains of the single arched

Gallicano nel Lazio

Ponte del Fico and *Ponte Lupo*, with two arches and made out of blocks of stone – both date back to ancient Roman times. There is also the imposing **Castello di Passerano** which used to belong to the abotts of Subiaco and later passed from the domain of the Orsini to that of the Colonna family. Today it belongs to the Regione Campania and cannot be visited. Continuing along the Prenestina and before reaching Palestrina, we reach that which was in the past *Praeneste*, as the archaeological remains in the area testify, today called **Castel San Pietro Romano**. The historic centre is still typically medieval with its pavings in white stone slabs. The *Rocca*, which belongs to the Colonna family, was in part destroyed during the attacks by Pope Boniface VIII who was an arch enemy of this powerful noble family. It is where illustrious prisoners such as St. Bernard the Archbishop of Marsi, Corradino di Svevia and Jacopone da Todi, who composed his *Stabat Mater* there, were jailed. In the centre of the village there is the **Church of San Pietro**, originally an oratorium, which is said to have been built by Constantine in the IV Century in memory of the Apostle who had stopped off in the area to preech the Gospel. Despite the continuous flow of pilgrims across the ages, including, it is said, St. Benedict, the church was saved from total ruin only in the XVIII Century thanks to Pope Clement XII (1730-1740). Inside it there is an altar-piece by Giacinto Gimignani called *Cristo che Affida il Gregge a San Pietro* dated 1633. Thanks to the beauty and the charm of the place, which is still as it was in origin, Castel San Pietro has often been chosen as a film set in the '50s, famous films such as *I Due Marescialli* with Totò and Vittorio De Sica and *Il Federale* with Ugo Tognazzi were shot there. We now go down to **Palestrina** where the various ages of history seem to blend together into

The Rocca Colonna at San Pietro Romano

Palestrina: the village and the area of the temple of the Fortuna Primigenia

one fascinating testament which includes them all: the Palazzo-Museo Barberini, easily spotted by the visitor situated as it is at the summit of the Temple of Fortune. Set on the southern slopes of the Prenestini Mountains, for ancient people Palestrina had legendary origins. Certainly it is one of the earliest inhabited centres in Lazio and of strategic importance. The place was also famed for the *Sanctuary of the Fortuna Primigenia*, one of the most important of ancient times, brought back to light by the bombings of World War II which destroyed the buildings which in time had been built over it. Destroyed by the ancient Roman Silla, as vengeance for having given hospitality to his ri-

The Santuario della Fortuna Primigenia and Palazzo Colonna Barberini
Cicero wrote extensively about this Hellenic sanctuary (II Century B.C.), telling of the discovery of the "Prenestian Fortunes", wooden tablets indispensable for the interpretation of the oracles of the goddess Fortune, kept in the sacred area of the temple, where there was the Cavern of Fortunes, the cave in which the Fortunes were found in an arc made of olive wood, considered to be miraculous in that it was said to transpire honey. The sacred area is in the lower sanctuary which is about 16 m below the upper one, which is in turn built upon a series of artificial terracings which gives it a pyramidal appearance of great effect. At the top there is the Palazzo Barberini which, with its exedra shaped façade follows the contours of the staircase below,

at the centre of which there is a a XVI Century well with two architraved columns. Built by the Colonna family, the palace was many times modified and it was at the end of the XV Century that its integration with the older buildings was begun, later completed by will of Taddeo Barberini (1640).

Palestrina: the cavea of the theatre, today the entrance staircase to the museum

The Museo Archeologico Nazionale

The National Museum of Archaeology has been recently restored and contains findings from excavations at the temple and the nearby necropolis: sculptures, reliefs, inscriptions, objects in terracotta, funerary trappings and portraits. Well known is the sculpture called the *Triade Capitolina* (Minerva, Jove and Juno) at the entrance to the museum, as is the large polichrome mosaic called l'*Inondazione del Nilo* and which must have been the paving to the floor of the hall of the apse in the lower temple. A work dating back to the II Century B.C., which survived the bombings of the last war because it had prudentially been taken to Rome in 1943, it is of exceptional importance for the understanding of ancient art.

The nilotic mosaic (detail) of the end of the II Century B.C.

The Triade Capitolina, 160-180 A.D.

val, Marius, and then again in 1298 and in 1437 in the course of battles between Popes and noble families, but always rebuilt, Palestrina still has ancient edifices in its historic centre, like the **Cathedral of Sant'Agapito** the youthful martyr who is the local patron saint. Built in the IX Century and later modified, the church still has its romanesque XII Century steeple and a portal of the XV Century with the coats of arms of the Colonna and Della Rovere families. Inside there are paintings by Girolamo Siciolante, Carlo Saraceni and Andrea Camassei, and frescoes by Bruschi. Next to the Palazzo Barberini is the **Church of Santa Rosalia** which was consacrated by Maffeo Barberini in 1660, and where many members of his family are buried. In the sacresty there used to be the so called *Pietà di Palestrina* by Michelangelo which, since 1938, has been removed to the Gallerie dell'Accademia in Florence. Palestrina is also where the famous composer of religious music called Giovanni Pierluigi da Palestrina (1525-1594) was born, inventor of polyphony and to whom we owe over 900 pieces between masses, madrigals and lithanies.

We now carry on South in order to reach Labico and Valmontone and then into the area of the Lepini Mountains. The name **Labico** comes from the ancient citadel of *Labicum* situated at the XV mile of the Via Labicana. Very little is known as to the origins of the citadel, apart from a few ancient Roman villas and a great cistern known as **Grotta Mamosa**, whilst it is certain that in 700 A.D. there already was a castle there around which a "borgo" grew up. In any case most of the older buildings belong to the XVII Century. Amongst these are: the **Parrocchiale di Sant'Andrea Apostolo**, built upon an ancient church of which there

M. Preti, detail of the ceiling of the stanza dell'aria representing Diana with the sleeping Endimion and, on the left, Father Time, Palazzo Doria Pamphili, Valmontone

is only a marble column left which acts as a base for the baptismal font, and **Palazzo Giuliani**, once a postal station. The origins of **Valmontone** are also uncertain and probably to be connected to those of *Labicum*. Its name appears in records dated 1100 in connection with the castle which stood over the valley of the River Sacco and is recorded as being the property of the Counts of Valmontone and Segni. Sacked and destroyed by the Lansquenets in 1527, this feudal estate passed from the Barberini to the Pamphili family in 1651. To Camillo Pamphili, nephew of Pope Innocent X, we in fact owe the layout which the village today has despite heavy bombing during the last war, this was the plan of the *Città Pamfilia* which had a nucleus of Palace-Church-Piazza as its generating fulcrum. This nucleus is still visible in the form of the Palazzo Doria-Pamphili (1651-1662) the construction of which is difficult to attribute and which incorporated parts of Taddeo Barberini's Palazzo Grande. It was always he who had the frescos painted in the halls of the first floor, floor which in italian palaces is known as the "piano nobile" which means noble floor, a job which was carried out between 1657 and 1661 and comissioned to some of the greatest artists of the time such as Pier Francesco Mola, Guglielmo Cortese, Gaspard Dughet, Francesco Cozza, Giambattista Tassi and, later, Mattia Preti. The decoration of the halls is based on the theme of the four elements: Water, Air, Earth, Fire, and of the Four Continents in the main hall called the *Sala dei Principi* where the landscapes are illusionistic. The **Collegiata dell'Assunta** (1685-1688), next to the palace, is instead the work of Mattia de' Rossi. It has a concave façade flanked by two steeples and has a great octagonal dome. The interior, eliptic in shape, contains an organ of the Seicento and several paintings, amongst which are the *Vergine Assunta in Cielo* by Gramiccia, *San Francesco di Assisi* by Andrea Pozzo and the *Annunciazione* by Ciro Ferri. In the lower part of the village there is instead the small XI Century **Church of Santa Maria delle Grazie**, with a steeple and beautiful polichrome stucco decorations inside.

Artena is of considerable historic and monumental interest. It looks down onto the Sacco valley from the edges of the Lepini mountains and, till 1873, was known as Montefortino. The historic cen-

Valmontone: Collegiata dell'Assunta

The Lepini Mountains

These mountains constitute an area of great naturalistic interest, where the phenomenon of carsism is predominant: gullies and dolinas are everywhere, creating a scenario of great effect. The vegetation, which is typical of the Appenines of Lazio, varies according to the altitude and to the vicinity to the sea, so that on the southern and western side one walks amongst woods of beech, holm-oak, arbutus and heather, whilst on the northern and eastern face there are oak trees, maples and elm. Between 400 and 700 metres the vegetation is dominated by chestnut trees. A place so rich in vegetation and relatively untouched by man is an ideal habitat for animals such as wolves, foxes, wild cats and small mammals such as hares, weasels and martens, without counting eagles and kites. And during the night the woods are alive with the twinkle of the eyes of various species of owls and night birds. But these mountains are also rich in chestnuts, berries, mushrooms, truffles, all typical of the area and to which are dedicated "sagras". Given the abundant production of chestnuts – Montelanico, Segni and Carpineto alone produce about 300 tons a year – the "sagras" dedicated to them are the most common. They are held in October and November and are a good occasion for tasting local recipes such as the famous "ravioli" of Segni, the "morettini" of Montelanico, a true gastronomic sin made with rhum and chocolate, and Carpineto's "jo puzzollaneve" with cream and vanilla flavoured sugar. The first festivities are at Segni, Montelanico and Cave in October, followed by those of Carpineto and Rocca di Cave in November.

Truffles also have their "sagras" on the first weekend of February at Artena, Carpineto, Gavignano, Gorga, Montelanico and Segni where one can taste excellent traditional local recipes prepared with this singular product of the soil. Further, the beauty of the surroundings offer an excellent pretext for excursions on foot, by mountain bike or on horse back, perhaps to the summit of Mount Semprevisa, which is the highest in the area (1,536 m.), and from whence one can admire a splendid view of the province of Rome, the peninsula of Sorrento and the Pontine Islands.

View of Artena from the South-West

Artena: a view of palazzo Borghese

tre is still medieval and picturesque with its cob-web of stairs that impede the use of cars and oblige one to walk or use mules for the transportation of goods and people. Above the "borgo", 600 m. above sea level, there is *Civita* of Artena, built there in order to control the Ariana valley and what was once the Via Latina and is now called the Anagnina-Casilina. Its enormous poligonal walls, with two entrance gates, encompass an area of about 30 hectares in which there are the remains of the ancient city built by the romans after the definitive defeat of the Volscians (IV-III Century B.C.). The place was inhabited as long ago as the VII Century B.C. and this testifies to the fact that the Volscians expanded their territory towards Rome and that there were continual wars between these two peoples until the Romans finally brought definitive defeat. The remains can be visited by climbing up in the direction of Santa Maria delle Grazie for about two kilometres. Instead, in the historic centre we find the austere *Palazzo Borghese*, built in the XII Century and restructured by the Colonna family in the XVI Century. Between 1614 and 1615 Cardinal Scipione Borghese took control of this fief and modified the citadel extensively. He unified into one residential palace the pre-existing buildings, one of the Colonna family, one of the Massimo family, by connecting them with a three floor gallery designed by the dutch architect Jan Van Santen also known as Giovanni Vasanzio (1550-1621), who also designed the staircase and the fireplace adorned by a medusa's head which some believe to be the work of Bernini. Of the same period are the *Palazzetto del Governatore, Porta Nuova* and *Porta Borghese*, and several churches amongst which the *Parrocchiale of Santa Croce*. There are also the *Church of Santa Maria delle Letizie* or delle Grazie, the oldest and which was semi-destroyed during bombings in the last war, the *Church of the Rosario*, that of *Santa Maria di Gesù* with its Franciscan convent, and finally the *Church of Santo Stefano* which dates back to the XII-XIII Century. We now leave Artena in order to enter the Sacco Valley and visit that part of the Province which forms a sort of peninsula between the provinces of Frosinone and Latina. The first citadel we meet is **Colleferro**, of recent origin in that it was built in the 1900's around a weapons factory, although the area was inhabited as long ago as the Paleolithic. There are numerous remains of that period and of roman villas, the excavations of which have brought to light a number of interesting artifacts now kept at the *Antiquarium Comunale* together with others which trace the history of the Sacco valley until the XVI Century. Not far from Colleferro there are the remains of the **Castello Conti** (XIII C.) built on the sight of a benedictine monastery and of which we can still see the walls, the tower and the central part of the structure, and **Castello di Piombinara** (XI C.). Both were destroyed in 1431 and subsequently rebuilt only to be definitively abandoned later. Of special interest is the *Parrochia of Santa Barbara*, built in 1936 in a severe rationalist style and which, on its alter, has a bronze copy of the Crucifix by Donatello and, on the back wall, a rather singular mosaic in which the saint is represented as an ancient Victory, surrounded by light as she holds a torch above her head, and rising above an industrial city as if she were some kind of modern deity. St. Barbara became the patron saint of the workers there above all after a terrible explosion in the Bombrini-Parodi Delfino factory, as a clock with its hands blocked at the time of the tragic event reminds us. One should also visit the **Rifugi**, from the last war, obtained by exploiting the tunnels of the pozzuolana quarries in the area. These modern catacombs, memory of still recent tragedy, have been opened to the public periodically since 1990. Continuing our itinerary southward we reach **Segni**, where the remains of a very distant past are still visible. There are the remains of cyclopean walls which date back to to the times of the ancient city of *Signa* which cross part of today's citadel. There are three entrance gates of

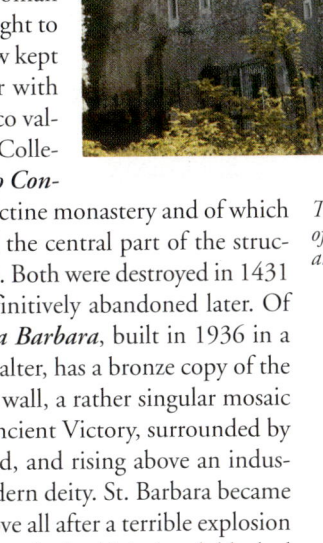

The façade of castello Conti at Colleferro

Segni

Segni: part of the cyclopean walls

which the most imposing is **Porta Saracena**. In 513 B.C. the ancient city became roman and the new occupants "borrowed" a local construction technique known as *opus signinum* which is a technique for making the walls of cisterns waterproof with a mixture composed of lime and ground terracotta. An episcopal seat since the V Century, so much so that it was here that Thomas Beckett, Archbishop of Canterbury, and Brunone D'Asti, who later became its patron, were canonized, the city suffered the feuds between Papacy and Empire until, allying itself with the former, it was destroyed at the end of the XVI Century by Philip II of Spain's ally Marcantonio Colonna. Of ancient Signa there is now only the **Acropolis** left. Of the remains still visible, the central cell has been utilized for the construction of the small **Church of San Pietro Apostolo** (XIII C.) which was restructured in the XVIII and XIX Century. Inside there are frescos which date back to the XIII and XVI Century and a painting of the Cinquecento called *Il Conferimento delle Chiavi a San pietro*. Behind the church there is a **Roman Cistern** of the III Century B.C. In the village there are the **Palazzo Cremona** with a renaissance loggia which crosses the street, the **Church of Santo Stefano Protomartire** with a romanesque steeple, the baroque **Church of Gesù**, and the romanesque **Cathedral of Santa Maria Assunta**, as is clearly visible from the steeple which was rebuilt in the XVII Century, and to the façade of which Valadier made modifications in the XIX Century. Inside it there is the *Madonna con Bambino e i Santi Domenico e Caterina da Siena* by Pietro da Cortona, the *Glorificazione della Croce* by Borgognone, the caravagesque *Incredulità di San Tommaso*, and the silver reliquiary-bust of *San Bruno* which contains the skull of the saint

View of Gavignano

who died in 1123. Those who love walks can venture up Mount Lupone (1.378 m.) amongst woods of chestnut and beech in order to reach the little lake called *Lago di Collemezzo* and the *Fonte Meo*, a mineral water spring. Here one might perhaps stop in a local "trattoria" for a "ganascione" a sort oven backed local pizza which is stuffed with local cheese and ham or, if they are in season, figs. Moving farther East, we reach **Gavignano**. A fortress in the XIII Century, it was destroyed at the end of the XV Century by Charles VIII King of France's troops, but rebuilt a few decades later. The "borgo" is still typically medieval. The most important monument is *the Palazzo Baronale*, also called Corte, the style of which is today that of the XVI Century because of the changes made by Cardinal Pietro Aldobrandini who transformed it from a fortress into a stately home. Also of some beauty are the *Palazzo Traietto* with its frescos by Federico Zuccari and the many times restored *Church of St. Rocco* (1656) which contains the statue of the *Madonna delle Grazie*, much venerated by the local population because it is said to have saved the citadel from the plague of 1679. Outside the village there is the *Abbey of Rossilli* (VIII-IX C.), built by the Benedictines and now alas abandoned. Heading even further South we can stop off at Gorga, then at Montelanico and at Carpineto Romano. On the slopes of Mount Volpinara there is **Gorga**. This village has historic connections with nearby Anagni, from whence probably came the people who founded this new "borgo" around the fortifications of the *Castello*. It was first the property of the Anagni family and then of the Benedictine monks (XII C.), destroyed in the XVII Century and rebuilt by the Doria Pamphili family as a stately home incorporating what was left of the old building. In the "borgo", still medieval, there are the romanesque churches of *San Michele Arcangelo* (XIV C.), alas badly restored in the last century (even the frescoes were white-washed), *the Church of Santa Maria Assunta* with two fine XVIII Century altarpieces, and the XIX Century *Church of the Vergine del Rosario*, incorporated into *Palazzo Santucci*. **Montelanico** also became a fortified "borgo" in the XII Century and, like, Gavignano followed the fate of Segni and of the Conti family, suffering sackings and destruction to the extent that there is little left of the medieval period apart

Gorga

The Oenological Itinerary

"Baccus amat colles" said the Latin poet Virgil, and which "colles" or hills could be better than those of the Castelli Romani which have all the right components, from the composition of the soil to the climate, for the production of excellent wine grapes. It is thus impossible not to propose an oenological itinerary in an area so rich in the production of wines. Where ever we look in the area of the Castelli we see vineyards and the signs cellars as well as signs put up by farmers who sell there own production directly. The choice of which wine to try is easy as all the wines produced in the area, all of which are D.O.C. wines, as are the "Prenestini", are excellent both for flavour and quality. To trace oenological itineraries in this area would be to retrace the ones already written about and so we shall limit ourselves to mentioning the areas of production and the various types of wine produced, leaving the reader to combine, according to personal interest, a stop in a cellar or one of the local "dives" where wine alone is served – there are many such places in Marino – with an excursion in the hills or a visit to a museum, castle or abbey. This combination will prove to be easy in that all the local wines carry the name of the place in which they are produced, names which are often connected to their long history. For example, the *Colli Albani* was the ancient Roman *Albanum*, the *Velletri* was the *Veliternum* and *Frascati* the *Tusculum*, from the name of the city the remains of which we can see on the hill by the same name. The wines of the Castelli have in fact been lauded for centuries, ancient Roman poets and writers wrote about them, as did more recent authors such as Gioacchino Belli and Trilussa, and the production of wine in the area was so important that Saint Francis himself, who stopped off in the area in 1222, upon request of the local peasants, is said to have miraculously freed the vines from parasites which menaced their existence. A DOC wine which is produced in the whole of the area of the Castelli as well as in the Province of Latina is the *Castelli Romani*. It is a white straw coloured wine, like most of the wines produced in the area and which are made from the fruits of Malvasia di Candia and Trebbiano vines. Other common characteristics, the few reds produced apart, are the alcohol content which ranges from 10.5° to 11.5° and the fact that these wines go well with virtually any type of meal. Let us then start this "drinking tour" with *Frascati*, certainly the best known abroad, produced in the areas of Frascati, Monteporzio Catone, Grottaferrata, Montecompatri and Colonna. In the last two of these areas another wine is also produced, the *Montecompatri-Colonna*, made also with grapes grown in the area of Zagarolo and Rocca Priora. Further East, in the area of the Prenestina, we can taste *Zagarolo* DOC, made in the area of Zagarolo and Gallicano. Also rich in vineyards is the area crossed by the Appian Way and the Via dei Laghi. Here we find *Marino*, sung by Ettore Petrolini in his song "Una gita ai Castelli", *Colli Albani*, made in the area of Castel Gandolfo, Albano, Ariccia, Lanuvio and Pomezia, and *Colli Lanuvini*, from the area of Genzano. Finally, two wines which can be either red or white: *Velletri*, made in the area of Velletri and Lariano, and *Genazzano*, from the Prenestina area, including those of Genazzano, Olevano Romano, San Vito Romano and Cave.

These are the only two reds produced in the area, and amongst the few reds made in the Province of Rome. They are ruby red in colour, as they are made from Sangiovese and Cesanese grapes, and go well with roast meats and the more robust dishes of Roman cuisine such as "coda alla vaccinara" (oxtail in tomato sauce), "trippa alla romana" (tripe with tomato sauce), fettuccine with porcini mushrooms, "spaghetti alla carbonara", "rigatoni con la pajata", "penne all'arrabbiata" or the excellent home made "gnocchi" with a meat or mushroom sauce.

from *Palazzo Doria*. On the main square, where we can admire the beautiful *Fontana con Putti* by Ernesto Biondi (1891), there is the sixteenth century church of the Gonfalone, now **Chapel of the Caduti**, inside which there is a painting of the XVI Century known as the *Salvatore*. Also worthy of mention is the **Church of San Pietro**, entirely rebuilt in 1750, with a tabernacle of the XV Century attributed to the school of Mino da Fiesole and, in a chapel on the left, the *Madonna del Soccorso*, an oil painting by Vincenzo Camuccini (1771-1844). Lastly we must also mention the **Chiesa "Tigri"**, built by the Marquis of Tigri at the beginning of the 1700's, and the **Church of Santa Maria del Soccorso** near the Rio torrent, in which is worshipped an anonymous image of the Madonna of the beginning of the 1400's. We now carry on to **Carpineto Romano** which looks down onto the Sacco Valley and the Pontine plains and from whence we can easily reach the highest peeks of the Lepini mountains: Mount Lupone (1378 m.), and Mount Semprevisa (1500 m.), as well as the plateau of the Faggeta from whence one can admire a splendid view. Inhabited since paleolithic times, the area was soon discovered by the Romans who built many villas in the area, then, in the XI Century, we find records of a castle called Karpineta which was the property of those same monks from Villamagna who owned Gorga. Its period of greatest splendour was that under the Aldobrandini family (XVII C.), and that under Pope Leo XIII (1878-1903), who made important changes in that he was born there in the *Palazzo dei Conti Pecci*. Inside this edifice, built at the highest point of the village between the end of the XVI Century and the beginning of the XVII Century, there is the **Museo Leoniano** which contains heir-looms connected to the life of the Pope. In the village there are several churches worthy of mention such as that of **Santa Maria del Popolo** (XIII C.), many times restructured, with a fine renaissance portal with a *Madonna in Trono col Bambino* bas-relief on the gable, and another *Madonna* attributed to Mino da Fiesole under an arch. Inside there are a large fresco of the *Battle of Lepanto*, a high-relief in local stone and the triptych *San Rocco e due Angeli*. The **Church of Sant'Agostino**, of the gothic part of which only the façade and portals are left due to the fact that it was restructured by Leo XIII, is of the 1300's. The **Church of San Michele Arcangelo** is also medieval and contains a painting known as the *Flagellazione* attributed to Giulio Romano (ca.1499-1546). In the centre of the citadel there is the **Collegiata** (1769-1770), restored during the reign of Leo XIII by Augusto Bonanni, then director of the Vatican Museums, which contains a large statue of the father of Giuseppe Lucchetti (1891) and a series of mosaics on cardboard by Carlo De

The fontana dei Putti (1891) by Ernesto Biondi, at Montelanico

The village of Carpineto Romano

Angelis. A special characteristic of Carpineto is the presence of many cartoons and proverbs on the walls of the older houses all of which are decidedly linked to peasant culture.

The Wine Feasts

Feasts have been dedicated to wine since the times of the ancient Roman *Vianalia*, this given the great importance which wine has always had in the area. The tradition has been handed down across the centuries, so that today there are many "sagre" where, together with wine tasting and processions of allegorical floats decorated with grapes, one can enjoy music and shows of various types. The most famous is the *Sagra dell'Uva* at Marino, which was started in 1925 by the poet Leone Ciprelli and is held on the first Sunday of October. The feast starts with a procession with the statue of the Madonna del Rosario, the patron saint of Marcantonio Colonna's expedition against the Turks (1571), and thus the re-evocation of the Battle of Lepanto in renaissance costumes skilfully made by local craftsmen, and then a procession with floats decorated with grapes and the baroque Fontana dei Mori. The festivities for the gathering of grapes however begin in September with "sagre" at Lanuvio and San Cesareo, and continue in Ocotber at Colonna, which also produces excellent grapes to be eaten, Genazzano, Frascati, Zagarolo and Velletri, this last held in connection with the *Palio delle Decarcie*, the six ancient wards into which the city used to be divided. The "palio", preceded by a procession in period costumes, is based on horse riding skills, riders must try and put their lance through rings which a dummy made to look like a Moor holds in its hand. During the occasion there are also exhibitions of crafts and antiques, traditional shows, and stands where one can eat local products and, of course, drink local wine. Lastly, there are also festivities for the new wine, with a "sagra" at Genzano in November and one at Frascati in December, with an event which is significantly called *Una fojetta a Frascati* in honour of the ancient "fojetta", the wine measure once used.

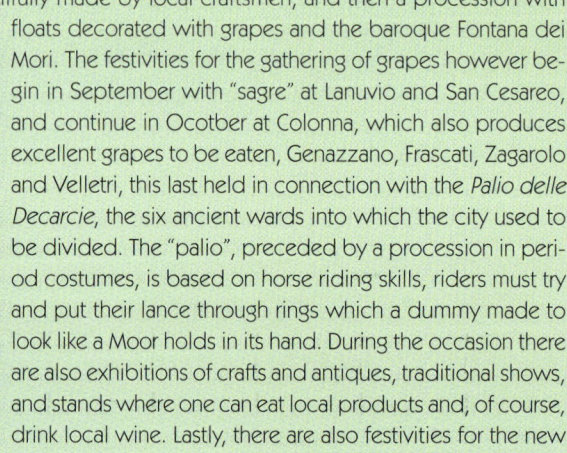

The religious itinerary

In this area too, as in almost all of the Province, after the fall of the Roman Empire, in the place of the ancient temples abandoned to the devastation of time and of the Barbarians, many monastic centres sprang up in the quiet of the woods or on cliff tops, often becoming fortresses and centres of power where Knowledge was preserved thanks to the patient work of monks. We will therefore follow a spiritual itinerary which will take us from the Tuscolo to the Prenestini Mountains, visiting convents, abbeys and churches tied to miraculous events, where we can, over and above enjoying incredibly beautiful works of art and taking pleasure in the quiet charm of the places we shall visit, also buy the wholesome products made by the monks. We shall start from Tuscolo where, not far from the remains of a medieval church covered in brambles and where there probably once was the castle of the citadel, there is a charming *Edicola* which contains a reproduction of the Madonna *Theotokos* of the abbey of Grottaferrata. Not very far away, along the last part of the Via Tuscolana, we will find the **Convent of the Capuchines** (1575) which, together with the church, was built in homage to St. Francis by Martino Longhi the Elder. It was Pope Gregory XIII who chose the artists who were to decorate the church: Girolamo Muziano painted two alter-pieces, *Cristo in Croce tra i Santi Francesco e Antonio da Padova* and *San Francesco che Riceve le Stimmate*, both markedly austere in style as was typical of this painter and, in general, of the period of the Catholic Counter-Reformation; the frescoes known as the *Evangelisti* are instead the work of Cesare Nebbia (1531-1614). The convent is one of the first examples of convent-villas together with those of Camaldoli and of San Silvestro, as its garden includes the pre-existing ancient Roman villas. In the convent there is also a small *Etheopian Museum* which gathers the objects collected by Cardinal Guglielmo Massaia, who was a missionary to Etheopia and died there in 1889. On the Tuscolo there is also the **Hermitage of Camaldoli**, one of the camaldolian hermitages founded by St. Romualdo (952-1029). Here members of an enclosed order of monks have lived since the XVII Century, their rule only once broken in 1660 in occasion of the consacration of the church wanted by Cardinal Aldobrandini, time when women were also admitted and amongst which, guest of honour, there was Queen Catherine of Sweden who was able to visit the hermitage thanks to papal dispensation. From Camaldoli to **Monteporzio Catone** the journey is short, it is surrounded by vines and olive groves and was, again, a favourite resort for the ancient romans who built many villas there. It was amongst these ruins that the famous statue of *Leda with the Swan*, now at the Museo Borghese, was found. First records of the citadel date back to 700 B.C., and it is known that in the XII Century it belonged to the Counts of Tuscolo but, these having been annihilated, it was involved in the bloody battles between the Papacy and

View of Monteporzio Catone

the Colonna family. This until the end of the XVI Century when it found stability first under the Altemps family and then the Borghese family. Of charm is the ancient nucleus of the citadel which one enters from the gates of *Palazzo Borghese*, which dates back to the 1600's as does the **Church of San Gregorio Magno** by the architect Rainaldi, built upon a church of the XVI Century. Outside the village there is the **Church of Sant'Antonio Martire**, which on the alter dedicated to Sant'Antonino has a fresco which portrays the saint, probably datable around 900, whilst the XVII Century frescoes on the walls portray, giant sized, St. Rocco and St. Anthony Abbot and are by some attributed to the school of Domenichino. Lastly, at Monteporzio there is an **Astronomical Observatory**. Always on the Tuscolo, within the confines of **Montecompatri**, there is the *Carmelite Convent of St. Sebastian* which dominates the citadel (668 m.), which has across the centuries changed function many times all be it within the context of religious activities. Tradition has it that it was St. Francis who first set up a community of friars, in this place where in late medieval times there had been an edifice dedicated to the worship of St. Sylvester, a comunity which stayed there until the XIV Century. In 1604, Clement VIII gave the place to the Carmelites who kept up its tradition of austerity. Amongst the many works in the choir and the sacresty, we must mention the painting donated by the Marquis of Villena Viceroy of Sicily, *the Vergine in Trono con i due San Giovanni*, of the school of Caravaggio, the austere style of which fits in well with the tone of the convent, and paintings by the mid-century painter Domenico Cerrini. The church we see today was built in 1660 and decorated by the Carmelite monk of flemish origin Lucas de la Haye. A legend relates that Montecompatri was founded by a group of Cretan refugees captained by Glaucus, son of Minos and that it was destroyed first by the Romans in 418 B.C. and later by the Saracens in the XI Century, forcing the inhabitants to flee to the mountains where they rebuilt the citadel using materials from the old one. The centre is still in part medieval and to be

The countryside in the area of Montecompatri with the village in the background

seen are the bronze **Fontana con il Genio Alato** which commemorates the miners who worked on the acqueduct tunnel (1889), and the **Parrocchiale of Santa Maria Assunta** (1633), the steeple of which, collapsed in the 20's and replaced by the Chapel of the Madonna of Loreto, was infact one of the square towers of the castle. Inside it there are some ancient doric columns, a fine painting of the venetian school (XVI C.) called the *Santi Antonio Abate, Rocco e Sebastiano*, a painting by Domenico Crespi known as the Passignano (1560-1636) called *Morte di San Francesco*, and one by Franceso Vanni (1563-1610) called *Vergine con Bambino e Santi*. Lastly, near San Silvestro, there is the small **Church of the Madonna del Castagno** (1605) built in order to house a painting called the *Vergine*, now in the enclosed convent and therefore impossible to see. It takes only a few minutes to go from here to **Colonna** and the citadel is easy to recognize because it has an enormous water tower which stands over the ancient part. Built upon the ruins of *Labicum Quintanense*, founded by the inhabitants of ancient *Labicum* who had fled after its destruction, Colonna took its name from a column of that ancient city so much so that in the past it was called "La Colona". A protagonist in the battles which involved the Colonna family, the castle was destroyed in 1298 and rebuilt shortly after, which is when the "borgo" started forming round it. Worth visiting are: the **Parrocchia of San Nicola di Bari**, built in the second half of the XVIII Century, in which there are a polichrome alter dedicated to the saint, an alter-piece painted by Carlo Ciappini called the *Vergine col Bambino e Santi Filippo e Nicola*, and a painting which depicts the most important monuments of Colonna; the **Church of San Rocco** (1566) which was rebuilt in 1665. Our next stop, always within the area of the Tuscolo hills, is **Grottaferrata**, where there is the **Abbey of San Nilo** which is worth visiting with care. The history of this citadel is closely connected to that of the abbey in that it would seem that the name of both places derives from *Crypta Ferrata*, in other words the steel grate one can still see today which belongs to an ancient Roman building later turned into a Christian oratorium upon which the church of Santa Maria was built. Of particular interest are: the **Catacombs of Ad Decimum** (IV Century A.D.), with many tunnels and disseminated with burial niches and epigraphs in greek and latin; and some villas such as **Villa Cavalletti**, **Villa di Campovecchio** of the XVI Century, and **Villa Montalto Grazioli** of the end of the XVI Century, probably designed by Mascherino. In the adjacent valley, near the sight of an ancient roman villa the remains of which can still

Colonna: the church of San Nicola di Bari

The Abbey of San Nilo at Grottaferrata

The central nave

The Abbazia di San Nilo

This abbey is the only one in the Province of Rome to be Greek-Orthodox. It was founded between 1004 and 1018 by the Basilian monks from Calabria called Nilo and Bartolomeo, and the land for it, where there was an oratory built upon the ruins of an ancient Roman building for a long time thought to be Cicero's and from which many of the materials for the construction of the abbey were taken, was donated by the Counts of Tuscolo. Thanks to the protection of the Tuscolo family and the popes, the power of this abbey grew rapidly and extended to the territories of Albano, Labicano and Tuscolano. Given its strategic position and the position of power it had acquired, the abbey with time came to be more a military headquarters for the battles between the Papacy, local lords and the Empire. It was for this reason that in the course of the second half of the XV Century Cardinal Giuliano della Rovere, later Pope Julius II, turned it into an imposing fortress with the mighty bastions which still today strike visitors. It was eventually handed back to the monks and then became a national monument in 1874. Today it is a place of prayer of charm and full of works of extraordinary beauty. The complex, situated inside a grandiose **castello** with towers, moats and battlements which are perhaps the work of Baccio Pontelli, has two courtyards, one with the Palazzo Abbaziale or abbey palace, the printing works, a "borgo" and the **cortile giardino** or walled garden of Sangallo, and the other with the **Basilica Abbaziale** the original aspect of which has been seriously compromised in time. Indeed, Santa Maria, which was extensively modified in the XVIII Century, is now late baroque in style, although it still shows interesting works dating back to the XI and XII Century such as the relief work marble portal and the mosaic above it which represents the *Redentore in Cattedra con il Vangelo*, or the baptismal font also in relief work. Inside the church we can see the XIII Century mosaic known as the *Pentecoste* set upon the Triumphal Arch and some frescoes which depict stories drawn from the Bible, by some attributed to Pietro Cavallini. Next to the church is the XII Century steeple. A remarkably striking work of art is the *Theotokos* Madonna which dates back to the XII-XIII Century. Sober and severe, it may have been brought there from the castle of Tuscolo and has been the object of pilgrimages ever since. In the Abbey there are also the **Raccolta Artistica Abbaziale**, which contains archaeological findings found during excavations within the complex of the Abbey and also in surrounding areas, the **Biblioteca** or library, with codicils which date back to the XI Century that were written by Saint Nilo and his disciples as well as the most ancient collection of byzantine liturgical music, the **Laboratorio di Restauro** or restoration laboratory which, in 1931, took the place of the alas destroyed *Scriptorium*. Of considerable interest and of great beauty is the chapel known as the **Cappella dei Santi Fondatori**, rebuilt by Odoardo Farnese, the then commendatory abbot, in 1608, and entirely executed by Domenichino, pupil of Annibale Carracci. The frescoes re-evoke the foundation of the Abbey, with particular attention to its dedication to the Virgin, symbol of the Catholic Church. In them the artist puts to fruit the experience gained as an assistant of Annibale Carracci at the Galleria Farnese in Rome, recreating the same alternation between frescos executed within a well defined architectural and decorative structure, and others which seem to illusionistically free themselves in space.

The chapel of Santi fondatori with frescoes by Domenichino

be seen, a prehistoric necropolis has been found.
From Grottaferrata we will now head in the direction of two sanctuaries: that of the Madonna del Tufo at Rocca di Papa, and Santa Maria di Galloro at Ariccia. Under the peek of Mount Cavo, **Rocca di Papa** has stood isolated in its position since the XI Century and it owes its name to Pope Eugene III (1145-1152) who was the first to stay in this massively fortified *Rocca,* built on the ruins of an acropolis which could have been the ancient city of *Cabum*. Still today one can see the ruins of the Rocca rise at a height of 700 m. above the village with its medieval historic centre composed of steep little streets which run down to the main square. Next to the rocca, in the neighbourhood called dei Bavaresi in memory of the of the attack on the part of the troups of Ludovico il Bavaro (1328) is the **Church of the Crocifisso**, the oldest in the village, which collapsed in the XVIII Century and was rebuilt in the XIX Century by Guglielmo Teodoro Achtermann, a Westphalian artist who died in the citadel. Started in 1664, the **Duomo** is dedicated to the Assumption and designed by Antonio del Grande but was only completed about a century later by Domenico Gregorini. Having collapsed during the earthquake of 1806, it was rebuilt in 1849 to a design by Domenico Palmucci, whilst the neoclassic façade is by Luigi Bracci. Inside there are a painting by Corrado Giaquinto (1739) called *l'Assunta*, the *Redentore*, probably of the school of Raphael, and one of the Senese school called *Madonna col Bambino* (XIV C.). The place of worship of major interest is however the **Sanctuary of the Madonna del Tufo**, not far from the village and tied to a miracle. It is in fact told that, a wayfarer having invoked the Madonna, she stopped a block of stone from falling onto him and crushing him. The man decided to put the block of tufa stone in a chapel and to have an image of the *Madonna with Child* painted on it, which some today attribute to Antoniazzo Romano. The church we see today, neoclassical in aspect, is the result of additions which date back to the XVIII and XIX Century. From here we head in the direction of Ariccia where, near the village, is the **Sanctuary of Santa Maria di Galloro**, designed in 1624 by the CapuchineFather Michele da Bergamo and restored at the beginning of the seventies, on commission from Alexander VII, by Bernini with the help of Mattia de' Rossi. Inside, in the two chapels which the Pope had especially built and which he dedicated to St. Francis of Sales and St. Thomas of Villanova, there are two altar pieces, one called *San Tommaso da Villanova Risana lo Storpio* by Giacinto Gimignani (1661) and the other *Francesco di Sales Predica agli Svizzeri* by Guglielmo Cortese (1663). On the main alter there is the "Tempietto", per-

Lake Albano with Rocca di Papa in the background

Ariccia: detail of the santuario di Santa Maria di Galloro

haps a work by Bernini in his youth, which contains the Holy Image, and an enormous block of peperino stone with an image of the Madonna painted upon it and said to have been found by a boy in a ditch in the valley below Ariccia (1621) which is also known as Valle d'Oro, from which perhaps the name "Galloro". However the image is more probably of the X Century and it is supposed to have belonged to the Basilian monks of Grottaferrata, who owned the castle of Ariccia. Since then the sanctuary has always been a destination for pilgrims, all the more so because the image it contains are considered to be miraculous. On the day of the Immaculate Conception there is a procession called of the procession of the maiden in that it is led by a young girl in memory of the plague of 1657 from which the citadel would seem to have been saved by the sacred image. We must now move on towards the Prenestini Mountains in order to visit the last sanctuary of this spiritual itinerary, the **Sanctuary of the Madonna del Buon Consiglio** at Genazzano. Along the way we shall however stop off and visit the villages of Cave and Rocca di Cave. **Cave**, so called because of the many tufa quarries in the area since the times of ancient *Praeneste*, is recorded as a castle in the X Century and then as part of the domains of the Colonna family in the XV Century, like most of the surrounding area.

One of the most important monuments is the **Palazzo Mattei**, where in 1557 the peace treaty which put an end to the war between Philip II King of Spain, sustained by the Colonnas, and Pope Paul IV was signed. The event is every year re-evoqued with the *Palio della Pace* which is held in the second week of September and includes a procession in renaissance dress. Then there is **Villa Clamenti**, with its beautiful XIX Century garden which contains the ruins of a roman villa, and numerous churches, amongst which the very Settecento style **Santo Stefano** where one can see the remains of two pre-

---

The Representation of the Passion of Christ

Re-evocations of the Passion are held on Good Friday in almost all the municipalities in the Province, but some are particularly interesting be it for no other reason than a cultural one. The sacred representation at Cave, which has been held for now more than a hundred years, has various scenes which are narratives of the Passion and involve as many as 500 people in costume and the whole of the village as a setting. But certainly full of atmosphere is also the re-evocation at the Abbazia di San Nilo as it is performed according to Greek-Orthodox right; lighting their way by torch and candle light, the monks carry the dead Christ in procession as they chant hymns.

ceding medieval churches in the basements, the XVII Century *Santa Maria Assunta*, the XIV Century *Santa Maria in Plateis* or "della Cona", many times restored and with frescos which range from the XV to the XVII Century, *San Carlo*, built in the Cinquecento, with a painting by Giuseppe Puglia, known as il Bastardo, called *Madonna di Caravaggio* on the alter, and the XV Century *Sant'Anatolia*. The three naved **Church of San Lorenzo** is also worthy of a visit, it is the oldest, it was built in the XI Century with the remains of Roman villas and restored in the XVI Century, it contains frescoes of the period from the XIV to the XVII Century. Lastly there is the XVII Century **Sanctuary of the Madonna del Campo**, built in the place where a crypt containing frescoes on the walls known as the *Vergine e gli Apostoli Pietro e Paolo* was found. If we know climb farther up 6 klms we can reach **Rocca di Cave** at over 900 m. above sea level. Part of Cave until 1909, it has a historic centre gathered around the Castello, property of the Benedictine monks of Subiaco in the X Century and then of the Colonna family since the XIV Century. Still imposing in its external appearance, with its walls and quadrangular towers, this manor, thought to be one of the oldest in Lazio, is almost completely in ruins.

Also nearby **Genazzano** is immersed in chestnut woods vineyards and olive groves, and its origins are just as ancient as they date back to the X Century even though as far back as roman times many villas were built in the area. A fief of the Colonna family, it is where Oddone Colonna was born, who was later to become Pope Martin V (1417-1431), as well as Brancaleone, who is today better known for the series of burlesque films inspired by him

A view of Cave

Genazzano:
detail fo the "borgo" with the castle keep

Genazzano: the northern lodge of the castello Colonna

rather than for the heroic challenge of Barletta (1503) where, together with other twelve Italian knights he challenged as many French knights to a duel. It is in his honour that at the end of May there is *the Palio Brancaleone*. At the very end of the "borgo" there is the dominant presence of the grandious **Castello Colonna**, the basic element of which dates back to the X Century, but upon which a "U" shaped building was constructed in the central courtyard in the XV Century, and upon which there is an elegant loggia said to be the work of Antonio Del Grande. Marcantonio Colonna further modified the castle at the end of the XVI Century, changing it from a castle into a stately home, opening out the northern loggia which was connected to the gardens opposite and decorated with fescoes, depicting the properties of the Colonna family, which are today no longer decifarable. It was indeed this area which was most damaged by the bombings of World War II, today completely rebuilt after a lengthy process of restoration for the whole palace. The frescoes in the chapel, attributed to an artist close to Cavalier d'Arpino and representing the battle of Lepanto, are instead in a good state of conservation. A few hundred metres from the castle, near the **Porta Romana,** there is a nymphaeum in the style of Bramante. This complex of buildings would seem to have been built for parties and theatrical representations. One should also visit: the **Church of San Pio** and its convent, built between the XV and the XVII Century on the remains of a Roman villa, and where in the cloyster there are still frescos by Vincenzo Manetti depicting the life of St. Francis; the **Church of San Nicola** (XIII Century), with its fine cosmatesque floors, which was restructured in the XVII at the expense of most of its gothic elements. Below the castle there are: the **Church of San Giovanni** where there is a holy-water font of the 1400's; the XIII Century **Church of San Paolo Apostolo** with a fine romanesque steeple, which was restructured in the XVII and XVIII Century and decorated in the

The Sanctuary of the Madonna del Buon Consiglio

Dating back to the XIII Century, the appearance of the Sanctuary today is the result of a series of changes. It was rebuilt by Domenico D'Ottavio between 1621 and 1629 and then again restored in the course of the XIX Century, so that today it is neo-classical in appearance, although the medial portal is of the XV Century. Its fame dates back to 1467, when a miraculous event which is recounted in chronicles of the 1600's took place. It is told that on 25 April, during vespers, an image of the Madonna with Child, which had disappeared from the Church of Scutari in Albania upon the arrival of the Turks, appeared on one of the walls of the church (actually, the image has since been attributed to the painter Gentile da Fabriano). Of interest, apart the museum of sacred works of art, is the balustrade by Bernini in the presbytery and, in the right hand aisle, a fresco known as the *Crocifisso*, of the Roman school of the XV Century. The coming of the Madonna del Buon Consiglio is celebrated at Genazzano on 25 April and 8 September with mass and a procession, but also with music shows and theatre, games and fireworks.

XIX Century by Cesare Caroselli of Genazzano. Inside it, the triumphal arch reminds one of the decorative motifs of the nymphaeum. A short distance from Porta Romana there is instead the small medieval *Church of Santa Croce*, today Sacrarium to the Fallen, with some interesting frescos which date back to the XIII, XV and XVI Century. Lastly, along the main road of the village and only a short distance from the most famous monument in Genazzano, the Sanctuary of the Madonna del Buon Consiglio, there is *Casa Apolloni* which dates back to the XIII-XIV Century, as is evident from the fine mullioned windows and the aragonese style portal.

Excursions on Horse Back

At Palestrina there is the **Centro Ippico Colle Fornaro**, in Via Colle Fornaro, tel. 06-9586392, whilst at Genazzano there is the **Azienda Agricola Santopietro**, in Località Santopietro, tel. 06-9579030.

Useful information

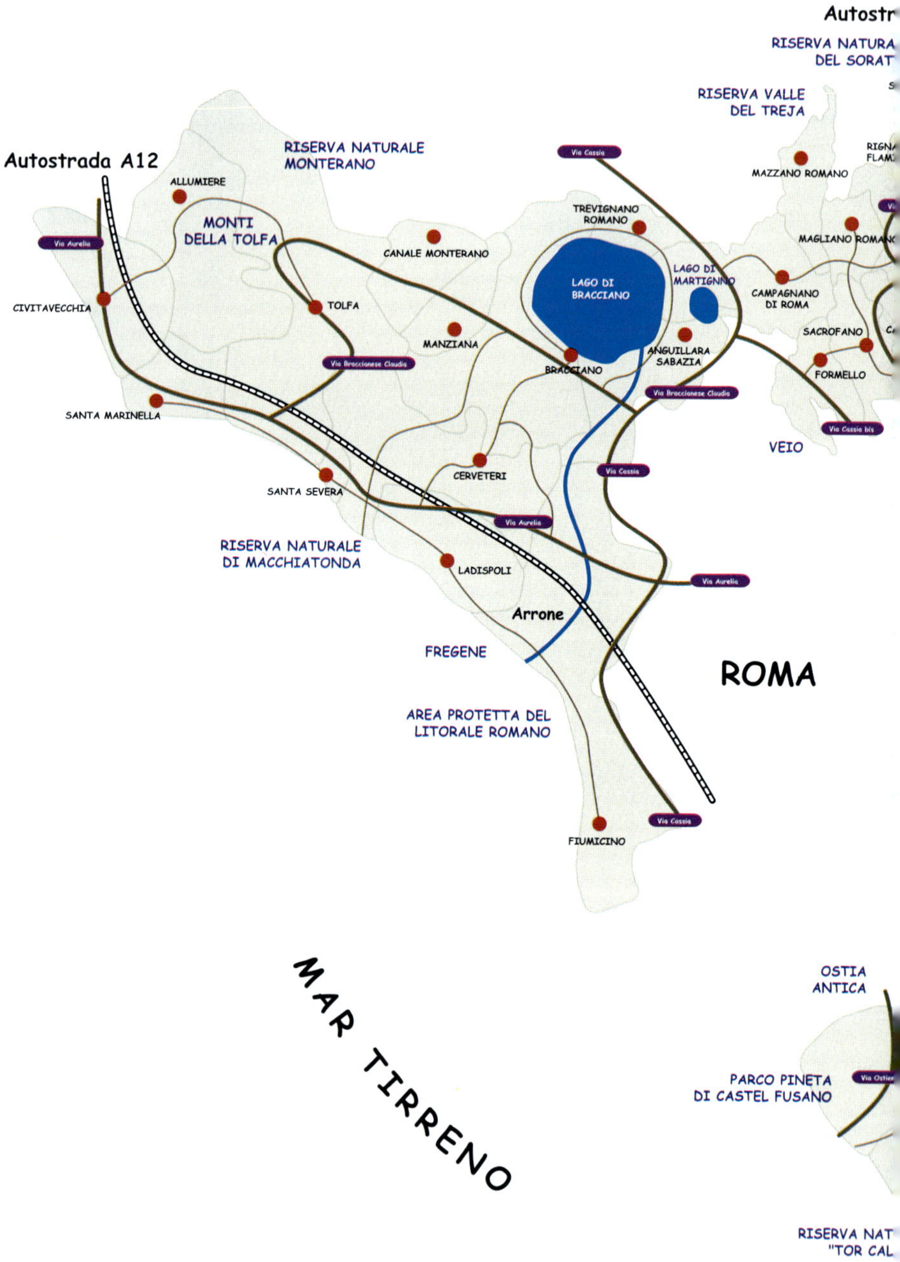

Autostrada A12
RISERVA NATURALE MONTERANO
RISERVA VALLE DEL TREJA
ALLUMIERE
MONTI DELLA TOLFA
Via Aurelia
CIVITAVECCHIA
TOLFA
CANALE MONTERANO
MANZIANA
Via Braccianese Claudia
SANTA MARINELLA
Via Cassia
TREVIGNANO ROMANO
LAGO DI BRACCIANO
LAGO DI MARTIGNANO
BRACCIANO
ANGUILLARA SABAZIA
MAZZANO ROMANO
CAMPAGNANO DI ROMA
SACROFANO
FORMELLO
Via Cassia bis
VEIO
CERVETERI
SANTA SEVERA
RISERVA NATURALE DI MACCHIATONDA
LADISPOLI
Arrone
FREGENE
ROMA
AREA PROTETTA DEL LITORALE ROMANO
FIUMICINO
MAR TIRRENO
OSTIA ANTICA
PARCO PINETA DI CASTEL FUSANO

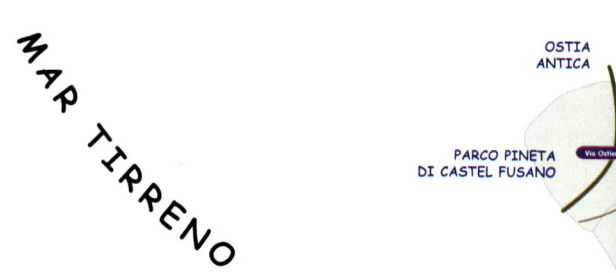

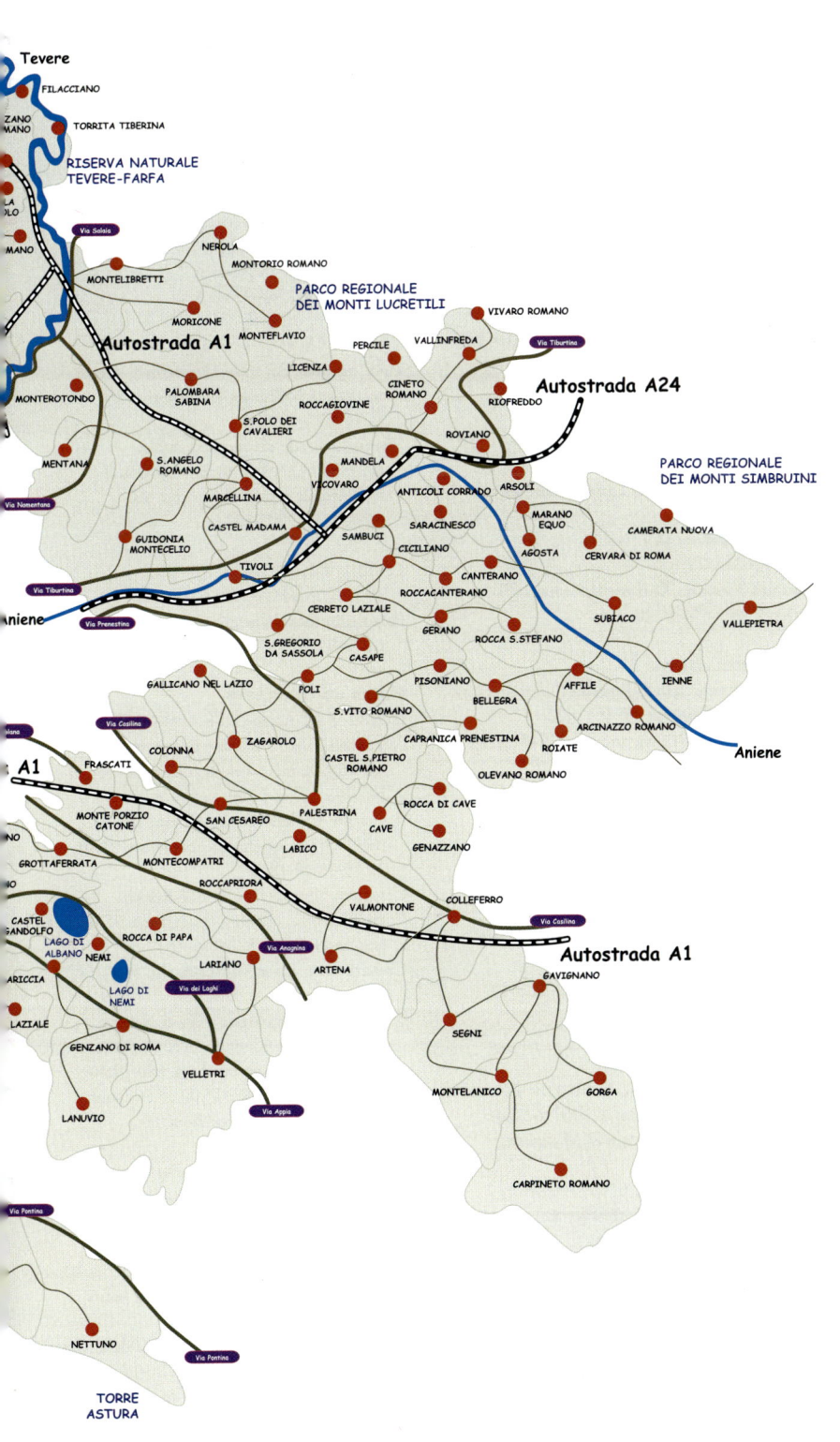

Useful information
PROVINCE OF ROME - TOURIST SERVICE
E-mail: servizioturismo@provincia.roma.it
A.P.T. provincia di Roma: tel. 06421381

I.A.T. (Tourist Information and Reception)
Albano Laziale: v.le Risorgimento, 1 tel. 069324081
Anzio: p.zza Pia, 19 - tel. 069845147
Civitavecchia: v.le G. Garibaldi, 42 tel. 076625348
Frascati: p.zza G. Marconi, 1 - tel. 069420331
Santa Marinella: via Aurelia, 363 - tel. 0766537376
Subiaco: via Cadorna, 59 - tel. 0774822013
Tivoli: l.go G. Garibaldi - tel. 0774334522
Velletri: via dei Volsci, 8 - tel. 069630896
Comunità Montana III Monti della Tolfa (Allumiere): tel. 076696290
Comunità Montana X del Lazio (Subiaco): tel.0774822431
Comunità Montana IX (Tivoli): tel. 0774314712
Comunità Montana XI Castelli Romani (Rocca Priora): tel. 069470820

TOURIST ASSOCIATIONS
Agenzia Turistica Castelli Romani (Grottaferrata): tel. 0694547046 - fax 0694547422
Aniene Valley (Tivoli): tel. and fax 0774319094
CON. TUR (Anzio): tel. 069870354 fax 069865386
CON. TUR (Nettuno): tel. 069805205
Consorzio Lago di Bracciano: tel. 0699895462/67662201
Consorzio Promo Alto Lazio (Civitavecchia): tel. and fax 076623806 - 03683609184
Consorzio Ecetra (Gavignano): tel. 069703386 fax 0697030536
Hotel Reservations (Roma): tel. 0669942042

Parks and Natural Reserves
NORTH-WESTERN AREA AND SOUTHERN COASTLINE
Riserva naturale Monterano: tel. 069962724
Monumento naturale Caldara di Manziana: tel. 069964104
Oasi di Macchiatonda: tel. 0766571097
Monumento naturale di Torre Flavia: tel. 063723644 (WWF Lazio)
Oasi del bosco di Palo: tel. 069911641
Oasi WWF di Macchiagrande: tel. 066876333/0691010350
Riserva naturale di Tor Caldara: tel. 069864177

TIBER VALLEY
Parco naturale di Vejo (Comune di Campagnano): tel. 069042774

Parco suburbano Valle del Treja: tel. 069049295
Riserva naturale del monte Soratte (Comune di Sant'Oreste): tel. 0761578185/579924
Ass.ne Avventura Soratte: 0761579895
Riserva naturale di Nazzano (Tevere-Farfa): tel. 0765332533/335121

TIBURTINO-SUBLACENSE AREA
Parco naturale dei monti Lucretili: tel. 0774637027; for excursions 077466779/634303
Riserva naturale del monte Catillo: tel. 0667663301 (Provincia di Roma)
Parco naturale monti Simbruini: tel. 0774827219/827221

CASTELLI ROMANI AND PRENESTINA-MONTI LEPINI AREA
Parco suburbano Castelli Romani: tel. 069495253/5

Places worth visiting
NORTH-WEST AREA AND SOUTHERN COASTLINE
Anguillara Sabazia: **Palazzo Baronale and Torre**, tel. 069996582; week days by appointment, holidays 10.00-12.00/15.00-18.00
Bracciano: **Castello Orsini Odescalchi**, tel. 0699804348; opening hours hours 10.00-12.00/15.00-18.00
Cerveteri: **Necropoli della Banditaccia**, tel. 9940001; opening hours hours 9.00-18.00 (summer), 9.00-16.00 (winter)
Civitavecchia: **Forte Michelangelo**, tel. 07665901 (Comune)
Anzio: **Parco archeologico Villa di Nerone**, tel. 069831420 (Comune di Anzio Ass.to Pubblica Istruzione); open on Sundays; 9.00-20.30 (summer), 9.00-13.00/15.00-17.00 (winter)
Ardea: **Giardini della Landriana**, tel. 0691010350/6876333
Nettuno: **Forte Sangallo**; opening hours 9.00-12.00/16.00-20.00, closed Mondays

Places of worship
Allumiere: **Eremo della Trinità**, tel. 07669620; only the church can be visited, opening hours 9.00-12.00/15.00-19.000
Allumiere: **Santuario della Madonna delle Grazie**; opening hours 9.00-12.00/15.00-19.00
Allumiere: **Chiesa della Madonna di Cibona**, tel. 0766967414
Canale Monterano: **Eremo di Monte Virginio**,

tel. 0699837167; opening hours 8.30-12.00/16.00-19,30

TIBER VALLEY
Civitella San Paolo: **Castello**, tel. 0765335121
Fiano Romano: **Castello ducale**, tel. 0765407218 (Comune)
Riano: **Castello Boncompagni-Paradisi**, tel. 069031001 (Comune)
Sant'Oreste: **Palazzo Canali**, tel. 0761579021 (Comune)

Places of worship
Campagnano: **Madonna del Sorbo**, tel. 069042924
Ponzano Romano; **Abbazia di Sant'Andrea in Flumine**, tel. 0765338065; ask permission to visit the abbey to the family living there
Sant'Oreste: **Eremo di San Silvestro**, tel. 0761578185; ask the Comune during week, holidays 8.30-19.00

TIBURTINO-SUBLACENSE AREA
Anticoli Corrado: **Palazzetto Brancaccio**, tel. 0774936318 (Comune); opening hours 10.00-13.00, Saturdays and holidays also in the afternoon 15.00-18.00
Arsoli: **Castello Massimo**, tel. 0635453677
Capranica Prenestina: **Palazzo Barberini**, tel. 069584126 (Comune); open Saturdays and Sundays only
Casape: **Palazzo Baronale**, tel. 0774489000 (Comune)
Castel Madama: **Castello Orsini**, tel. 077445001(Comune)
Cervara di Roma: **Rocca**; free access
Ciciliano: **Villa Manni**, private property, tel. 066787718 - 0774790041
Ciciliano: **Castello Theodoli**, tel. 0774790775
Guidonia-Montecelio: **Rocca medievale**, tel. 07743012 (Comune)
Licenza: **Palazzo Orsini**; opening hours 16.00-18.00 (summer), 10.00-12.00/15.00-17.00 (winter), closed Mondays
Mentana: **Palazzo Baronale**, tel. 069091851 (Comune)
Monterotondo: **Palazzo Ducale**, tel. 06906741 (Comune)
Palombara Sabina: **Castello Savelli**, tel. 077466779; open Saturdays and guided tours on Sundays, 10.00-12.00/16.00-19.00 (summer), 10.00-12.00/15.00-17.00 (winter)
Poli: **Palazzo Conti**, tel. 069551026/20
Roviano: **Castello Brancaccio**, tel. 07747903008 (Comune)
Sambuci: **Palazzo Theodoli**, tel. 0774797006, (Comune)
San Gregorio da Sassola: **Castello Brancaccio**, tel. 06739739002
Sant'Angelo Romano: **Rocca**, tel. 0774420002 (Comune)

Subiaco: **Rocca Abbaziale**, tel. 07748240205 (Comune)
Tivoli: **Villa Adriana**, tel. 07743908739; opening hours 9.00-one and a half hours before sunset, in summer also in the evening
Tivoli: **Villa d'Este**,.tel. 0774312070; opening hours 9.00-one hour before sunset
Vivaro Romano: **Rocca Borghese**, tel. 0774923002; opening hours 9.00-18.00

Places of worship
Bellegra: **Ritiro di San Francesco**, tel. 069566148; open by request
Capranica Prenestina: **Santuario della Mentorella**, tel. 0695471899; opening hours 8.30-19.00
Gerano: **Chiesa di Sant'Anatolia**, tel. 0774798254; opening hours Saturdays 16.00-20.00, during week days open by request
Palombara Sabina: **Abbazia di San Giovanni in Argentella**, tel. 077466093; open Saturdays 16.00-18.00, Sundays 10.00-12.00/16.00-18.00
Subiaco: **Monastero di Santa Scolastica**, tel. 077485525; opening hours 9.00-12.30/15.30-19.00 (week days), 9.00-10.00/11.30-12.30/15.30-18.30 (holidays). The Museum has the same opening hours
Subiaco: **Monastero di San Benedetto**, tel. 077485039, open daily 9.30-12.30/15.30-18.30
Vallepietra: **Santuario della Santissima Trinità**, tel. 0774899051; opening hours 7.00-20.00
Vicovaro: **Convento di San Cosimato**, tel. 0774492391; opening hours 8.30-12.00/15.30-19.00
Vicovaro: **Santa Maria delle Grazie**, tel. 0774498201; opening hours in week days 6.30-12.00

CASTELLI ROMANI AND PRENESTINA-MONTI LEPINI AREA
Albano: *Castra Albana*, tel. 069325759 (Museo Civico)
Ariccia: **Palazzo Chigi**, tel. 069330230
Artena: **Palazzo Borghese**, tel. 069515381; visits by appointment only
Carpineto Romano: **Palazzo and Torre Aldobrandini**, tel. 0774489000 (Comune)
Castel Gandolfo: **Ninfei and Emissario**; visits by request via fax to the Soprintendenza Archeologica per il Lazio, tel. 063214300/3265961, fax 3214447
Castel San Pietro Romano: **Rocca Colonna**, tel. 069538481 (Comune); opening hours 9.00-24.00 (summer), 9.00-21.00 (winter, Saturdays and Sundays)
Frascati: **Villa Falconieri**; visits by request via fax to the Segretario Generale del Centro Europeo dell'Educazione, tel. 0694185205
Frascati: **Villa Sora**, tel. 069421831; visits by appointment only

169

Genazzano: **Castello Colonna**, tel. 069579010 (Comune); opening hours 9.00-12.00/15.00-18.00

Grottaferrata: **Castello**; part of it can be visited free, for the remaining parts, guided tours by Gruppo Archeologico Latino, tel. 069459854

Grottaferrata: **Villa Grazioli**, tel. 06945400; visits by request

Monteporzio Catone: **Villa Mondragone**, tel. 06942831 (Comune)

Palestrina: **Palazzo Colonna-Barberini**, tel. 069538100; opening hours 9.00-19.00 (summer), 9.00-16.00 (winter)

Valmontone: **Palazzo Doria Pamphili**, tel. 069591152; opening hours 10.00-12.30/15.00-18.30, guided tours on Saturdays and Sundays or by request

Zagarolo: **Palazzo Rospigliosi**, tel. 06957691/217/212 (Comune, ufficio cultura); visits by appointment only

Places of worship

Albano: **Convento dei Cappuccini**; opening hours 7.00-12.00/15.00-sunset

Ariccia: **Santuario della Madonna di Galloro**, tel. 069330704; opening hours 8.30-11.00 (week days), 15.30-19.00 (holidays)

Frascati: **Convento dei Cappuccini**, tel. 069428661; opening hours (church and Ethiopian museum only) 9.00-12.00/15.30-18.30

Genazzano: **Santuario della Madonna del Buon Consiglio**, tel. 069579002; opening hours 9.00-12.00 (week days), 15.30-19.30 (holidays)

Grottaferrata: **Abbazia di San Nilo**, tel. 069459309; opening hours 16.00-17.00 (week days, closed Mondays), 8.30-12.30 (holidays)

Montecompatri: **Eremo di San Silvestro**, tel. 069485023; opening hours 9.00-12.00/16.00-19.00

Monteporzio Catone: **Eremo di Camaldoli**, tel. 069447528; opening hours 8.30-12.30/15.30-17.00

Rocca di Papa: **Santuario della Madonna del Tufo**, tel. 069799012; opening hours 15.30-17.00 (week days), 8.30-12.30 (holidays)

Sagras and fairs, musei, ricettività

North Western Area and Southern Coastline

Sagras and fairs

Allumiere
Easter
Good Friday, procession of the dead Christ
April
Spring Festival with Giostra dell'allume
May
Spring in Maremma (1st to 10th)
July
Beer Festival (from 15th to 19th)
August
Palio of the Contrade (first Sunday after 15th)
September
Madonna delle Grazie (8th)
October
Autumn Festival and pangiallo Sagra (dates to be confirmed)

Anguillara
Easter
Good Friday Procession
June
Anguillara produces (dates to be confirmed)
Palio of San Biagio (dates to be confirmed)
Un libro per amico/book as a friend (dates to be confirmed)
July
Fish Sagra (1st weekend)
September
Madonna delle Grazie with Palio of the Rioni (8th)
Christmas
Underwater crib

Anzio
March
International Sailing Week (end of the month)
June
Fish Sagra (2nd o 3rd weekend)
July-August
"Anzio Spettacoli": prose, concerts e ballets
August
"Il Padellone", gastronomic festivals (13th)

Ardea
April
Spring at the Landriana, gardening fair (dates to be confirmed)
May
Palio of the Contrade (1st Sunday)
December
"Natale in Coro" Poliphonic Review (The two Sundays before 25th)

Bracciano
Easter
Good Friday Procession
May
Fair dei Terzi (1st weekend)
Game Fair Italia (last weekend)
May-June
Corpus Domini Infiorata
June
Music Festival (21st)
July
Concerts e ballets (between 2nd and 18th)
Festa dell'assedio (between 22nd and 25th)
30th-31st July-1st August
"Faciolata" (bean tasting fair)
August
Antiques fair (2nd Sunday)
Concerts e ballets (in the period of Ferragosto)
September
Sagra del cinghiale (dates to be confirmed)
Christmas
Live crib

Canale Monterano
Jaunuary
"Arriva la Befana" (6th)
February
Carnevale canalese with "veglione mascherato" (7th)
May
Festa del Riarto and of the butteri with lasso (2nd Sunday in the month)
Festa Campestre della Madonnella (25th)
June-July
Soccer Tournament of the Rioni
August
"Corsa del Bigoncio", Palio delle Contrade (1st° Sunday of the month)
September
Sagra del fungo porcino (1st Sunday of the month)
December
Sagra dell'olio e del vino novello (penultimateSunday of the month)
Christmas
Preparation of the crib

Cerveteri
Easter
Good Friday Procession
Infiorata (last Sunday of the month)
June
Carosello storico dei Rioni (4thSunday of the month)
15th July -15th August
Estate cerite
August
Sagra dell'uva (last Sunday of the month)
September
Steak and Sausage Sagra (1st and 2nd Sunday of the month)

Civitavecchia
February
Salone del mare/Boat Show (dates to be confirmed)
Easter
Good Friday Procession
July
Estate civitavecchiese
August
Palio marinaro with 'Padellone' -

giant fish fry-up and city feast day (day of Ferragosto)

Fiumicino
March
Carneval parade (dates to be confirmed)
May
Sagra della tellina at Passoscuro (last Sunday of the month)
Festa degli aquiloni at Passoscuro (dates to be confirmed)
August
Children's festival at Passoscuro (dates to be confirmed)
September
Fish sagra (24th and 25th)
Christmas
Live crib

Ladispoli
February
Carneval parade (last Sunday of Carneval)
Easter
Good Friday Procession
April
Sagra del carciofo romanesco (a weekend to be confirmed)
May
Fiera Campionaria 'Mania' (dates to be confirmed)
Fiordimaggio (dates to be confirmed)
July
The "Giochi Panetruschi" heritage parade (dates to be confirmed)
"Vorrei cantare insieme a voi..." concert on the beach (dates to be confirmed)
July - August
Il bazaar di Simbad (oriental market and arab cuisine)
August
Etruscan dinner (1st Sunday of the month)
"Una magica notte etrusca" (8th)
"I concerti della Posta Vecchia" (dates to be confirmed)
Festa dell'arrivederci (last Sunday of the month)
September
Sagra del fungo porcino (dates to be confirmed)
October
Palio degli anelli per la Madonna del Rosario
November

Halloween Party (1st)
Christmas
Live crib in the woods at Palo

Manziana
Market fair (1st Sunday of every month)
February
Carnevale Parade
June
Spring Festival (last weekend of the month)
June - July
Estate manzianese festival with cinema in the square
October
Ecological bike ride to the oasi di Macchiagrande (dates to be confirmed)
December
Fiera di santa Lucia (12th)
La Pasquella (24th)

Nettuno
February
Carnevale nettunese
Easter
Good Friday Procession
April
Premio Caruso (dates to be confirmed)
May
Processione delle "Priore" per la Madonna delle Grazie (1st)
Memorial Day, commemoration of the american soldiers fallen during World War II (last Sunday of the month)
Summer
Maremusica estate
Christmas
Live crib in the medieval borgo

Pomezia
February
Carneval parade
Easter
Good Friday Procession
June
Festa del grano (23rd)
August
Festa dell'Assunta: Procession on the sea at Torvaianica (during Ferragosto)
December
Live crib (from 24th December to 6th January)

Santa Marinella
June
Palio dell'autopedale (first weekend)
July-August
Nights at the castle of Santa Severa
August
Festa dell'Assunta and of the mare (Ferragosto)

Tolfa
Easter
Good Friday Procession
July
Truffle Fair (2nd weekend)
August
Sagra del prosciutto (the Sunday before the 15th)
Torneo dei butteri (dates to be confirmed)
December
Festa del cavallo tolfetano Horse Fair (3rd weekend)
La Pasquella (23rd)

Trevignano
May
Sagra del pesce marinato (3rd Sunday)
August
Festa del lago (procession with the Madonna on the lake, the day of Ferragosto)
December
Live crib

MUSEUMS

Allumiere
MUSEO CIVICO ADOLFO KLITSCHE DE LA GRANGE
Palazzo della Reverenda Camera apostolica
Piazza della Repubblica, 29
Tel. 0766967793 fax 076626634
Open:
Tuseday to Sunday 9.00-13.00/15.00-18.30
Closed mondays and Thursday afternoons

Anguillara
MUSEO STORICO DELLA CIVILTÀ CONTADINA E DELLA CULTURA POPOLARE
Rocca Medievale
Tel. 069996582
Open:

Sundays 9.00-12.00 e 15.00-19.00
Other days by request

Anzio
Museo dello Sbarco di Anzio
Villa Adele
Via di Villa Adele, 2
Tel. 0698499411 fax 069848392
Open, winter hours:
Tuesdays, Thursdays, Saturdays and Sundays 10.00-12.30/16.00-18.00
Open, summer hours:
Tuesdays, Thursdays, Saturdays and Sundays 10.00-12.30/17.00-19.00
Museo Civico di Anzio
Villa Adele
Via di Villa Adele, 2
Tel. 0698499411 fax 069848392
Opening soon

Ardea
Museo Raccolta Giacomo Manzù
Via Laurentina Km. 32, 800 - Via Sant'Antonio, 1
Tel. 069135022
Open:
Tuesday to Sunday 9.00-19.00, Mondays 14.00-19.00

Bracciano
Museo Storico dell'Aeronautica Militare
Aeroporto L. Bourlot
Via Circumlacuale, Loc. Vigna di Valle
Tel. 0699801156 fax 0699806176
Open:
Tuesday to Sunday 9.30-16.30 (in summer, until 17.30)

Cerveteri
Museo Archeologico Nazionale Etrusco
Piazza Santa Maria
Tel. 069941354
Open:
Tuesday to Sunday 9.00-19.00
Closed Mondays

Civitavecchia
Museo Archeologico Nazionale
Largo Cavour, 2
Tel. 076623604

Open:
Tuesday to Sunday. 9.00-13.00
Closed Mondays

Fiumicino
Museo delle Navi
(Aeroporto di Fiumicino)
Via Guidoni, 36
Tel. 066529192
Tel. 0656358099
(Soprintendenza Archeologica di Ostia)
Open:
Tuesday to Sunday 9.30-13.30, Tuesdays and Thursdays also 14.30-16.30
Closed Mondays

Nettuno
Antiquarium Comunale
Forte Sangallo
Via Gramsci, 5
Tel. 069807114
Open:
From Monday to Saturday 10.00-12.00
Closed Sundays
Museo dello Sbarco Alleato 22 gennaio 1944
Forte Sangallo
Via Gramsci, 5
Tel. e fax 069803620
Open:
Monday to Friday 14.00-20.00, Tuesdays and Thursdays also 10.00-13.00
Closed Saturdays, Sundays and public holidays

Santa Marinella
Antiquarium di Pyrgi
Via del Castello
Località Santa Severa
Tel. 0766570194
Open:
Tuesdays, Thursdays, Saturdays and Sundays 9.00-14.00
Other days on request
Museo civico di Santa Marinella
Castello di Santa Severa
Tel. e fax 0766570077
Open, winter hours:
Tuesday to Sunday 9.30-12.30/15.00-18.00
Open, summer hours:
Tuesday to Sunday 9.30-12.30/17.00-20.00, in July and August also 21.00-24.00
Closed Mondays

Tolfa
Museo Civico
Ex convento dei padri Agostiniani
Via V. Veneto, 12
Tel. 0766939040
Open:
From Tuesday to Saturday 8.00-13.00, Wednesdays and Fridays also 15.00-17.30, Sundays 7.30-13.30
Closed Mondays

Trevignano
Museo Civico Etrusco-Romano
Piazza V. Emanuele III, 1
Tel. 069991201
Open:
Saturdays and Sundays 10.00-13.00, other days on request

Accommodation

Allumiere
Hotels
Profumo al faggeto **
Via del Faggeto s.n.c. (Loc. Faggeto)
Tel. 076696041 fax 0766967541

Anguillara
Hotels
Corte dei Principi *** (Località Vigna di Valle)
Tel. 0699607082 fax 069968440
Da Massimino ***
Viale Anguillarese Km 4,200
Tel. 069994558 fax 069995316
Da Vittorio ***
Via Reginaldo Belloni, 23
Tel. 069968030 fax 069968330
*La Villa****
Via degli Oleandri, 7
Tel. 0699900591 fax 0699900357
Poggio dei Pini ***
Via Beethoven, 10
Loc. Marchione
Tel. 069995609 fax 069995603
Relais 2 Laghi *** (Loc. Le Cerque)
Tel. 0699607059 fax 0699607068
*Bruna**
Via Po s.n.c.
Tel. 069968819
*Roma**

173

Via di Domenico, 10
Tel. 069968055
ROOMS FOR RENT
Montori Claudio & Roberto
Via degli Oleandri, 9
Tel. 069969884
B&B
Il Cancelletto
Via M. Pendola, 26/e
Tel. 03384089650
Prati della Rena
Prati della Rena, 47
Tel. 03395228912
Sabazia
Via Ponte Valle Trave
Tel. 069995705
Villa Gemma B&B
Via Augusto, 8/b
Tel. 0699900317
Villa Giulia
Via G. Mazzini, 6
Tel. 069996287
CAMPEGGI
Parco del Lago
Str. Prov. Anguillara-Trevignano, Km. 4,100
Lungolago di Polline, 75
Tel. 0699802003
Vigna di Valle
Str. Prov. Anguillara-Sabazia
Loc.Vigna di Valle
Tel. 069968645 fax 0699609048

Anzio
HOTELS
Dei Cesari****
Via Mantova, 3
Tel. 06987901 fax 0698790835
Dei Cesari (dipendenza)***
Via Ardeatina, Km 38,500
Tel. 06987901 fax 0698790835
Golfo***
Piazza della Pace, 20
Tel. 069846141 fax 069845715
La Bussola***
Via Aldobrandini, 10
Tel. 069831477 fax 069848333
Lido Garda***
Piazza Caboto, 8
Tel. 069870354 fax 069865386
Parco dei Principi***
Via Nettunense, 63
Tel.069875109 fax069875109
L'Approdo**
Via Ardeatina, 64
Tel. 069870965
La Tavernetta**
Via Catilina, 7
Tel. 069846104 fax 069830455

Riviera**
Viale Mellozzi, 37
Tel. 069846127 fax 069848082
Villa Marina**
Via Severiano, 3
Tel. 069846607 fax 069847756
B&B
B&B
Via Casal di Claudia, 9
Tel. 0360993866
Le Querce
Via Cavallo Morto, 5
Tel. 069890766
Piccolo Rifugio
Via Stella, 57
Tel. 069862677
Villa Tizy
Via delle Viole, 63
Tel. 067802327
Villa Umberto
Via delle Viole, 41
Tel. 069813950

Anzio-Lavinio-Lido di Enea
HOTELS
Belvedere***
Viale delle Sirene, 14
Tel. 069822554 fax 069813336
La Sirenetta***
Passeggiata delle Sirene, 12
Tel. 069820273 fax 069815873
Succi***
Via Portofino, s.n.c. (Loc. Tor Materno)
Tel. 069873923 fax 069871798
Barone**
Via Acqua Marina, 21
Tel. 069822665
Betlemme**
Viale del Sole, 38
Tel. 069814006
La Playa**
Passeggiata delle Sirene, 92
Tel. 069822611 fax 069815611
Villa Anna**
Via San Francesco, 159
Tel. 069820306 fax 069822872
Il Pioniere*
Vicolo del Pioniere, s.n.c.
Tel. 069820278
Tropical*
Viale delle Camelie, 36 - Cincinnato
Tel. 069820330 fax 069877925
ROOMS FOR RENT
Boccuccia Carlo
Loc. Lavinio Scalo
Via Giove, 1
Tel. 069870567

Anzio-Lido dei Pini
HOTELS
Lido dei Pini***
Via Litorenea, Km 28,600
Tel. 069890131 fax 069890550
Villa delle Camelie**
Via delle Cammelie, 39
Tel. 069890164
fax 069890552
CAMPSIGHTS
Internazionale "Lido dei Pini"
Via Litoranea Ostia-Anzio, km. 28,800
Tel. 069890101 fax. 069890197
Internazionale "Lido delle Ginestre"
Via Ardeatina, Km 28,800
Tel. 069890101

Ardea
HOTELS
La Pineta dei Liberti***
Lungomare della Pineta, 140
Tel. 069141917
fax 069141920
Calypso**
Via Litorenea, Km 22,200
Tel. e fax 0691011606
Al Tavolaccio**
Via Laurentina, 86
Tel. 0691969025 fax 0691821534
Piccola Capri**
Via Litorenea, Km 23,300
Tel. 0691010642 fax 0691010996
Tirreno**
Via Litorenea, Km 19,500
Tel. 069133257
La Veranda*
Lungomare Ardeatini, 271
Tel. 069133249
B&B
La Casa nel Bosco
Via dei Lecci, 36
Tel. 069332292
Mara 1
Via C. di Pitagora, 2
Tel. 069137024
Mara 2
Via C. di Pitagora, 2
Tel. 0655284982
Mara 3
Via C. di Pitagora, 2
Tel. 0655284982
Puccetti B&B
Via Legnano, 21
Tel. 069135567

Bracciano
HOTELS
Alfredo Hotel ***
Via Circumlacuale (Loc.
 Sposetta)
Tel. 0699802168 fax
 0699805455
Da Alfredo**
Loc. Sposetta Vecchia
Tel. 0699805585
Casina del Lago**
Via del Lago, 4
Tel. 0699805475
Villa Maria**
Via del Lago, 20
Tel. 0699803015 fax
 0699803034
Villa Maria II**
Via del Lago, 17
Tel. 0699803015
Della Posta*
Via Agostino Fausti, 29
Tel. 0699804556
Vitello d'Oro *
Via Braccianese Km 18 (Loc.
 Vigna di Valle)
Tel. 0699801118
ROOM FOR RENT
Bastianini Rossana
Via San Celso, 14
Tel 069986270
B&B
The Ranch
Via Santa Lucia, 2
Tel. 069987189
CAMPSIGHTS
Azzurro
Via Settevene Palo, 16
Tel. e fax 0699805050
Porticciolo
Via del Porticciolo
Tel. 0699803060
Roma Flash Sporting
Via Settevene Palo, Km 19, 800
 (Loc. Vigna Grande)
Tel. 0699805583

Canale Monterano
B&B
L'Oasi
Via Fontericcio, 22
Tel. 069963657
Tatiana
Via Gramsci, 6
Tel. 069962723

Cerveteri
HOTELS
El Paso**
Via Settevene Palo, 293

Tel. 069943033 fax 069943582
AGRITURISMI
La valle di Ceri
di Umberta Gregori
(Loc.Piancerese - Pod. 1021-
 Fraz. Ceri)
Tel. 0699207007
B&B
Al Villino
Via Vetulonia, 59
Tel. 0360292053
Elisa B&B
Via Donnini, 3
Tel. 069951182
Las Primas
Via G. Marini, 4
Tel. 0621701108
Le Querciole
Via Scarlatti, 36
Tel. 069908101
Valcanneto Taverna Nova
Via A. Corelli, 3/a
Tel. 03358309857
Villa Silvana
Via M. Clementi, 76
Tel. 064424248
Villino Chantal
Via Veio, 44
Tel. 069901269

Civitavecchia
HOTELS
Sunbay Park Hotel****
Via Aurelia sud, 67
Tel. e fax 076622801
Hotel de la Ville***
Viale della Repubblica, 4
Tel. 0766580507 fax 076629282
Mediterraneo-Suisse ***
Via Lungomare Garibaldi, 38/40
Tel. 076623156 fax 076629262
Sunbay (dipendenza) ***
Via Aurelia sud, 67
Tel. e fax 076622801
Traghetto***
Via Braccianese Claudia, 2
Tel. 076625920 fax 076623692
La Medusa**
Via Aurelia Sud, 73/c
Tel. 076624327 fax 076622775
La Palamite*
Via Aurelia sud, 6
Tel. 076623657
Ollolai*
Via Gazzometro, 3
Tel. 0766581040
Roma Nord*
Via Montegrappa, 27
Tel. 076622770

Samarcanda*
Via Aurelia nord Km 86
Tel. 0766560281
SERVICE FLATS
I Riflessi**
Via Terme di Traiano
Tel. 0766581084
Rosa Service**
Via Santa Fermina, 38
Tel. 0766581417
Soc. La Medusa**
Via Aurelia, Km 68,300
Tel. e fax 076622775
Vittoria Residence**
Viale della Vittoria, 6
Tel. e fax 0766501400
B&B
Casamica B&B
Via De Gasperi, 1
Tel. 076631182
I tre Bastioni
Via dei Bastioni, 9
Tel. 03395237172
Len House
Via Spinelli, 6
Tel. 0766540771
San Souci
Via Tirso, s.n.c.
Tel. 076632790
Villa Chiara
Via San Gordiano, 68
Tel. 03384981581
CAMPSIGHTS
Traiano (Loc. Sant'Agostino)
Tel. 0766560248

Fiumicino
HOTELS
Hilton Roma Airport****
Via A.Ferrarin
Tel. 06652584 fax 0665256525
Hotel Roma***
Via Tempio della Fortuna, 54
Tel. 0665029681 fax
 0665523713
Mach 2***
Via Portuense, 2465
Tel. 066507149 fax 066505855
Eden**
Via della Pesca, 38
Tel. 066505087
Golden River**
Viale Traiano, 97
Tel. 0665025391
Riviera**
Via L. Visentini, 30
Tel. 066580302 fax 066581024
Traiano**
Via Fiumara, 2

175

Tel. 066521659
La Perla*
Via Torre Clementina, 214
Tel. 066505038 fax 066507701
La Spiaggia*
Via Fiocene, 427
Tel. 066589975 fax 066589065
SERVICE FLATS
Cancelli Rossi*
Via R. La Valle, s.n.c.
Tel. e fax 066507221
Golden River**
Viale Traiano, 97
Tel. e fax 0665025391
ROOMS FOR RENT
Bed and Breakfast
Via Cesenatico, 129
Tel. 066680979
Forcellini Fernanda
Via C. Fecia di Cassato, 90
Tel. 0665881805
B&B
Belvedere
Via Portunno, 23
Tel. 066550524
Luisa B&B
Via U. Botti, 35
Tel. 03496664966
CAMPSIGHTS
Marina di Roma
Via Aurelia, Km 30 (Loc. Passoscuro)
Via San Carlo a Palidoro, 360
Tel. 066670082

Fiumicino-Fregene
HOTELS
Corallo***
Via Gioiosa Marea, 149
Tel. 0666560121 fax 0666560222
Golden Beach***
Via Gioiosa Marea, 63
Tel. 0666560250 fax 0666561095
La Conchiglia***
Via Lungomare, 4
Tel. e fax 066685385
Villa Fiorita***
Via Sestri Ponente, 12
Tel. 0666564590 fax 0666560301
Il Miraggio**
Via Sestri Ponente
Tel. 066560433 fax 066562284
Cervia*
Via Cervia, 38
Tel. 0666560657
B&B

Le Coin Vert
Via Porto Maurizio
Tel. 066685010

Fiumicino-Passoscuro
HOTELS
Venosta**
Via Carbonia, 230
Tel. 0666716240 Fax 066671613
ROOMS FOR RENT
Abacab
Via Villa Salto, 123
Tel. 066670331

Fiumicino-Torrimpietra
HOTELS
Motel Corsi***
Via Aurelia Km 27,700
Tel. 0661697021 Fax 0661697443

Ladispoli
HOTELS
La Posta Vecchia**** (Località Palo Laziale)
Tel. 069949501 fax 069949507
Miramare (V-IX) ***
Via Trieste, 3
Tel. 069946186 fax 069912829
Villa Margherita***
Via Duca degli Abruzzi, 147
Tel. 0699221155 fax 0699222171
Celestina*
Viale Italia, 12
Tel. 069946899
La Torretta (VI-XI) *
Via Odescalchi, 69
Tel. 069946022
SERVICE FLATS
Residence House**
Via Ancona, 48
Tel. 0688640081 fax 0688386637
B&B
Chicca d'Oro
Via Trapani, 23
Tel. 063207927
Le Naiadi
Via Orione, 6
Tel. 0635507350
Mary B&B
Via Trapani, 8
Tel. 03393269524
Villa Luciana
Via Georgia, 2
Tel. 067096591
CAMPSIGHTS
La Torretta

Via Roma
Località Torre Flavia
Tel. 069948243
Internazionale Riviera
Via dei Delfini, 9
Tel. 069911627
Queen
Loc. Torre Flavia
Tel. 069913681

Manziana
HOTELS
Degli Etruschi***
Via Roma, 101
Tel. 069964102 fax 0699674155
B&B
Il Tiglio
Via delle Grazie, 13
Tel. 0699674037
Silvia B&B
Via delle Spinare
Tel. 0699800142

Nettuno
HOTELS
Marocca***
Via della Liberazione, s.n.c.
Tel. e fax 069854241
Neptunus***
Via Corallo (angolo Via Eolo)
Tel. 069855930 fax 0698579005
Scacciapensieri***
Largo Giovanni XXIII
Tel. 069852628 fax 069852629
Villa Verdiana**
Via dello Scopone, 3
Tel. 069858169 fax 069858042
SERVICE FLATS
Nettuno**
Largo Santa Barbara, 5
Tel. e fax 069806198
B&B
Maria Paola
Via degli Oleandri, 1
Tel. 069803927
Vega
Via dei Laghi, 1
Tel. 0698988013
Villa Abete B&B
Via Accumuli, 2
Tel. 069804153
Villa Chiara
Via Aprilia, 6/a
Tel. 069882638
CAMPSIGHTS
Isola Verde
Via Nettunense, Km 30,500
Tel. 069819472
Sunset

Via Nettunense, Km 29
Tel. 0698989835

Pomezia
HOTELS
Antonella****
Via Pontina, Km 28
Tel. 06911481 fax 0691148700
Holiday Inn Pomezia****
Via Santo Domingo, 15
Tel. 0691601462 fax
0691601477
Enea****
Via del Mare, 83
Tel. 069107021 fax 069107805
Principe****
Via dei Castelli Romani, 14/a
Tel. 069122330 fax 0691602344
Selene****
Via Pontina, Km 30
Tel. 06911701 fax 069116015
Centrale***
Via Copernico, 30
Tel. 0691604043 fax 069104205
Facioni***
Via Palladio Rutilio, 9
Tel. e fax 0691601632
Golden Hotel***
Via Pontina, Km 27,500
Tel. 069108524
fax 0691602794
Green Park Hotel***
Via della Solfatara, 1
Tel. 0691604817 fax
0691620038
L'Aquila***
Via dei Castelli Romani, 16
Tel. 069121691 fax 069107240
Abruzzese**
Via dei Castelli Romani, 47
Tel.069107532
fax 069107533
B&B
Antonio House
Via dei Castelli Romani, 122
Tel. 03384231102
Camera con vista
Via Silvio Pellico, 49/c
Tel. 069110053

Pomezia-Torvaianica
HOTELS
Albatros***
Lungomare delle Sirene, 455
Tel. 0691903996 fax
0691903893
Italia**
Piazza Ungheria, 29
069155749 fax 069155749

La Vela**
Piazza Ungheria, 10
Tel. 069107240 fax 069157105
Le Caravelle (V-IX)**
Via Litoranea, Km 16,950
Tel. 0691903341
Miramare**
Piazza Ungheria, 24
Tel. 069157028 fax 069174221
Marechiaro*
Viale delle Muse, 38
Tel. 069157060 fax 069155529

Santa Marinella
HOTELS
Cavalluccio Marino ***
Via Capolinaro, 64
Tel. 0766534888 fax
0766534866
Del Sole ***
Via Aurelia, 64
Tel. 0766511801 fax
0766512193
Il Gabbiano **
Piazza Civitavecchia, 23
Tel. 0766513750 fax
0766513751
LA Medusa **
Via Aurelia sud, 73/c
Tel. 076624327
fax 076622775
Le Naiadi ***
Lungomare G. Marconi, 23
Tel. 0766537019 fax
0766537408
Le Palme ***
Via Capolinaro, 12
Tel. 0766534661
L'Isola***
Piazza Trieste
Tel. 0766512875 fax
0766518112
Miramare **
Via Francesco Crispi, 7
Tel. 0766537186
Portofina **
Via Aurelia, Km 56,300
Tel. 0766570159
SERVICE FLATS
Cavalluccio Marino**
Lungomare G. Marconi, 64
Tel. 0766534888 fax
0766534866
Mare e Sole**
Via del Carmelo, 9
Tel. 076624327
fax 076622775
B&B
Danny

Via L. Da Vinci, 10
Tel. 0766510538
Flower House
Via Lazio, 15
Tel. 0766510058
Il Rimessone
Via Lerici, 9
Tel. 0766510498
La Baia
Via Aurelia, 40
Tel. 0766513866
Villa Paradiso
Via Aurelia, 40/b
Tel. 0766511319

Santa Marinella-Santa Severa
HOTELS
Fenici***
Via Monacella, 35
Tel. 07666570851 fax
0766570852
Pino al Mare***
Via C. Domizio, 32
Tel. 0766570027 fax
0766571541
Santasevera***
Via Aurelia, 198
Tel. 0766572050 fax
0766572053
Pirgy Mare**
Lungomare Pirgy
Tel. e fax 0766570783

Trevignano
HOTELS
Il Casale***
Via Trevignanese, Km 6,500
Tel. 069985003
fax 069985157
Villa Clara***
Via Cipollini, 11
Tel. e fax 0699919937
Nuovo Torrione**
Via Settevene Palo, 1
Tel. 069999046
ROOMS FOR RENT
Bastianini Rossana
Via Romania, 16
Tel. 069999582
CAMPSIGHTS
*Internazionale "Lago di
Bracciano"*
Via Settevene Palo, Km 7,400
Tel. 069985032
Smeraldo di Trevignano
Via Trevignanese, Km 5,200
(Loc. Acquarella)
TEL. 069985180
FAX 069985178

Valley of the Tiber

Sagras and fairs

Campagnano di Roma
Easter Monday
Procession to the santuario del Sorbo
April
Sagra of the Baccanale (last ten days of the month)

Capena
Easter
Good Friday Procession
April
Feast of san Marco: procession of bambini with puppet charicatures (25th)
August
Feast of the Assunta (dal 13 al 15)
October
Vendemmiale (first Sunday of the month)

Castelnuovo di Porto
January
Palio della Stella in renaissance costume(first Sunday after 17th)
Easter
Good Friday Procession in costume
May - August
Estate castelnuovese
October
Sagra of polenta (3rd Sunday of the month)
Christmas
Live Crib

Civitella San Paolo
February
Sagra of the castagnola (Carnival Sunday)
May
Feast of the canestri (1st)
July
Feast of san Giacomo Maggiore with rain fall from the Castello (25th)

Fiano Romano
February
Carnevale fianese
Easter
Good Friday Procession
June
Sagra of Snails (last Sunday of the month)
Mid June to the beginning of August
Estate fianese

Filacciano
February
Carneval procession
Easter
Good Friday Procession
May
Sagra of broadbeans and pecorino with dancing and music (1st)
May - June
Infiorata for Corpus Domini
30th August - 2nd September
Feast of sant'Egidio with procession of the confraternities in costume
December
Sagra de' "u filaretto", typical local bread with aniseed (8th)

Formello
Easter
Feast of santa Maria del Sorbo (following Tuesday)
October
Sagra of wine and typical products(date to be confirmed)
December
Feast of olive oil (date to be confirmed)

Magliano Romano
April
Sagra of sheep (date to be confirmed)
October
Feast of the Cristo Re with sagra of the Raspellone (4th Sunday of the month)

Mazzano Romano
May
Feast for 1st May with fave and pecorino
September
Sagra of the bruschetta and sausages (1st Sunday of the month)

Morlupo
Antiques and Crafts Show "Tesori e Ricordi" (1st Sunday of every month)
February
Carneval Processions (Thursday, Sunday and Mardì Gras)
June-August
Estate morlupese; concerts and shows in the piazza
August
Palio morlupese (13th)
October
Sagra of sausages with horse races and bingo (last Sunday of the month)

Nazzano
October
Feast of san Francesco (4th)
Ponzano Romano
June
Festa della Transumansa with rodeo (dates to be confirmed)
August
Festival delle rocche and estate ponzanese (every weekend)
September
Maria Santissima and corsa della stella (6th-8th September)
December
Festa delle zitelle and sagra della bruschetta (7th-8th December)

Riano
May
Infiorata (last Sunday of the month)
September
Sagra of figs (dates to be confirmed)
December
Sagra del pangiallo (second Sunday of the month)

Rignano Flaminio
February
Carnival
June
Feast of Pentecoste with sagra della porchetta (Pentecoste Sunday)
1st August - 8th September
Estate rignanese

Sant'Oreste
February
Sagra della castagnola and bonfire del fantoccio (dates to be confirmed)
Easter
Feast of the montagna (second

week after Easter)
May
Torch light procession on mount Soratte in honour of the Madonna (last Sunday of the month)
August
Vicoli in festa and "Grattachecca" prize (from 10th to 20th)
September
Fair for the feast of san Nonnoso e Luminata (2nd and 3rd)
October
Feast of sant'Edisto with historic re-evocation of horse jousting (2nd weekend)
December
"Il tempo delle olive" feast with bruschetta (2nd Sunday of the month)

Sacrofano
Easter
Good Friday Procession
May
Palio of the Rioni (2nd Sunday of the month)
June
Festa patronale of san Biagio and san Geminiano with horse races (last Sunday of the month)

Torrita Tiberina
January
"Pasquarella", children's visits to the families
Easter
Good Friday Procession
May
Festa for 1st May, with fave and pecorino
May - June
Corpus Domini with Infiorata
August
Ferragosto Torritano
September
Festa del ponte and fair (2nd Sunday of the month)

Museums

Campagnano di Roma
Museo Civico
Palazzo Venturi
Corso V. Emanuele II, 2

Tel. 069042924
OPEN:
From Tuesday to Saturday 9.00-13.00, last Sunday of the month 10.00-17.00
Closed Mondays and remaining Sundays

Capena
Museo Archeologico di Lucus Feroniae e villa dei Volusii
Lucus Feroniae
Via Tiberina, Km 17
Tel. 069085173
Winter hours:
From Tuesday to Sunday 9.00-13.00
Summer hours:
From Tuesday to Sunday 9.00-18.00
Closed Mondays

Formello
Museo dell'Agro Veientano
Provisionally, at the Municipality
Tel. 06901491 (ufficio Cultura)

Nazzano
Ecomuseo del Parco Didattico
Casale Bussolini
Via del Fiume
Tel. 063216804
Open:
Saturdays and Sundays, other days by appointment
Museo del fiume
Piazza Regina Margherita
Tel. 0765332002
Opening soon

Accomodation

Campagnano di Roma
Hotels
Drive Park Hotel***
Via Sacrofano Cassia (Loc. Vallelunga)
Tel. 069077445 fax 069077468
Benigni**
Via della Vittoria, 13
Tel. 069042671
fax 069071760
Il Postiglione**
Via Cassia, Km 30
Tel. 069041214
Villa Celeste*
Via Cassia, Km 29

Tel. 069041026
B&B
Il Crepuscolo
Via M. Gemini, 21
Tel. 069042344
L'ulivo
Strada Sorgente, 17
Tel. 069044170
Orli B&B
Via A. Gramsci, 42
069041471

Capena
Hotels
Feronia***
Via Provinciale
(Loc. San Marco)
Tel. 069032682
fax 069032798
B&B
Le Cese
Via Provinciale, 41
Tel. 0689074173
Oasi 2000
Via Monte Serpente
Tel. 069085553
Villa Maria Pia
Via Morlupo, 118
Tel. 069032273

Castelnuovo di Porto
B&B
B&B
Via del Pascolo, 10
Tel. 069073380
Birdland
Via del Pascolo, 8
Tel. 069073380
Green House
Via Giammarile, 26
Tel. 069034466
Il Fagiano
Via Vallelunga, 1
Tel. 069085142
La Casa rosa
Loc. Valle Iorio
Tel. 069078655
Villino Serenità
Monte Funicolo, 18
Tel. 069079280
Rooms for rent
Roberti Giuseppe
Via Girardi, 3
Tel. 069085621

Fiano Romano
Hotels
Eurohotel**** (Loc. Bei Poggi)
Tel. 0765455611 fax 0765455333

Henry***
Via Milano, 19
Tel. e fax 0765455445
Hotel Sara***
Piazza Federico Fellini, 9
Tel. 0765389350 fax
   0765389819
Il Ruspante***
Via Procoio, 41
Tel. 0765455084 fax.
   0765455379
Angeletti*
Via Aldo Moro, 115
Tel. 0765389680 fax
   0765484005
B&B
Il Laghetto
Via del Laghetto
Tel. 0765480321
La Spighetta
Via Torino, 11
Tel. 0765455591
Pianeta Verde
Via V. Casale, 66
Tel. 0765480489

Formello
HOTELS
Da Giovanni*
Via della Rubbia, s.n.c. (Loc. Praticello)
Tel. 069088410
B&B
GQuattroG
Viale delle Rughe, 81
Tel. 069087077
Casa dei Girasoli
Via Leccino, 17
Tel. 069089049

Mazzano Romano
B&B
Il Sole e la Luna
Via Vallicelle, 10
Tel. 03392522117

Morlupo
HOTELS
Gran Sasso*
Via Flaminia,
Km. 28,700
Tel. 069079311/051
B&B
Il Monastero
Via Giovanni XXIII
069070860
Lady Joe
Corso Umberto I
Tel. 069071927

Ponzano Romano
AGRITURISMI
Monterone di Nunzio Di Pillo
Loc. Monterone, s.n.c.
Tel. 07653380019

Riano
HOTELS
Abruzzese**
Via Cerchiara, 1
Tel. 069081271 fax. 069081290
B&B
Villa Rosa
Via Parigi, 97
Tel. 069035127
L'Isola
   (Loc. Colle Romano)
Tel. 069081471
Il Roseto
Via Monte I, 1
Tel. 069034885
L'Uliveto
Via Monte I, 1
Tel. 0690131726
La Pineta
Via Monte I, 1/d
Tel. 069034686
P. Pascucci e Figli
Via Trieste, 1
Tel. 069034545

Rignano Flaminio
B&B
Friendly
Via L. Da Vinci, 15
Tel. 0761509130

Sant'Oreste
B&B
Il Covo
Via A. Farnese, 3
Tel. 0761578128

Sacrofano
HOTELS
Park Hotel Serenissima***
Via Sacrofano, Km 1,300
Tel. 069083001 fax 069084365
Fraterna Domus**
Via Monte Caminetto, 2
Tel. 06330821 fax 069084166
AGRITURISMI
Vivai Montecaminetto
Via del Bosco, 36
Loc. Montecaminetto
Tel. 0633615290
B&B
Centro Pagliarini
Loc. Paglierini
Tel. 0690834138

Casa Ester
Via Rimbomba, 7
Tel. 069083004
La Collina degli Ulivi
Via Monte Casale
Tel. 069083323
Villa dei Pini
Monte Caminetto
Tel. 069084202

TIBURTINO SUBLACENSE AREA

SAGRAS AND FAIRS

Affile
August
Festa of the Madonna del Giglio
   (1st weekend)
September
Sagra del Cesanese (1st weekend)
End October - early November
Sagra del Fallone (corn pizza
   with vegetables and sausages)

Agosta
February
Carneval Procession
Easter
Festa dei Lanternuni and Good
   Friday Procession
May
Infiorata and procession of the
   flowers for the Madonna del
   Passo (last Sunday of the
   month)
May-June
Feasta of Corpus Domini
August
Sagra of the fagiolo Regina (dates
   to be confirmed)
Festa dell'Inchinata (14th and
   15th)
October
Reposizione della Madonna del
   Passo (last Sunday of the
   month)
Christmas
Live crib

Anticoli Corrado
February
Carneval Procession, and tasting
   of frappe and castagnole
May
Folklore shows (1st)
August
Festa d'agosto (12th and 13th)
September
Festa della Madonna del Giglio

with ballo della Mammocchia
(2nd Sunday of the month)
December
Live crib in the medieval 'borgo'

Arcinazzo Romano
During summer, sports events at the altipiani di Arcinazzo
August
Walking and cycling races (penultime Sunday of the month)
November
Sagra del marrone (1st Sunday of the month)
24th December-5th January
Late XIX Century style live crib

Arsoli
Easter
Re-evocation of the Passione
May
Fiera di san Filippo (last Sunday of the month)
June
Palio dell'amico (last weekend)
July
Beer Festival (last weekend)
August
Inchinata (14th and 15th)
Settimana dell'arte e del folklore e Sagra della fagiolina arsolana (from 19th to 26th)
October
Fiera dell'Incoronata (last Sunday of the month)

Bellegra
May - June
Corpus Domini con Infiorata
July
Sagra del fico Fallacciano (last week)
August
Day of pardon of san Francesco (1st of the month)
Processione dell'Inchinata (15th)
October
"Ottobre al borgo" (dates to be confirmed)
Sagra della castagna (last weekend)

Camerata Nuova
January
Sagra della braciola (Sunday after 17th)
Easter
Good Friday Procession

June
Sagra del raviolo dolce (1st Sunday of the month)
August
Sagra della panzanella and cocomerata (14th and 15th)
October
Sagra of sausages (2nd Sunday of the month)
December
"Torna Babbo Natale"

Canterano
August
"La Suata", a non-competitive race (last Sunday of the month)
Sagre of hazel nuts, bread, panzanella, bruschetta and fregnacce (type of pasta) (dates to be confirmed)

Capranica Prenestina
June
Sagra della ricotta (1st Sunday of the month)
August
Sagra dei ciammaruchigli (snails) at Guadagnolo (dates to be confirmed)
Corsa delle conche at Guadagnolo (mid month)
September
Festa della Madonna delle Fratte (1st Sunday of the month)
December
Sagra della mosciarella (dried chestnuts) (Sunday closest to the 8th)

Casape
January
Sagra dell'olio d'oliva (dates to be confirmed)
Festa della Pasquella (6th)
Easter
Representation of Good Friday
July
Sagra del fico Fallacciano (dates to be confirmed)
November
Sagra della caldarrosta (1st)
December
Sagra della bruschetta (dates to be confirmed)

Castel Madama
EasterPasqua

Candle light Good Friday pilgrimage
May
Fiera di san Michele (9th)
May-June
Infiorata for Corpus Domini
June-July
"Castellestate"
July
"Castelli in Fiera" (1st° Sunday of the month)
Sagra della pera Spadona with palio di madama Margherita in XVI Century costumes (2ndSunday of the month)

Cerreto Laziale
Easter
Good Friday Procession
April
Festa della gatta with palio di sant'Agata (24th and 25th)
May
Sagra della bruschetta (3rd weekend)
September
Sagra delle pizzarelle (Sunday after 8th)
November
Sagra della castagna (1st)
December
Live crib

Cervara di Roma
August
Festa dell'Inchinata (14th)
Ballo della Mammocchia (16th)

Ciciliano
February
Good Friday Procession
May-June
Corpus Domini with Infioratella
July
Festa of the Madonna della Palla (14th)
August
Processione delle zitelle and Lumacata (mid month)
September
Sagra delle Sagne (1st Sunday of the month)

Cineto Romano
February
Sagra della polenta (1st half of the month)
Carnevale Cinetese
July

Sagra delle Sagne di farro (2nd Sunday of the month)
August
Band Festival (14th)
November
Fagiolata di san Martino (2nd Sunday of the month)

Gerano
April
Madonna del Cuore and Infiorata (first weekend after 25th)
June
Eve of Ascension
Festa dell'Illuminata
July
Agricultural and crafts fair (9th and 10th)
Sagra degli strozzapreti (last Sunday of the month)
October
Sagra delle zazicchie e veròle (roast chestnuts and sausages) (3rd weekend)
December
Crib in the piazza

Guidonia Montecelio
April
Propitiatory feast for the harvest (last Sunday of the month)
June
Palio degli anelli (last Sunday of the month)
August
Festa d'agosto (last Sunday of the month)
September
Sagra delle Pianciarelle (1st weekend of the month)
Sfilata delle Vunnelle (traditional costumes) (last Sunday of the month)
December
Sagra del pangiallo (22nd)

Jenne
August
Festa dell'Inchinata and san Rocco (15th and 16th)
Marcia della Transumanza (120 Klms - 3 days.) (mid month)
September
Festa della Madonna della Rocca with night time torch light procession and of the "Ndremmappi" (spaghetti) (3rd)
Ballo della Pantasema (3rd Sunday of the month)
24th December-6th January
Live crib with reconstruction of the old "Borgo vecchio"

Licenza
April
Festa della primavera; children plant trees (beginning of the month)
August
Trofeo "la Scuvella" (mid month)
August-September
Manifestazione oraziana in Horace's villa
September
Sagra della ciambella all'anice
November
Sagra della castagna and of the "Sagne e farre" with visit to Horace's villa (3rd° Sunday of the month)
Sagra della bruschetta (dates to be confirmed)
Sagra dell'olio d'oliva (dates to be confirmed)

Mandela
Easter
Good Friday Procession
May-June
Corpus Domini and Infiorata
December
Sagra della polenta, dell'olio e delle olive (1st Sunday of the month)

Marano Equo
August
Festa della Madonna della Quercia con marcialonga and treassure trove (5th)
Sagra dei fagioli Regina (last Sunday of the month)

Marcellina
March-April
Rassegna nazionale olio extra-vergine d'oliva (last Sunday in March and first in April)
May
Festa dei Butteri with Sagra della coppietta (3rd Sunday in the month)
Sagra della ciliegia (dates to be confirmed)
September
Rassegna internazionale di polifonia e canto popolare (last Saturday in the month)
October
Oktoberfest (2nd Sunday in the month)

Mentana
Every month
Tor Lupara-Mostra Mercato "l'Antica Torre" (4th Sunday of the month)
May
Sagra delle rose (last week of the month)
June
Palio dei rioni con sfilata in costume (2nd half of the month)
Lumacata a Casali (around 24th)
September
Festival del folklore (3rd week)
End September- beginning October
Sagra dell'uva e dell'agricoltura
October
Premio nazionale di poesia"Arturo Massimi" (2nd° week in the month)
November
Re-evocation of the meeting between Charlemagne and Pope Leo III (last week of the month)
1stOctober-10th December
Anniversary of the Repubblica Romana
December
Live crib

Monteflavio
September
Festa delle zitelle (dates to be confirmed)
December
Sagra dell'olio (3rd° Sunday in the month)

Montelibretti
February
Carnevale montelibrettese
May
Goods Fair (9th and 10th)
June
Festa della primavera with period costume parade and Palio degli anelli (last Sunday of the month)
July

Mercatino di merci antiche (1st Sunday of the month)
Estate montelibrettese (2nd Sunday of the month)
November
Sagra dell'olio (1st Sunday of the month)

Monterotondo
Every second Sunday in the month
"L'isola del tempo" antiques and crafts fair
February
Carnevale eretino
Easter
Good Friday Procession
May
Sagra delle fave e del pecorino at Borgonuovo (2nd° Sunday of the month)
May-June
Infiorata for Corpus Domini
June
Festa dell'estate di san Luigi (21st)
Festa di san Giovanni with "Ciumacata" (snails in sauce) (24th)
July
Sagra della panzanella (1st° Sunday in the month)
July-August
"Estate eretina" music, theatre, cinema, and dance review
November
Concert for santa Cecilia (21st)
Christmas
Natale monterotondese-New Year Concert

Montorio Romano
May
Festa di Santa Croce with torch light procession (1st to 3rd)
September
Corsa della stella (8th)

Moricone
January
Sagra della bruschetta (the Sunday after 17th)
February
Carnevel Procession
March
Sagra dell'olio (dates to be confirmed)
Easter
Good Friday Procession

Festa della primavera with agricultural fair (1st and 2nd May)
August
Sagra della pesca Reginella (2nd Sunday in the month)

Nerola
March
Sagra dell'olio d'oliva (dates to be confirmed)
April
Antiques fair (dates to be confirmed)

Olevano Romano
July
Festa di santa Margherita di Antiochia with medieval historic re-evocation called "Dies In Castro Olibani" (20th)
August
Sagra del cesanese (last week of the month)

Palombara Sabina
March
Festival of Italian cinema (dates to be confirmed)
Easter
Good Friday Procession
June
Sagra delle cerase (1st or 2nd Sunday of the month)
July
Sagra della Persica a Cretone (mid month)
August
Rassegna dell'olio extra-vergine della Sabina at Stazzano (29th)
October
Concerts at castello Savelli (dates to be confirmed)
Christmas
Live crib

Percile
Easter
Good Friday Procession
August
Festa dell'Inchianta (15th)
October
Sagra della bruschetta (dates too ve confirmed)
Sagra della castagna (last Sunday of the month)

November
Festa dell'albero (21st)
December
Sagra della Ramiccia (fettuccine) (Sunday nearest 13th)

Pisoniano
May-June
Infiorata for Corpus Domini
August
Sagra dei frittelli and festa della Madonna della Neve (1st°Sunday of the month)
Sagra delle Sagne (15th to 18th)
November
Sagra della castagna (1st)

Poli
January
Festa di sant'Antonio abate with fave (Sunday after 17th)
August
La Ciambellata (dates to be confirmed)
September
Festa di sant'Eustachio dating back to 1450 and antiques fair (Sunday after 20th)

Riofreddo
Easter
Good Friday Procession
November
Sagra del castagnone (1st Sunday of the month)
December
Live crib and Pastorella (24th)

Rocca Canterano
August
Sagra dei Cecamariti (local pasta) (Sunday after 15th)
November
Festa del Cornuto and Sagra delle 'Role' (weekend nearest 11th)
December
Fiaccolata torch light procession (24th)

Roccagiovine
February
Carneval
Easter
Good Friday Procession
May-June
Infiorata for Corpus Domini
August

Festa della Madonna della Neve (1st° Sunday of the month)
Festa dell'addio all'estate with dinner in the piazza (end month)
October
Sagra della castagna with various fairs (3rd Sunday of the month)
December
Festeggiamenti con balli e dolci locali (Capodanno)

Rocca Santo Stefano
May
Festa della Primavera (dates to be confirmed)
June
Sagra degli Gnoccacci (last Sunday of the month)
August
Festa di Santo Stefano in period costumes (3rd and 4th)
Festa dell'Inchinata (14th)

Roiate
August
Festa di san Benedetto (4th Sunday of the month)
September
Sagra dell'abbacchio (4th° weekend)
November
Sagra del vinello (2nd Sunday in the month)

Roviano
February
Carneval Procession
Easter
Good Friday Procession
May-June
Corpus Domini and Infiorata
June
Festa pagana della Marzella (beginning of the month)
August
Sagra degli Cuzzi co'j'ajju (maccheroni) - crafts market and Sagra degliu Salavaticu' (rustic frittelle) (dates to be confirmed)
"Panarda di san Giovanni", dinner in honour of the Patron (24th)

Sambuci
January
Sagra della bruschetta e dell'olio d'oliva (Sunday after 17th)
February
Carneval
May-June
Infiorata for Corpus Domini
September
Festa di santissima. Maria bambina with the ballo della Signoraccia (1st weekend)
October
Sagra della polenta (last Sunday of the month)

Sant'Angelo Romano
Easter
Night time Good Friday Procession
May
Sagra delle Cerase (last Sunday of the month)
June
Feast of Corpus Domini
July
Sagra dei Cellitti (pasta) (1st Sunday of the month)
Festival del folklore internazionale (1st week)
August
Sagra dello Strengozzo (pasta) (1st Sunday of the month)
September
Sagra della pizza fritta (1st° Sunday of the month)

Saracinesco
Easter
Good Friday Procession
September
Sagra della polenta (last Sunday of the month)
December
Sagra delle Sagne e dei Fasoli (beans) (3rd)

San Gregorio da Sassola
January
"La Pasquerella", procession for the dead in costume (5th)
March
Sagra delle Sagne "co jaju pistatu"
May
Sagra della bistecca (last Sunday of the month)
May-June
Infiorata for Corpus Domini
August
Sagra dell'oliva in salamoia and festa della Madonna della Cavata (last Sunday in August and first in Septembe)
October
Sagra della bruschetta (1st Sunday in the month)

San Polo dei Cavalieri
January
Festa di sant'Antonio abate and Sagra dell'olio d'oliva e della bruschetta (18th)
February
Festa della Candelora
July-August
Estate San Polese

Subiaco
May
International canoe ralley (1st half of the month)
June
Walking race (13th)
August
Natale di Subiaco (10th)
Subiaco rock blues festival (2nd week of the month)
Festa del fiume (dates to be confirmed)
Manifestazione Campestre (last Sunday of the month)
December
Night time torch light procession with Father Christmas in a canoe (4th)
December-January
"Tra Medioevo e futuro", crafts show (from mid December to early January)

San Vito Romano
June
Festa della primavera (17th to 19th)
August
Festa della Madonnina (25th)
December
Sagra della bruschetta (1st Sunday in the month)
Festa dell'Immacolata organized by a confraternity of men only (8th)

Tivoli
February
Carnevale Tiburtino
April
Birthday of the town with various events
May

Procession of the Madonna di Quintiliolo, protector of butteri (1st Sunday of the month)
June
Concerts and shows
July
Music Festival with jazz, ethnic music and Opera
August
Festa dell'Inchinata (14th and 15th)
September
"Pizzutellata", sagra dating back to 1845 (3rd Sunday in the month)
Settembre Tiburtino (dates to be confirmed)
December
Live crib

Vallepietra
Easter
Pianto delle zitelle on Good Friday
May-June
Pilgrimage to the Santissima Trinità (57th day after Easter)
July
Pilgrimage to the Santissima Trinità (25th and 26th)

Vallinfreda
January
Sagra della polenta (last Sunday of the month)
June
Pilgrimage to the ritiro di San Francesco at Bellegra (2nd Sunday of the month)
August
"Agosto a Vallinfreda" (all of the month of August)
Passeggiata gastronomica (2nd° Saturday in the month)
October
Sagra delle Sagne (last Sunday of the month)

Vicovaro
February
Carneval
Easter
Historic representation of Good Friday
September
Sagra della pagnotta (3rd° Sunday in the month)

Vivaro Romano
August
Festa di Maria Santissima con Illuminata (4th to 6th)
Cocomerata d'agosto (from 14th to 21st)
Sagra del fagiolo di Cincone (last Saturday of the month)
November
Sagra della castagna (1st Saturday of the month)

MUSEUMS

Anticoli Corrado
GALLERIA COMUNALE D'ARTE MODERNA
Piazza Santa Vittoria, 1
Tel. 0774936318 fax 0774936379
Open:
Every day: 10.00-13.00 and 16.00-19.00

Capranica Prenestina
MUSEO NATURALISTICO DEI MONTI PRENESTINI
Palazzo Barberini
Piazza A. Frezza, 4
Tel. 069584126
Winter hours:
Fridays and weekends 9.00-13.00 e 14.00-18.00
Summer hours:
Fridays and weekends 9.00-13.00 e 16.00-20.00

Cervara di Roma
MUSEO ARTE PER LA PACE
Via Aldo Moro, 1
Tel. 0774828275
Open:
Wednesday 16.00-18.00
On other days by appointment
MUSEO DEGLI EX VOTO DI SANTA MARIA DELLA PORTELLA
Via Verdi, 20
Tel. 0774828715
Opening soon

Licenza
MUSEO ORAZIANO
Palazzo Baronale
Piazza del Palazzo, 3
Tel. 077446031
Open:
Tuesday to Sunday 10.00-12.00 e 15.00-17.00
Mondays closed

Mentana
MUSEO NAZIONALE GARIBALDINO DELLA CAMPAGNA DELL'AGRO ROMANO PER LA LIBERAZIONE DI ROMA
Ara dei Caduti
Via delle Mura, 2
Tel. 0690627194
0360238984
Winter hours:
Tuesdays and Thursdays 10.00-12.00 (group guided tours only, by appointment), Sundays and holidays 10.00-12.00, Saturdays 16.00-18.00
Summer hours:
Tuesdays and Thursdays. 10.00-12.00 (group guided tours only, by appointment), Saturdays, Sundays and holidays 18.00-20.00; in August by appointment only
MUSEO DI SCIENZE NATURALI
Piazza della Repubblica, 22
Tel. 06/9090699
0639737009
By appointment only
MUSEO DELLE MASCHERE TEATRALI E DEL TEATRO DEI BURATTINI
Palazzo Borghese
Piazza San Nicola, 3
Tel. 069093885
0774365173
By appointment only

Guidonia Montecelio
ANTIQUARIUM COMUNALE
Palazzo Comunale
Piazza San Giovanni
Tel. 0774511482
Open:
Mondays, Wednesdays and Fridays 9.30-12.30/17.30-19.30, Sundays: from October to March 15.00-19.00, from April to September 18.00-22.00

Palombara Sabina
MUSEO NATURALISTICO
Castello Savelli
Tel. 077466004/3
Open:
Saturdays and Sundays 10.00-13.00 and 15.00-17.00
Other days by request only

Pisoniano
Museo dell a Canapa
Via Santa Maria, 27
Tel. 062184189
Open:
Saturdays and Sundays
in July and August 9.00-13.00
e 16.00-19.00, other days
and periods by request only

Riofreddo
Museo delle culture
Villa Garibaldi
Via C. Garibaldi
Tel. e fax 0774929116
Opening soon

Roviano
Museo della Civiltà
    Contadina dell'Alta Valle
    dell'Aniene
Castello Brancaccio
Via Mazzini, 1
Tel. 0774903143
Opening soon

Sant'Angelo Romano
Museo Preistorico
Castello Cesi Orsini
Tel. 0774420100
Opening soon

Tivoli
Museo Didattico e
    Antiquarium del
    Canopo di Villa
    Adriana
Area archeologica di Villa
    Adriana
Via di Villa Adriana, 204
Tel. 063908739
Open:
Every day from 9.00 till one
    hour before sunset

Accomodation

Agosta
Hotels
La Colonnetta*
Via Sublacense, 9
Tel. 0774878064

Bellegra
Hotels
San Camillo**
Località San Francesco
Tel. 069565037
    fax 069565960

Canterano
Hotels
Bell'Orizzonte*
Via delle Piaje, 12
Tel. 0774803213

Cineto Romano
Hotels
L'Oliveto**
Via IV Novembre, 14
Tel. 0774928023

Guidonia Montecelio
Hotels
Motel River***
Via Tiburtina, Km 25,400
Tel. 0774528448 fax
    0774528281
Jolie Ville**
Largo dei Tartari, 33
Tel. 0774378819 fax
    0774353823
Voi e Noi**
Via Colle Giannetta, 40
Tel. 0774341294 fax
    0774345028
Lupi*
Via Sant'Angelo Romano, 12
Tel. 0774340755
Service Flat's
Soc. Marco Simone*
Via Palombarese, km. 17,300
Tel. 077430591 fax 0774367435
B&B
Antares
Via Antares, 24/b
Tel. 0774573123
Flowers Hill
Via Orchidee, 15
Tel. 0774343032
La Magnolia
Via V. Monti, 39
Tel. 0774391223
Lola House
Via Frecce Tricolori, 11
Tel. 0774340765
R&D
Via Anticoli Corrado, 56
Tel. 0774366325
Tivoli
Via Primule, 16
Tel. 0774343605
Villa Diomira
Via Anticoli Corrado, 56
Tel. 0774366325
Villa Giubileo
Via Buonarroti, 7
Tel. 0774340605
Villa Marisa

Viale Trento, 201
Tel. 0774371719

Villanova di Guidonia
B&B
Gemma 2000
Via N. Sauro, 19
Tel. 0774325069

Licenza
Hotels
Fonte Bandusia**
Località Monte delle Torri
Tel. 077446030 fax 077446226

Mentana
Hotels
Barbados***
Via Nomentana, Km 23
Loc. San Salvatore
Tel. 069092869 fax 069094985
B&B
Centro Casa 2
Via Zanella, 14
Tel. 0699906611
Casa Karin
Via Santacroce, 39
Tel. 069093760
Santa Lucia B&B
Via Palombarese, 591
Tel. 069050056

Mentana-Santa Lucia
Hotels
La Brocca***
Via Palombarese, 309
Tel. 069050119 fax 0690531907

Mentana-Tor Lupara
Hotels
La Colonna***
Via Nomentana, 384
Tel. 069058110 fax 069058307
Tecla*
Via Nomentana, 460
Tel. 0690024459
B&B
Torlupara Federici
Via Platone, 60
Tel. 0690024662

Monterotondo
Hotels
Sette Archi***
Via Salaria, 264
Tel. 069004154 fax 069003986
Antico Hotel Palio Bianco**
Via Matteotti, 17/19
Tel. 069065523 fax 069065571

Dei Leoni**
Piazza del Popolo, 11
Tel. e fax 0690627394
La Conchiglia*
Via San Martino, 20
Tel. 069064612
fax 069064952
SERVICE FLATS
Valery**
Via Papa Lando I, 6
Tel. 069004369
ROOMS FOR RENT
Sogg. Villa Santa Maria di Alberto Fabri
Via Adda, 18/22
Tel. 069061054
B&B
Casa delle Rose
Via dell'Unione, 53
Tel. 069066334
Casa Rurale
Loc. Monte Mele
Tel. 069093144
Centro Casa 1
Via Sicilia, 4
Tel. 0699906611
Fantasia B&B
Via Sele, 15/c
Tel. 0690627636
Villa Francesca
Via G. di Vittorio, 68
Tel. 0690625493
Villa Simona
Via G. di Vittorio, 68
Tel. 03470195666

Nerola
HOTELS
Castello degli Orsini****
Via Aldo Bigelli, 54
Tel. 0774683107 fax 0774683272
Tre Palme**
Via Romana, 7
Tel. e fax 0774683135

Olevano Romano
HOTELS
Il Boschetto*
Via San Francesco d'Assisi, 27
Tel. 069564027/069562652

Palombara Sabina
AGRITURISMI
Lucretius di Pierfrancesco De Santis
Via Pozzo Badino, s.n.c.
Fraz. Stazzano
Tel. 077465392

Pisoniano
HOTELS
Residence del Colle***
Via Aldo Moro, 5
Tel. 069577385

Riofreddo
HOTELS
Villa Celeste**
Via Valeria, 147
Tel. 0774929146

Roiate
HOTELS
Mafalda*
Via Scalambra, 32
Tel. 069569013

Sambuci
B&B
La Quiete
Str. Prov. 42a, 4
Tel. 0774797081

Sant'Angelo Romano
HOTELS
Villa Alex**
Via Collelungo, 2
Tel. 0774420570
Sylvan*
Via Palombarese, Km 9
Tel. 0774420063
B&B
B&B Sant'Angelo
Via Oleandri, 30
Tel. 0774343097
Dany Home
Loc. La Selva
Tel. 0774420534
Domus Selvae
Loc. La Selva
Tel. 0774421427

San Polo dei Cavalieri
HOTELS
Mille Pini ***
Loc. Prato San Nicola
Tel. 0774416088 fax 0774416756

San Vito Romano
HOTELS
Ai Pini***
Via Giovanni XXIII, 46 (Loc. Arcatura)
Tel. 069571019 fax 069571839
La Sorgente***
Via Piave, 82
Tel. 069571653 fax 069571013l

Subiaco
HOTELS
Roma**
Via F. Petrarca, 38
Tel. 077484609 fax 0774822288
Aniene*
Via Cavour, 21
Tel. 077485565
Miramonti*
Via Giovanni XXIII (Loc. Le Verole)
Tel. 077810007 fax 06483243

Subiaco-Monte Livata
HOTELS
Italia***
Via C. Da Bandita (Loc. Montelivata)
Tel. 0774826128 fax 0774826014
Livata***
Via dei Boschi, 28
Tel. 0774826031 fax 0774826033
La Genziana**
Via dei Boschi, 16
Tel. 0774826059 fax 077486100
CAMPSIGHTS
Luisiana
Tel. e fax 0774826087

Tivoli-Bagni di Tivoli
HOTELS
Grand Hotel Duca d'Este****
Via Tiburtina Valeria, 330
Tel. 07743883 fax 07743885101
Adriano***
Via di Villa Adriana, 194 (Loc. Villa Adriana)
Tel. 0774382235 fax 0774535122
Aurora***
Via Manzoni, 19
Tel. 0774354214 fax 06354092
Delle Terme***
Piazza B. della Queva, 5
Tel. 0774371033 fax 0774371010
Marino al Pioppo**
Via C. Pascarella, 4
Tel. 0774373693
Delle Rose**
Via Tiburtina, 288 (Loc. Villa Adriana)
Tel. 0774357930 fax 0774371304
Grottino*
Via Paolo D'Egina, 1
Tel. 0774357834

Tivoli

Hotels
Il Maniero****
Via di Villa Adriana, 11
Tel. 0774530208 fax
 0774533797
Sirene****
Piazza Massimo, 4
Tel. 0774330605 fax
 0774330608
Torre Sant'Angelo****
Via Q. Varo, s.n.c. (Loc.
 Castagnola)
Tel. 0774332533
Cristallo***
Via Maremmana Inf., km 0,500
Tel. 0774381919 fax
 0774381990
Padovano***
Via Tiburtina Valeria, 130
Tel. 0774530807 fax
 0774531382
Monte Ripoli*
Via Colle Ripoli
Tel. 0774313238 fax
 0774311352
Rooms for rent
Affittacamere Igea
V.le Mannelli, 2
Tel. 0774335285
Passeretti Clara
Via Teatro Latino, 1
Tel. 0774531518
Agriturismi
La Cerra
Strada di San Gregorio da
 Sassola, Km 6,8
Tel. 0774411671
B&B
La Chiocciola
Via del Trevio, 9
Tel. 0774-317278
(Raccoglie vari B&B)
Da Luigia B&B
Via di Villa Adriana, 186
Tel. 0774531441
La Panoramica
Via Arnaldi, 45
Tel. 0774317278
Rocca Bruna
Via Rocca Bruna, 16
Tel. 0774530114
Trevio B&B
Via Trevio, 38
Tel. 0774314885

Vicovaro

Hotels
Lo Smeraldo**
Via Tiburtina Valeria, Km 39
Tel. 0774496214

Castelli Romani and Prenestina-Monti Lepini

Sagras and fairs

Albano Romano
Mercatino dell'artigianato
 (1stSunday of the month)
Mercatino dell'antiquariato (2nd
 Sunday of the month)
February
Carneval with puppet show
Easter
Good Friday Procession and
 sacred representation
October
Fiera di san Francesco (4th)

Ariccia
Mercatino dell'artigianato (3rd
 week of the month)
January
Palio dei somari (15th and 16th)
May-June
Fiera di Pentecoste and Madonna
 di Galloro
June
Festa di san Giovanni and
 lumacata (Saturday after 24th)
July
Sagra delle cannacce (last Sunday
 of the month)
September
Sagra della porchetta, del pane e
 del vino and piglet race (1st
 weekend)
December
Processione della signorina (8th)

Artena
January
Carnevale di sant'Antonio
 (weekend nearest 17th)
February
Truffle fair (1st weekend)
August
Palio delle Contrade (1st half of
 the month)
September
Festa di Montefortino (dates to
 be confirmed)
Sagra della polenta (dates to be
 confirmed)

Carpineto Romano
February
Truffle fair (1st weekend)
July
Festa della montagna (dates to be
 confirmed)
August
Teatro sotto le stelle and concerti
Palio della corriera (last Sunday
 of the month)
November
Sagra della castagna (1st Sunday
 of the month)

Castel Gandolfo
Antiques market (last Sunday of
 every month)
July
Sagra of peaches (last Sunday of
 the month)

Castel San Pietro Romano
August
Festa dell'Assunta e san Rocco
 (15th and 16th)

Cave
Easter
"Tragedia del Golgota" with 500
 extras in costume (Good
 Friday)
September
Rievocation of the treaty of
 peace of Cave (1557), with
 renaissance menù (2nd week)
October
Sagra of chestnuts
 and typical
 products
 (last week)

Ciampino
December
Anniversary of the Municipality
 (18th and 19th)

Colleferro
February
Carneval
Premio nazionale della canzone
 d'autore (dates to be
 confirmed)
May
Antiques market
August
Sagra delle fettuccine (15th)
Christmas
Live crib (from 26th December
 to 3rd January)

Colonna
Easter

Good Friday Procession
May
Festa della primavera and marathon (1st and 2nd Sunday of the month)
July
Palio degli asini and beginning of Estate colonnese (1st° weekend)
October
Sagra of uva Italia and of quality wines (1st decade)

Frascati
February
Tuscolano Carneval
April
Castles in flower
May
Maggio tuscolano
June
Festa di san Giovanni with lumacata or Festa delle streghe (23rd)
June-August
Festival delle Ville Tuscolane
October
Festa della cortesia (thanksgiving of the owners of the vineyards to their labourers at the end of the vendemmia; last weekend)
December
"Una fojetta a Frascati", tasting of the vino novello (2nd and 3rd° weekend)

Gallicano nel Lazio
January
Sagra del ciambellone (17th)
Easter
Rievocation of the Golgota on Palm Sunday

Gavignano
February
Truffle fair (1st° weekend)
Carnevale gavignanese
Sagra degli otti (end of the month)
Easter
Good Friday Procession
May
Festa del lavoro with crafts fair (1st)
Maggio gavignanese with photographic exhibition (dates to be confirmed)
June
Festa di sant'Antonio with horse races (dates to be confirmed)
July-August
Sagra dei maccheroni with treasure trove and sagra della bruschetta (dates to be confirmed)
August
Agosto gavignanese with exhibitions and shows (dates to be confirmed)
Christmas
Crib competition (from 25th December to 6th January)

Genazzano
February
Carneval
April
Festa della primavera (3rd decade)
May
Palio di Brancaleone (end of the month)
July
Opening of Summer music festival and festa del Sacro Cuore with Infiorata (1st Sunday)
September
Madonna del Buon Consiglio (8th)
October
"Vinaliae", ancient roman wine festival
December
Sagra of new wine and oil (from 6th to 10th)
Live crib (24th)

Genzano
February
Carneval
April
Festa of violettes (dates to be confirmed)
May
Sagra of strawberries at Landi (dates to be confirmed)
Easter
Good Friday Procession
May-June
Corpus domini with Infiorata dating back to 1778
June
Sagra del vino and Concorso enologico "Grappolo d'Oro" (dates to be confirmed)
September

Sagra of home made bread (2nd Sunday in the month)
November
Sagra del Novello (dates to be confirmed)

Gorga
February
Truffle fair (1st weekend)
July
Festa della montagna (dates to be confirmed)
August
Festa di Ferragosto (15th)
Sagra del castrato (dates to be confirmed)

Grottaferrata
February
Carneval
March
Fiera nazionale Grottaferrata (last decade)
Easter
Rievocation of Good Friday in the Greek-Orthodox tradition in the abbey of San Nilo and fiera dell'Annunciazione
June-July-August
Festival delle Ville Tuscolane
September
Festa di san Nilo in Greek-Orthodox tradition (26th)
'Na Vota C'era' ancient fair in the Abbey (dates to be confirmed)

Lanuvio
Antiques fair (1st° Sunday of every month)
September
Sagra of grapes and wine (4th Sunday of the month)

Lariano
April
Sagra del carciofo alla matticella (1st)
July
Sagra dell'agnello (dates to be confirmed)
September
Sagra of porcino mushrooms (3rd° and 4th° weekend)

Labico
Anno domini 1312 (dates to be confirmed)

Marino
June
Festa di san Giovanni with lumacata (17th)
October
Sagra dell'uva with rievocation in costume of the battle of Lepanto (1st decade)
Sagra delle ciambelle al mosto (2nd Sunday of the month)
December
Natale marinese

Montecompatri
March
Festa delle fraschette
May-June
Corpus Domini and Infiorata
August
Sfida dei borghi and agosto monticiano (last week)

Montelanico
February
Truffle fair (1st weekend)
May-June
Corpus Domini and Infiorata
October
Sagra of chestnuts (3rd Sunday of the month)

Monteporzio Catone
February
Carnevale monteporziano
May-June
Corpus Domini and Infiorata
March
Sagra delle orchidee (dates to be confirmed)
June
Sagra of apricots (last week)
June-July-August
Festival della Ville Tuscolane
December
International exhibition of cribs and Christmas arts

Nemi
June
Sagra of strawberries and flowers and theatre in dialect (1st or 2nd Sunday of the month)
Festa of gladiolas (dates to be confirmed)

Palestrina
Easter
Good Friday
May
Sagra of strawberries at Carchitti (dates to be confirmed)
June
Processione delle zitelle (13th)
August
Palio medievale di sant'Agapito and Sagra del giglietto (typical biscuit) (17th, 18th, 19th)
September
Sagra of hazelnuts and of the giglietto at Carchitti (dates to be confirmed)
Christmas
Live cribs

Rocca di Cave
January
Festa del "Magnarone", dating back to the tradition of exchange food during periods of famine (1st)
May-June
Infiorata for Corpus Domini
13th August-8th September
Palio delle contrade
November
Sagra of chestnuts (1st Sunday of the month)

Rocca di Papa
Mercatino dell'antiquariato (1st Sunday of every month)
July-August
Estate roccheggiana
August
Palio dei rioni (dates to be confirmed)
October
Sagra of chestnuts (3rd Sunday of the month)
September
Sagra del fagiolo Regina (4th and 5th)
"Vivi il Vivaro" with equestrian show (dates to be confirmed)
November
Festa di san Carlo Borromeo with historic procession (4th)
December
Christmas festivities

Rocca Priora
May
Sagra del narciso with 'passatella' and 'scottone' (wine and ricotta cheese) (2nd Sunday of the month)
August
Madonna della Neve (dates to be confirmed)

San Cesareo
February
Carnival floats in procession
September
Sagra of grapes (last weekend)
Christmas
Cribs (25th Decemberl 6th January)

Segni
February
Truffle fair (1st weekend)
July
Palio delle contrade with giostra del Saracino (18th)
October
Sagra del marrone (3rd weekend)

Valmontone
February
Carneval processions
Easter
Representation of the Passion of Christ
June
Fiera merci a Pentecoste
Infiorata for Corpus Domini
Sagra delle lumache (24th)
July-August
Estate valmontonese
December
Natale valmontonese and live crib (26th)

Velletri
January
La Pasquella (4th)
Festa dei carrettieri e dei mulattieri (4th)
February
Carnevale Veliterno
March
Festa delle camelie (2nd half of the month)
Easter
Good Friday Procession
April
Gold crafts exhibition (dates to be confirmed)
Fiera Campionaria (dates to be confirmed)
May
Carciofolata (1st)
Festa della Madonna delle Grazie with candle light procession and walk round the vineyards

(1st Sunday of the month)
Viliternian spring music festival
(dates to be confirmed)
Summer
Jazz concerts and theatre
October
Festa dell'uva and Palio delle
Decarcie with procession in
costume (2nd week)
December
Live crib and crib show

Zagarolo
February
Carneval Processions
25th April-1st May
Primavera a palazzo Rospigliosi
(crfts and foods)
June
Sagra del tordo matto (horse
meat) (week of the 13th)
October
Sagra of grapes (1st weekend)

MUSEUMS

Albano Laziale
MUSEO CIVICO DI ALBANO
Villa Ferrajoli
Viale Risorgimento, 3
Tel. 069323490 fax 069320534
Open:
Every day 8.00-12.30,
Wednesdays and Thursdays
also from 16.00-19.00

Artena
MUSEO CIVICO ARCHEOLOGICO
Complesso Corsetti
Viale 1° Maggio
Tel. 069517014
Opening soon

Castel Gandolfo
ANTIQUARIUM DI VILLA
BARBERINI
Villa Barberini
Via C. Rosselli
Tel. 0669883411
Opened upon request to be sent
by fax to Direzione Ville
Pontificie 0669883437

Cave
MUSEO DELLA CIVILTÀ
CONTADINA
Convento di San Bartolomeo
Piazza Marconi, 5

Tel. 069580423
Open:
1st Sunday of the month, or by
appointment

Colleferro
ANTIQUARIUM COMUNALE DI
COLLEFERRO
Via dell'Artigianato, 9
Tel. 069781169
Open:
Tuesdays, Thursdays, and
Saturdays 17.00-20.00, or by
appointment

Frascati
MUSEO SCUDERIE
ALDOBRANDINI
Piazza G. Marconi, 6
Tel. 069417195
Open:
Tuesday to Friday 10.00-18.00;
Saturdays Sundays and
holidays 10.00-19.00
Closed Mondays

Genazzano
POLO MUSEALE INTERNAZIONALE
ARTE CONTEMPORANEA
Palazzo Colonna
Tel. 069579745 (biblioteca
comunale)
Opening soon (currently
showing temporary
exhibition)

Lanuvio
ANTIQUARIUM COMUNALE
Via Roma, 1
Tel. 0693789228
Opening soon

Marino
MUSEO CIVICO "UMBERTO
MASTROIANNI"
Ex Chiesa di Santa Lucia
Tel. 06936621
Opening soon

Montecompatri
PINACOTECA DI SAN SILVESTRO
Convento dei Padri Carmelitani
Via San Silvestro
Tel. 069485023
Opened by request only

Nemi
MUSEO DELLE NAVI ROMANE
Via del Tempio di Diana, 15

Tel. e fax 069398040
Winter hours:
Tuesday to Sunday 9.00-14.00
Summer hours:
Tuesday to Sunday 9.00-18.00
Mondays closed

Palestrina
MUSEO ARCHEOLOGICO
NAZIONALE
Palazzo Barberini
Piazza della Cortina
Tel. 069538100
Open:
Every day 9.00-19.00

Segni
MUSEO ARCHEOLOGICO
Via Lauri, 1
Tel. 0697262235
Open:
guided tours by appointment
only

Velletri
MUSEO CAPITOLARE DELLA
CATTEDRALE
Cattedrale di San Clemente
Largo della Repubblica, 347
Tel. 069642095
Open:
Every day 10.00-13.00/15.00-
19.00
MUSEO CIVICO
Via G. Mameli, 7
Tel. 0696158239
Opening soon

ACCOMODATION

Albano Laziale
HOTELS
Villa Maria***
Via del Mare, 263 - Loc. Pavona
Tel. 0693123914
Miralago**
Via dei Cappuccini, 12
Tel. 069321018 fax 069322253
L'oasi della pace*
Via dei Tulipani, 50 - Loc.
Pavona
Tel. 069343253
ROOMS FOR RENT
Fini Maria teresa
Via Sicilia, 12
Loc. Cecchina
Tel. 069342439
Haggar Giuseppe
Via del Mare, 34

Loc. Pavona
Tel. 069311453
Reali Giuliana
Via del Mare, 20
Loc. Pavona
Tel. 069315083
AGRITURISMI
Tor Paluzzi
Di Enrico Pellini (Loc. Tor Paluzzi)
Via Tor Paluzzi, 184 - Cecchina
Tel. 069341171
B&B
Il Bosco
Via Tibullo, 12
Tel. 03383115419

Ariccia
HOTELS
Appian Hotel***
Via Appia Nuova, Km 28,350
Tel. 069333026 fax 069332387
Villa Aricia***
Via Appia Nuova, Km 26,200
Tel. 069321161 fax 069320065
Motel Fontana di Papa al 12°**
Via Nettunense, Km 12 (Loc. Pavona)
Tel. e fax 069340922
B&B
Casa Bianca
Via Campo Leone, 14
Tel. 069278301
Diana Aricina
Via Cerquette, 6
Tel. 069332532
La casa nel bosco
Via dei Lecci, 36
Tel. 069332292
La quiete
Via Muracce, 5
Tel. 069333374

Artena
HOTELS
Chicchio**
Via Santa Maria, 28
Tel. 069517096 fax 069515861

Carpineto Romano
HOTELS
Il Faggio* (Loc. Semprevisa)
Tel. 06979031

Castel Gandolfo
HOTELS
Castel Vecchio****
Viale Pio X, 23
Tel. 069360308 fax 069360579

Culla del Lago***
Via Spiagia del Lago, 36
Tel. 069360047 fax 069360425
La Mongolfiera***
Via Spiaggia del Lago, Km 4,300
Tel. 0693668241 fax 0693668251
Pagnanelli Lucia**
Via A. Gramsci, 2
Tel. 069361422
Belvedere*
Viale B. Buozzi, 4
Tel. 069324205
Bucci*
Via degli Zecchini, 27
Tel. 069360018 fax 069322244

Castel San Pietro Romano
ROOMS FOR RENT
Le Cannuccette (Loc. Cannuccette)
Tel. 069535811

Cave
HOTELS
La Fonte**
Piazza G. Venzi, 3
Tel. 069580057 fax 069508948
B&B
Villa M. Celeste
Via della Selce, 271
Tel. 069581556

Ciampino
HOTELS
Dany***
Via A. Grandi, 2
Tel. e fax 0679321151
Louis II***
Via Monti, s.n.c.
Tel. 0679321937 fax 0679329728
Villa Giulia ***
Via Dalmazia, 9
Tel. 0679321874 fax 0679321994
Laura**
Via San Francesco d'Assisi, 58
Tel. 067914501 fax 067914970
Louis**
Via Montegrappa, 33
Tel 067918095 fax 067918096
Anna*
Via San Francesco d'Assisi, 34
Tel. 067910144
Maria Alessandra
Via Adamello, 4
Tel. 067911792
ROOMS FOR RENT

Gentile Maria
Via Renzo Bersani, 25
Tel. 067923236
B&B
Ciampino B&B
Via Coldilana, 18
Tel. 067915830
Danys
Via R. Bersani, 26
Tel. 067915690
Pellegrini B&B
Via R. Vecchia, 52
Tel. 067963772
Vigna Fiorita
Via del Sassone, 8
Tel. 067960051
Villa Valentino
Via Errico, 5/b
Tel. 069332292

Colleferro
HOTELS
Astoria***
Via Savoia, 71
Tel. 06974724
Il Grottino*
Via Artigianato, 67
Tel. 06975168

Frascati
HOTELS
Villa Tuscolana****
Via del Tuscolo, Km 2
Tel. 06942900 fax 069424747
Bellavista***
Piazza Roma, 2
Tel. 069426320 fax 069421068
Flora***
Viale V. Veneto, 8
Tel. 069416110 fax 069416546
Hotel Colonna ***
Piazza del Gesù, 12
Tel. 0694018088 fax 0694018730
Villa Icidia***
Via Tuscolana Vecchia, 81
Tel. 069408604 fax 069408013
Villa Mercede***
Via Tuscolana, 20
Tel. 069424760 fax 069416461
Villa Pina '92***
Via Carlo Lucidi, 2
Tel. 069421063 fax 069417711
Eden Tuscolano**
Via Tuscolana, 15
Tel. 069408589 fax 069408591
Giardina**
Via Diaz, 15
Tel. 069419415 fax 069420440

Il Pinocchio**
Piazza del Mercato
Tel. 069417883 fax 069417884
Panorama**
Piazza Carlo Casini, 3
Tel. 069421800
Villa Maria Luigia**
Via delle Cisternole, 204
Tel. 069464430
ROOMS FOR RENT
Camera con vista
Di Nofri Carlo
Piazza Roma, 2
Tel. 069419954
B&B
Casa Branchi
Via Tuscolana, 22
Tel. 069425038
Merum alia
Vicolo Prata Porci, 8
Tel. 069456687
Villa Chiara
Via delle Cisternole, 50
Tel. 069464036
Villa delle Acace
Vicolo Prata Porci, 6
Tel. 069424732

Frascati-Vermicino
HOTELS
Da Bottaccio**
Via G. Luzi, 32
Tel. 069408173 - fax 069408663

Gallicano nel Lazio
ROOMS FOR RENT
Belvedere di Betti C.
Via Europa, 6
Tel. 0695460063

Genazzano
HOTELS
Cremona***
Via Palmiro Togliatti, 19 (Loc. Tofali)
Tel. 069579603 fax 069578234

Genzano
HOTELS
Grand Hotel Primus****
Via G. Pellegrino, 12
Tel. 069364932 fax 069364231
Villa Vittoria****
Via Rosselli, 29
Tel. 069364333 fax 069364277
Villa Robinia**
Via Rosselli, 19
Tel. 069398617 fax 069396409
AGRITURISMI

J.J.M.R.S.
di Jacqueline Franca Balzarini
Vicolo Sant'Antonio (Loc. Selvotta)
Tel. 069342264
Tre Palme
di Ernesto Lercher
Via Muti, 75 (Loc. Landi)
Tel. 069370286
Monte due Torri
Via Monte Giove, 119
Tel. 069363276
ROOMS FOR RENT
Villa Emanuela
di D'Achille Mauro
Colle San Gennaro
Tel. 069370335
Gentile Anita
Il Stradone Muti, s.n.c.
Tel. 069370512
B&B
Garden House
Via Dott. Francavilla, 20
Tel. 069399494

Grottaferrata
HOTELS
Park Hotel Villa Grazioli****
Via U. Pavoni, 19
Tel. 06945400 fax 069413506
Villa Florio****
Viale Dusmet, 25
Tel. 0694548007 fax 0694548009
Villa Ferrata***
Via Tuscolana, 287
Tel. 0694548049 fax 0694548050
Villa Letizia***
Via XXIV Maggio, 110
Tel. 069411103 fax 069411098
I Locandieri**
Via Tuscolana, 285
Tel. 069456375 fax 069410522
Centro**
Via 1° Maggio, 98
Tel. 069415151
Conca d'Oro*
Via Vecchia di Marino, 6
Tel. 0694 59822
SERVICE FLATS
Il Residence**
Via Roma, 84
Tel. 0694315443 fax 0694315749
B&B
Casa Daniela
Piazza Vittime del Fascismo
Tel. 069410317

Villa Flavia
Via Anagnina, 165/167
Tel. 03388940089

Lariano
HOTELS
Nespolo d'oro**
Via G. Garibaldi, 76
Tel. e fax 069655050
Villa Rosa*
Via Colle Manzoni, 17
Tel. 069655039
B&B
Casa di Angela
Via D. Alighieri, 59
Tel. 069648131
Friend Home
Via della Pace, 3
Tel. 0696498499

Marino
HOTELS
Helio Cabala****
Via Spinabella, 15
Tel. 0693661235 fax 0693661125
Grand Hotel Villa dei Papi****
Via Selva Ferentina, 15
Tel. 069367224 fax 069367493
Park Hotel***
Via Appia Nuova, Km 19,200
Tel. 069300254 fax 069300332
Ai vecchi tempi**
Via Nettunense, Km 3 (Loc. Pavona)
Tel. 069310575 fax 069310579
Villa Svizzera**
Via B. Buozzi, 53
Tel. e fax 0693660231
Dei Pini*
Via Nettunense Vecchia, 116/bis (Loc. Frattocchie)
Tel. 0693547028
B&B
Domitilla 2000
Via T. Speri, 42
Tel. 0693546413
Le Betulle
Via C. Picchione, 61
Tel. 0693541088
Nebli
Via dei Canneti, 15
Tel. 0669311125
Santa Chiara
Via dei Canneti, 15
Tel. 03498017381
Spallone
Via dei Laghi, km 8.6
Tel. 03478102922

Vigne del Sole
Via Vivaldi, 9
Tel. 069384342
Villa Monia I
Via C. Picchione, 71
Tel. 069352337
Villa Monia II
Via C. Picchione, 71
Tel. 03475306898
Villa Monia III
Via C. Picchione, 71
Tel. 03388113916

Montecompatri
HOTELS
Il Castagneto***
Via Tuscolana, Km 27,700
Tel. 069406292 fax 069406101
Le Terrazze***
Via Oberdan, 25
Tel. 069487108 fax 069487632
L'Ottava***
Via Frascati Colonna, 62
Tel. 0694730018 fax
 0694730156
Paradiso***
Via Campo Gillaro, 19
Tel. 069487531 fax 069487533
Belsito*
Via Tuscolana, Km 26,700
Tel. 069406293 fax 069406665
Forchetta d'Oro*
Via Casilina, Km 23,500
Tel. 069462072
Nuova Campagnola*
Via Casilina, Km 21,300 (Loc. Laghetto)
Tel. 069476065
B&B
La Torre B&B
Via P. Martini, 98
Tel. 069485140
Oliveto
Via del Romito, 10
Tel. 069486824

Monteporzio Catone
HOTELS
Giovannella***
Piazza Trieste, 1
Tel. 069449038 fax 069449109
Villa Sciarra**
Via Montecompatri, 22 (Loc. Palocci)
Tel. 069449272
B&B
Pennacchiotti
Via Costa Grande, 42
Tel. 069448746

Villa Lia
Via Frascati, 12
Tel. 069449176

Nemi
HOTELS
Diana Park****
Via Nemorense, 44
Tel. 069364041 fax 069364063
Al Bosco**
Via Nemorense, 1
Tel. 069368085
Al Rifugio**
Via Nemorense, 22
Tel. 069368686 fax 069368656

Palestrina
HOTELS
Le Meridienne****
Loc. San Agapito
Tel. 069536859 fax 069536653
Stella***
Piazzale della Liberazione, 3
Tel. 069538172 fax 069573360
B&B
La Dea Fortuna
Via Prenestina, 311
Tel. 069536608
Praeneste
Via B.ca Piana, 10
Tel. 069573170
Via Verdi
Via Verdi, 1
Tel. 069574070
Villa Mara
Via Stella, 96
Tel. 069535905

Rocca di Papa
HOTELS
Angeletto***
Via del Tufo, 32
Tel. 06949020 fax 069499973
Europa***
Piazzale della Repubblica, 20
Tel. 069498652 fax 06949361
Villa Ortensie***
Via Ariccia, 19
Tel. 0694749108 fax 069495155
La Locandina**
Via Calcare, 18
Tel. 06949202
Polentone**
Via Vecchia di Velletri, 1
Tel. 069496984 fax 069497331
ROOMS FOR RENT
Locanda il Giardino
Via delle Barozza, 53
Tel. 069499938

B&B
Il Mosaico
Via E. Fermi, 71
Tel. 069498733
In Villa
Via Barozze, 51
Tel. 0696196009
Ortensie
Via Ortensie, 20
Tel. 069497111
The Holiday House
Via Valle Vergine
Tel. 069497386

Rocca Priora
HOTELS
Villa La Rocca****
Via dei Castelli Romani, 1
Tel. 069471594 fax 069471750
Villa Margherita*
Via Tuscolana, Km 29,100 (Loc. Il Pratone)
Tel. 069406155 fax 069406277
B&B
Casa Carlotta
Via Tuscolana, km 30
Tel. 0694436119
Casa Giafredda
Via A. Moro, 19
Tel. 03393621840
Green B&B
Via dei Ciliegi, 27
Tel. 0694436466
La Rocca
Via IV Novembre, 9
Tel. 069461482
Villa Praticello
Via Vicinale Prati, 21
Tel. 03473480856

San Cesareo
HOTELS
Motel Belvedere***
Via Maremmana Inferiore, Km 2,200
Tel. 069589200 fax 069587841
B&B
Villa Pina
Via C.le Farinaccio
Tel. 069586144

Segni
HOTELS
La Noce***
Via Casilina, Km 53,900 (Loc. La Noce)
Tel. 069770475 fax 069770282
La Pace***
Via dei Cappuccini, 9

Tel. 069767125 fax 069766262

Valmontone
HOTELS
Alla Fonte*
Via Formale Nuovo, 3
Tel. 069598040
Jolly Car santandrea*
Via Adriana, Km 18,300
Tel. 069598086 fax 069598043

Velletri
HOTELS
Da Benito al Bosco***
Contrada Morici, 20
Tel. 069633991
Al Falchetto**
Via Appia Nuova, Km 32
Tel. 069631321
Monte Artemisio**
Via dei Laghi, Km 14,500 (Loc. Pratoni di Nemi)
Tel. 069634206 fax 069634207
Roma*

Viale Roma, 26
Tel. 069631225
AGRITURISMI
Iachelli Elio-Armando e figli
Via dei Laghi, Km 15 (Loc. Pratone)
Tel. 069633256
ROOMS FOR RENT
Arena Savo Anna Maria
Via Cannetoli, 23
Tel. 069630839
Mastrantonio Roberta
Via Arcioni, 24
Tel. 069647421
B&B
Castelli Romani
Colle Ottone, 108
Tel. 069627928
In Villa
Via del Boschetto, 32
Tel. 069632952
Santa maria
C. da Paganico
Tel. 069626022

Villa Alba
C. da Cigiolo Nord
Tel. 069641601

Zagarolo
HOTELS
Al Pozzo***
Via Apollinaria, s.n.c.
Tel. 069549280
Albio Tibullo**
S.P.S. Apollinaria, Km 1
Tel. 069575510
fax 069575510
Dei Platani*
Via Prenestina Nuova, Km 17,900
Tel. 069524115
B&B
Il Pero
Via c.le del Pero, 10
Tel. 069524389
La Villa
Via Colle Ripa, 7
Tel. 03471544902

Index of places

Affile 84
Agosta 109
Albano 125, 126
Allumiere 24, 39
Anguillara Sabazia 18
Anticoli Corrado 101
Anzio 31
Arcinazzo Romano 85
Ardea 31
Ariccia 128, 160
Arsoli 99
Artena 148
Bellegra 107
Bracciano 19
Camerata Nuova 112
Campagnano di Roma 49
Canale Monterano 23, 39
Canterano 108
Capena 58
Capranica Prenestina 106
Carpineto Romano 153
Casape 95
Castel Gandolfo 124
Castel Madama 96
Castelnuovo di Porto 57
Castel San Pietro Romano 143
Cave 160
Ceri 36
Cerreto 108
Cervara di Roma 111
Cerveteri 37
Ciampino 123
Ciciliano 93
Cineto Romano 97
Civitavecchia 26
Civitella San Paolo 60
Colleferro 149
Colonna 157
Fiano Romano 59
Filacciano 62
Formello 47
Fiumicino 34
Frascati 139, 140
Gallicano nel Lazio 142
Gavignano 151
Genazzano 161
Genzano di Roma 130
Gerano 107

Gorga 151
Grottaferrata 157
Guadagnolo 106
Guidonia Montecelio 82
Jenne 110
Labico 145
Ladispoli 28
Lanuvio 131
Lariano 134
Licenza 90
Lucus feroniae 59
Magliano Romano 52
Mandela 92
Manziana 22
Marano Equo 109
Marcellina 80
Marino 136
Mazzano Romano 50
Mentana 73
Montecompatri 156
Monteflavio 77
Montelanico 151
Montelibretti 74
Monteporzio Catone 155
Monterotondo 72
Montorio Romano 75
Monumento naturale di Torre
    Flavia 28
Moricone 77
Morlupo 56
Nazzano 60
Nemi 125, 135
Nerola 74
Nettuno 30, 41
Oasi faunistica di Palo 29
Oasi di Macchiagrande 29
Olevano Romano 83
Palestrina 144
Palombara Sabina 78
Parco naturale dei monti
    Lucretili 76
Parco naturale dei monti
    Simbruini 111
Parco regionale dei Castelli
    Romani 123
Parco suburbano della valle del
    Treja 51
Parco di Vejo 47

Percile 92
Pisoniano 105
Poli 95
Pomezia 33
Ponzano Romano 62
Riano 57
Rignano Flaminio 53
Riofreddo 98
Riserva naturale di
    Macchiatonda 28
Riserva naturale
    Tevere-Farfa 61
Rocca Canterano 108
Rocca di Cave 161
Rocca di Papa 158
Roccagiovine 91
Rocca Priora 140
Rocca Santo Stefano 107
Roiate 84
Roviano 97
Sacrofano 48
Sambuci 100
Sant'Angelo Romano 81
San Cesareo 141
San Gregorio da Sassola 94
Santa Marinella 28, 36
San Polo dei Cavalieri 80
Sant'Oreste 54
Santa Severa (castello) 35
San Vito Romano 105
Saracinesco 101
Sasso 36
Segni 149
Subiaco 112
Tivoli 87
Tolfa 24, 39
Tor Caldara 29
Torre Astura 29, 30
Torrita Tiberina 61
Trevignano Romano 21
Tusculum 138
Vallepietra 116
Vallinfreda 99
Valmontone 146
Velletri 132
Vicovaro 103
Vivaro Romano 99
Zagarolo 141

Bibliography

S. Ardito, *A piedi nel Lazio*, vol. III, Subiaco 1998
AA.Vv., *Bracciano e gli Orsini nel '400*, Roma 1981
AA.Vv., *L'arte per i Papi e per i Principi nella campagna romana*, Roma 1990
AA.Vv, *Il Lazio paese per paese*, 3 voll., 1993
AA.Vv., *Atlante storico politico del Lazio*, Bari-Roma 1996
AA.Vv, *I Principi della Chiesa*, Milano 1998
Assessorato alla Cultura della Provincia di Roma, *Montegelato*, Roma 1998
Assessorato alla Cultura della Provincia di Roma, *Progetto Vie*, Roma 1999
Assessorato allo Sport e Turismo Provincia di Roma, *Percorsi Archeologici*, 10 voll., Roma 1993
Assessorato al Turismo della Provincia di Roma, *I Volsci*, Roma 1997
Assessorato al Turismo della Provincia di Roma, *Le vie dell'Olio della provincia di Roma*, Roma 1998
Azienda Romana per i Mercati, *Materiali per la strada dei vini dei Castelli Romani*, Roma 2000
G. Bove, *Il Francescanesimo nel Lazio*, Provincia di Roma Settore Cultura, Roma 1994
R. Cavalli-N. Messina, *Lazio a cavallo*, Supplemento a «Lazio ieri, oggi e domani» n III, 1994
G. Censi, *S. Anatolia a Gerano*, Gerano 1993
M. Ciampani-P. Tojati-F. Zozi-S. R. Redwan, *Quaderni di storia e di ricerca dell'agro falisco capenate*, Comune di Sant'Oreste 1999
IX Comunità Montana del Lazio, *Patrimonio Artistico e Monumentale dei Monti Sabini, Tiburtini, Cornicolani e Prenestini*, Tivoli 1995
F. Coarelli, *Dintorni di Roma*, Bari 1981
M. De Carolis, *Il Monte Soratte e i suoi santuari*, Roma 1950
R. Del Nero, *Guida storica ed archeologica alla città di Tuscolo*, Cecchina (Roma) 1985

70 itinerari all'aria aperta, Subiaco 1989
C. Feliciani, *Genzano e l'infiorata*, Comune di Genzano 1996
J. G. Frazer, *Il ramo d'oro*, Roma 1992
La Valle dell'Aniene, Subiaco 1999
L. Iannattoni, *La cucina romana e laziale*, Roma 1998
M. A. Lozzi Bonaventura, *Abbazie, boschi, castelli*, 2 voll., Subiaco 1996
Feste sagre e mercatini nel Lazio, Subiaco 1999
V. Mannucci, *Il parco archeologico naturalistico del porto di Traiano*, Roma 1999
B. Martinis, *Il Lazio prima di Saturno*, Roma 1995
G. Massimi, *Scoprire i dintorni di Roma*, Roma 1992
G. Mezzetti, *Origini e storia del carnevale tiburtino*, Tivoli 1995
D. Moretti-F. Maffei-E. Mazzarini-A. Gelderman, *Il lago di Martignano*, Assessorato al Turismo, Comune di Campagnano 1990
S. Moscati, *Nuove passeggiate Laziali*, Roma 1996
M. Quercioli, *Le città perdute del Lazio*, Roma 1992
A. Ravaglioli, *Alla scoperta del Lazio*, Roma 1995
Regione Lazio, *I parchi e le riserve naturali del Lazio*, Roma 1992
G. Silvestrelli, *Città, castelli e torri della regione romana*, 2 voll., Roma 1993
Touring Club Italiano, *Lazio*, Guida d'Italia 1991
O. Zanini De Vita, *Il Lazio a tavola*, Assessorato alle politiche per la promozione della Cultura dello Spettacolo e del Turismo della Regione Lazio, Roma 1997

Further, leaflets, brochures and various other documents, published by Municipalities, Visitors', Offices and other bodies concerned with tourism on behalf of the Province of Rome, have been consulted.

Printed in november 2000
for Fratelli Palombi Editori